MW01028158

Charles Pickering, Sr. has written an extraordinary book, a healing book at a time when that is what we all need. Senator Chuck Schumer should pay special attention to Chapter Thirteen.

MIKE WALLACE

60 Minutes

Having known Charles Pickering for more than thirty years, I watched with frustration and anger as far left groups and liberal senators falsely smeared him and insulted Mississippi. But what he and other conservative judicial nominees endured actually hurt Democrats at the polls and helped assure confirmation of John Roberts and Sam Alito to the Supreme Court. In *A Price Too High* Judge Pickering shares an intriguing story that every Mississippian and everyone interested in good government should read.

HALEY BARBOUR

Governor of Mississippi

and former Chairman,

Republican National Committee

Unlike those who attacked him in Washington, D.C., I know Charles Pickering personally; and I know his positive record on race relations, civil rights, and equal protection for all. *A Price Too High* tells a captivating and compelling story of a young man who came of age in the segregated South, and at the age of 26, fought the Ku Klux Klan when they were strongest. Washington liberals attempted to portray him as a racist, they sickened me. I've been in the fight. I have the wounds. I know the truth. If you are interested in promoting better race relations, you should read Charles Pickering's story.

CHARLES EVERS

Civil Rights Leader

Brother of slain Civil Rights Leader Medgar Evers,

And former Mayor of Fayette, Mississippi

My friend, Judge Charles Pickering, a much respected jurist, was in a very real sense martyred for his faith. Senators shockingly refused his confirmation largely because of his expressed Christian views.

CHARLES W. COLSON
Founder, Prison Fellowship

Charles Pickering's four-year confirmation fight gave him a unique perspective of how liberal politicalization of the judiciary seriously threatens the third branch of government. The recommendations in *A Price Too High* are both reasonable and provocative and will make a positive contribution toward solving a problem that gravely endangers the Judiciary and undermines comity and collegiality in the Senate. This is a must-read for all who are serious about fidelity to the Constitution.

DAVID LIMBAUGH
Attorney and author of *Persecution*

Let's see if I have this right: White northern liberals, who knew absolutely nothing about the real Charles Pickering, maligned him as a bigot who was soft on cross burners. But African-American civil rights workers in Mississippi know Judge Pickering is a man of great moral courage who took on the KKK back when it was dangerous and who to this day stands for decency and fair play. This tells you a lot about Pickering — but even more about his enemies. For some, public service is a price too high, but not for Charles Pickering.

BERNARD GOLDBERG
Journalist and author of several books including
Bias, and most recently, *Crazies to the Left of Me,*
Wimps to the Right: How One Side
Lost Its Mind, And The Other Lost Its Nerve.

A PRICE TOO HIGH

Stroud & Hall Publishers
P.O. Box 27210
Macon, Ga 31221
www.stroudhall.com

©2007 Stroud & Hall

All rights reserved.
Printed in the United States of America
First Edition

The paper used in this publication meets the minimum requirements
of American National Standard for Information Sciences—
Permanence of Paper for Printed Library Materials.
ANSI Z39.48–1984. (alk. paper)

Library of Congress Cataloging-in-Publication Data

Pickering, Charles Willis, 1937–
A price too high : the judiciary in jeopardy / by Charles Pickering.
p. cm.
ISBN 978-0-9745376-9-6 (hardcover : alk. paper)
1. Pickering, Charles Willis, 1937– 2. Judges—United States—Biography. 3. Judges—Selection and appointment—United States—History—Sources. 4. Political questions and judicial power—United States. I. Title.

KF373.P53A3 2007
347.73'14—dc22

2007013820

A PRICE TOO HIGH

The Judiciary in Jeopardy

BY JUDGE CHARLES PICKERING, SR.

STROUD & HALL

DEDICATION

I dedicate this book to my wife Margaret Ann and our four
children: Paige Dunkerton, Chip Pickering, Allison Montgomery,
and Christi Chapman. Margaret Ann has been my helpmate,
supporter, best friend, loving companion, and wife for more than
forty-seven years. Our four children have all brought us joy and
made us proud. During my confirmation battle, and throughout
my life, they could not have been more supportive.

—Charles W. Pickering Sr.

Contents

Prologue

IN 1990, THE United States Senate unanimously confirmed my lifetime appointment to the federal district court. In 2001, President George W. Bush nominated me to the Fifth Circuit Court of Appeals. Eleven years after my first federal nomination, a ferocious, highly partisan, bitter, and mean-spirited confirmation fight (a product of the culture war raging in America) consumed my life for almost four years. This unprecedented battle for supremacy of the federal courts threatens the quality, independence, diversity, and integrity of the American judicial system. It erodes civility and collegiality in the Senate, creating roadblocks for senators who wish to discharge their responsibilities to the American people. The politicization of the judiciary threatens our democratic processes, our separation of powers, and the rule of law as envisioned by our Founders.

During the confirmation process, nominees are discouraged from speaking out to the media or the public. In part, this protects the integrity of the judiciary by ensuring sitting or potential judges do not prejudice themselves in cases that may come before them. However, this policy also prevents nominees from defending themselves against vicious attacks and precludes them from addressing concerns raised by opponents before the American people. No longer a nominee and no longer a judge, I can now speak out on the circumstances of my struggle as well as address the larger confirmation fight and the culture war that created it. I can advocate reform.

This book presents my fight for confirmation from initially learning of my recommendation to the Fifth Circuit, through my Senate Judiciary Committee hearings and the obstruction therein, President Bush's re-nomination following the return of the Republican majority in

2002, the unprecedented filibuster by Senate Democrats, and finally a recess appointment. I served on the Fifth Circuit and retired. I will share my reflections and observations of this journey and make suggestions for solutions to the confirmation struggle that I believe will benefit the nominees of any party, strengthen the independence of the federal judiciary, and fortify our nation's commitment to the rule of law.

Shortly after I began writing this book in earnest, Hurricane Katrina hit my home state of Mississippi and delayed the project. When the confirmation battle over the nomination of Sam Alito to the Supreme Court heated up, my publisher and I decided it would best serve the cause of trying to strengthen the rule of law and improve the confirmation process if we divided my writing into two books and rushed the first part to publication. As a result, we published my first book, *Supreme Chaos: The Politics of Judicial Confirmation & the Culture War*, in January 2006.

Supreme Chaos provides a background and history of the judicial confirmation process, describes the flaws in the current procedure, and outlines remedies. It relates the history and defines the filibuster as well as gives details of its unprecedented and unconstitutional use in defeating judicial nominees with majority support. It discusses the culture war including the role of special-interest groups and the media and shares how judicial activism—a product of this battle for the hearts, souls, and minds of the American people—affects not only our country but also each individual American. It gives a historic review of the nature and impact of religion on the American experience, how modern secularism challenges that tradition, and the relation of this sacred/secular fight to the judiciary, the Constitution, and the confirmation process.

My previous book explains the "mystery Constitution"—also known as the "living Constitution"—and discusses how players fight the battle for this document in the halls of the Senate and the chambers of the Court. I review and make observations on the 2005 compromise (the Gang of Fourteen) that provided a Band-aid for the hemorrhaging confirmation process, and I analyze how the nominations of John Roberts, Harriet Miers, and Sam Alito evolved in the current atmosphere of the politics of judicial confirmation. If you desire a complete panorama of the confirmation battle and a compliment to this book, I believe you will find *Supreme Chaos* a worthy read.

Throughout this book, I discuss extensively my record in protecting civil rights and seeking equal rights for Americans regardless of race. I am proud of my civil rights record, but was reluctant to emphasize this portion of my life as much as I did. However, because opponents used race as a central attack against me, I thought
it necessary to present it in some detail.

Senator Chuck Schumer criticized me because I am from Mississippi, and he and other opponents attacked me and other nominees because of our faith. I discuss those matters briefly in the epilogue.

As I describe my personal odyssey traveling through the quagmire of judicial confirmation, I hope I clearly present an insider's perspective on the nature of the struggle. I hope you find the solutions I recommend appropriate remedies to the confirmation chaos and the politicization of the judiciary. I hope you will join me in the fight to preserve the rule of law. How we resolve this battle for the judiciary will produce consequences with an enormous impact on the America in which our children and grandchildren will live.

—Charles W. Pickering Sr. (September 2006)

Time Line of Events

May 11, 1990—Nominated to Federal District Court

September 20, 1990—Unanimously Confirmed by U.S. Senate for Federal District Court

January 7, 2001—Recommended for Fifth Circuit Court of Appeals

May 24, 2001—Senator Jim Jeffords Leaves Republican Party

May 25, 2001—Nomination Forwarded to U.S. Senate

June 6, 2001—Democrats Take Control of U.S. Senate

October 18, 2001—First Hearing on My Nomination

February 7, 2002—Second Hearing on My Nomination

March 14, 2002—Blocked by Committee Vote

November 5, 2002—Republicans Net Two Senate Seats in Mid-term Elections

January 2003—Republicans Take Control of U.S. Senate

January 7, 2003—Re-nominated for Fifth Circuit Court of Appeals

October 2, 2003—Third Hearing; Voted out of Committee

October 30, 2003—Filibustered

January 16, 2004—Recess Appointment to Fifth Circuit Court of Appeals

February 17, 2004—*60 Minutes* Interview Conducted

March 28, 2004—*60 Minutes* Interview Airs

November 2, 2004—President Bush Reelected and Republicans Net Four Senate Seats

December 8, 2004—I Retire from Fifth Circuit Court of Appeals

May 23, 2005—Gang of Fourteen Agreement Provides Confirmation of Appellate Nominees

September 29, 2005—John Roberts Confirmed as Chief Justice of the United States

A PRICE TOO HIGH

October 31, 2005—Sam Alito Nominated to Supreme Court

January 2006—*Supreme Chaos: The Politics of Judicial Confirmation &
the Culture War* Released

January 31, 2006—Sam Alito Confirmed to Supreme Court

Nominated: 2001

IT WAS ONE of those father/son things. My only son Chip and I were duck hunting in the marshlands of south Louisiana. It had been a mild winter and this early January day in 2001 was great for outdoorsmen. When Chip was growing up, I taught him to enjoy hunting and fishing and appreciate the wonder of the natural world. However, since his election to Congress in 1996, we had to work harder at finding moments like this to share. Now in the outdoors, we were ages away from the political fights of our nation, though it had been but a few weeks since George W. Bush had been declared president-elect following the Florida debacle.

Chip and I were hunting at a duck camp built in the 1920s on an island in the marshes southwest of Lafayette. Surrounded by marsh grass and a few scrubby trees, it is accessible only by boating across the inter-coastal waterway and winding through channels and canals of the marshland for about an hour.

In the morning, we and the other hunters divided into groups, dispersed in different directions, and hunted in separate blinds round about the camp. Chip and I hunted together. The ducks were flying that morning but not in large numbers. Still, we had a good hunt despite not quite killing our limit. That afternoon we fished and shot skeet.

We gathered at the camp for the evening meal to swap stories and enjoy the company of fellow hunters away from the hustle and bustle of everyday life. Chip answered his cell phone, grinned after a few minutes, and handed it to me. It was Senator Trent Lott, Mississippi's junior U.S. senator and a political and personal friend to both Chip and me. Trent told me he and Mississippi's other U.S. senator, Thad Cochran, were recommending that President Bush nominate me to the Fifth Circuit Court of Appeals in New Orleans. (The White House selects the nominees but traditionally relies on recommendations from leaders of its own party in the nominee's home state. In Mississippi, Republican presidents turn to Cochran and Lott. Each state and circumstance work out this informal procedure to fit local protocol.)

Ten years earlier, Trent had asked if I would like a recommendation to the Fifth Circuit. At that time, I was fifty-three years of age with an active trial practice and heavy involvement in civic, political, and church activities. I viewed a circuit court appointment too sedate, too drastic of a change, too difficult for me to adapt to the cloistered life of an appellate judge reading briefs and drafting opinions. I instead opted for the more active district court judgeship where I could preside over the trial of cases and interact with lawyers. This more energetic judgeship better suited me in 1990. But in 2001, I was approaching sixty-four years of age and thought I could adjust. I had a lifetime appointment, but in just three years, whether I remained on the district bench or moved up to the Fifth Circuit, I would have been eligible to take a reduced workload (senior status) or retire. Trent's call was good news. This would be a promotion, another opportunity for service, and a capstone to my judicial career.

The morning after I returned from south Louisiana—before breakfast—I received a call from a longtime friend who heard about Trent and Thad's recommendation. Grady Jolly, a judge on the Fifth Circuit, asked, "Charles, have you lost your mind? You've got the best possible job you can have. You hear a matter and you can decide, but if you come on the Fifth Circuit you are going to have to convince at least one other judge on a three-judge panel and if en banc [the entire Fifth Circuit] seven or eight other judges. You won't have nearly as much independence or freedom." He told me a heavy workload was causing Fifth Circuit judges to work fifty to sixty hours a week. At that time, my district court docket was up to date, and I did not have to work more than a forty-hour week. Sometimes when cases settled, I had free time with my family on the farm.

I thought about the change. I had a good life, a familiar routine, a comfortable job. Many of the lawyers who practiced before me supported my nomination but said they preferred I remain on the district bench as a trial judge. I had second thoughts and seriously considered not going forward. But after careful consideration, prayer, conversations with my family, and discussions with Trent and Thad, I decided if the president offered the nomination, I would accept.

The Constitution empowers the president of the United States to "nominate, and by and with the Advice and Consent of the Senate" appoint the judges of the Supreme Court. Congress under constitutional authority created lower federal courts. The president submits the nomination of all federal judges to the Senate, where typically the Senate Judiciary Committee conducts hearings. After the committee reports the nomination to the full Senate, a nomination requires the vote of a majority of senators for confirmation.

The nomination process required a tremendous amount of paperwork. The White House and Justice Department provided an extensive form, and the Senate requested a detailed response to a lengthy questionnaire. The Bush Administration decided not to let the American Bar Association (ABA) vet its judicial nominees before nomination. Democratic senators stated they would not consider a nominee without the ABA evaluation, which they praised as "impartial" and the "gold standard." This produced additional forms and paperwork.

The FBI conducted an extensive background check, interviewing people who had known me to verify each phase of my life. Both FBI and ABA representatives interviewed lawyers who appeared before me and judges who worked with me. As standard practice, the FBI and ABA inquired into my record of protecting civil rights and discovered nothing of concern. (I learned later that one FBI agent asked a former business partner whether he ever heard me tell jokes with racial overtones. The partner said no, but he had heard me ask someone else not to do so.)

February, March, and April were busy months as I tried to keep up my district court docket, complete my nomination paperwork, and prepare for an eventual confirmation hearing. It was a time-consuming process, so much so I postponed elective prostate surgery.

In Washington, the Republican control of the Senate rested on a one-vote margin and the majority leadership was concerned about Republican senator Strom Thurmond's failing health (he was nearly a hundred years old). Had Thurmond passed away, Governor Jim Hodges of South Carolina—a Democrat—would have appointed his successor, shifting the Senate majority and putting Democrats in control of the Senate and its committees, including the Judiciary Committee. Republicans urged President Bush to move rapidly on his judicial nominees.

As it turned out, Strom Thurmond's health was not what really should have worried Republican leadership. After two months of secret meetings, courtship, and whispers, Vermont senator Jim Jeffords left the Republican Party, became an independent, and gave control of the Senate to the Democrats, surprising and stunning Republicans. He caucused with the Democrats to elect Senator Tom Daschle of South Dakota majority leader. The immediate impact on my nomination was shifting control and chair of the Senate Judiciary Committee from Republican senator Orrin Hatch of Utah to Democratic senator Patrick Leahy of Vermont.

President Bush submitted my nomination for a seat on the Fifth Circuit on May 25, 2001, the day after Senator Jeffords made his announcement. With more than a dozen previously named circuit court nominees pending, I assumed other hearings would come ahead of mine. In the meantime, I had plenty of district court work (in addition to preparing for my hearing) to keep me busy.

On Monday, June 4, some ten days after the president submitted my name to the Senate, a severe pain in my lower abdomen woke me in the morning. Instead of court, I went to the hospital. I had a severe case of diverticulitis (an inflamed and infected pocket in my colon). I required immediate and emergency surgery. I awoke with eighteen inches of my colon removed and in its place the most excruciating pain I had ever experienced. I had a temporary colostomy and required reconnective surgery in sixty to ninety days.

As I lay in the hospital, I thought about what was ahead—about facing the Senate Judiciary Committee. Being sixty-four years of age and facing two additional surgeries, I wondered if the committee would think I was not physically up to the job. (Had I known then what was in store for me, the Senate's perspective on my health would have been of lesser concern.) I asked my family physician to call my urologist to see if I could have my previously postponed prostate surgery the day after the hospital discharged me from the colon surgery; then I would be facing only one additional surgery. Dr. Randy Ross, remembering I had earlier postponed the surgery, joked, "Judge Pickering likes continuances." When he heard I wanted to recover from both surgeries at the same time, Dr. Ross again quipped, "So Judge Pickering wants concurrent sentences, not consecutive sentences." He was right.

Over the next few months, due to reconnective surgery and complications, I made numerous trips—some planned, some not—to the hospital. I recovered at home on the farm where my staff would bring me work in an attempt to help me keep up with my docket. On Labor Day weekend, an inflamed incision sent me back to the hospital once more. While recovering at home a few days later, I turned on the television news and watched as a plane crashed into the second of the Twin Towers at the World Trade Center, another into the Pentagon, and another into a field in Pennsylvania. I watched President Bush visit firefighters at Ground Zero; I observed the prayer service at the National Cathedral; and I grieved with the families in New York searching for their loved ones. Our nation mourned and prepared for a war against the forces of terror. Congress united against terrorism, but partisan fights would continue on judicial confirmations.

I lost thirty pounds due to my three surgeries, but I was feeling better and my doctors sent letters to the Judiciary Committee advising I had recovered, I was healthy, and I was physically capable of doing the job. I let Senators Lott and Cochran know I would be ready for a hearing anytime after September 15. By this time, special-interest groups had attacked some twelve or fifteen of the Bush nominees, but no opposition had surfaced to my nomination.

While serving on the board of directors for the Federal Judges Association, I developed a friendship with Judge Larry Piersol of South Dakota, a close friend (and former personal lawyer) of Senator Daschle.

He had inquired of Daschle's staff whether I had any problems or opposition and reported that I was not even on their radar screen. Another friend, Judge Fred Parker from the Second Circuit Court of Appeals, served with me on the Judicial Branch Committee of the Judicial Conference of the United States. He gave me a similar response from Senator Leahy's office, which confirmed a prior report I had received. I naively thought and told people I was a noncontroversial nominee. I was unaware of things going on beneath the radar screen. Things were about to change. Reality would soon confront my naivety.

With a Republican president and a Democratic Senate, judicial confirmations were moving at a snail's pace. Senator Lott, now minority leader, criticized Senator Leahy for the slow progress, referring to confirmation under Democratic control as a "black hole of inactivity."[1] Lott threatened to slow down legislation to call attention to the Democrats' inaction on judges.

In response, Senator Leahy scheduled a hearing on me and four district court nominees for October 18, 2001, moving me ahead of more than a dozen previously submitted nominees. On October 16, Leahy faxed me a request to furnish him a list of all cases in which I had rendered unpublished opinions as quickly as possible. My hearing was only two days away.

I advised Senator Leahy that during my ten years on the bench, I had decided between 4,000 and 4,500 cases and had rendered about 1,000 unpublished opinions. I told him I wanted to be responsive, but my staff did not have the technical capability to provide this information on such short notice. I suggested he share "any specific area or subject matter that [was] of specific interest" and I would provide all of the information in those areas I could obtain. Leahy revised his request and asked me to produce copies of all available unpublished opinions relative to civil rights in four specific areas: Title VII (race and gender), the Americans with Disabilities Act, the Age Discrimination Employment Act, and the Equal Pay Act.

I forwarded to Senator Leahy copies of all opinions we could reproduce that day. The next day while my wife and I were traveling to Washington, my staff furnished copies of the remaining requested

opinions. Many of the opinions were unsigned copies from our computers because the court had already forwarded the originals to archives in
Atlanta.

When we arrived at Baltimore-Washington International Airport on
the day before my hearing in the Hart Senate Office Building, I learned
Senator Daschle's office had opened a letter laced with anthrax. Security
sealed the entire Hart facility, and it was unclear whether the hearing
would go forward.

Another bit of information was troubling as well. The previous day,
People for the American Way, Alliance for Justice, and other Far Left
groups had sent out an e-mail attacking my nomination. I had
wondered why Senator Leahy was requesting a list of my unpublished
opinions, but I was still surprised at this opposition. Regardless, I did
not think my nomination was in trouble. After all, I had been unanimously confirmed by the Senate ten years previously, and I now had the
ABA's highest rating, which I did not have at the time of my previous
confirmation. The Democrats had proclaimed the ABA an "impartial"
evaluator: its recommendation the "gold standard." But I failed to
comprehend how partisan politics had escalated during my decade on
the bench. I failed to understand the stranglehold Far Left secularist
groups held over the Democrats in the Senate, especially those on the
Judiciary Committee. I soon discovered just how nasty politics can be.

I traveled to the Department of Justice (DoJ) and met with White
House and DoJ officials assigned to work with President Bush's judicial
nominees. Four nominees to federal district courts scheduled for the
same hearing were also present: Christina Armijo of New Mexico, Karon
Bowdre of Alabama, Stephen Friot of Oklahoma, and Larry Hicks of
Nevada. We discussed the process and types of questions expected. I left
DoJ and went to visit Chip in the Cannon House office building.

The Third District of Mississippi had elected Chip to Congress
three times: in 1996, 1998 and 2000.[2] As the underdog, he won a hotly
contested Republican Primary effectively securing his first election in
1996. Voters handily reelected him the next two times. However, the
2000 census reflected a Mississippi that had failed to grow in population
as much as other states and so would lose a congressional seat. For the

2002 election, Mississippi would have only four congressional seats but five incumbent congressmen; someone was going to lose.

Politicos and newspaper pundits prognosticated that legislators would combine Chip's Third District with the Fourth District represented by Ronnie Shows, a folksy, popular, "good old boy" Democrat. Ronnie won his first election to Congress in 1998. Voters had previously elected him circuit clerk in his home county, state senator from a five-county district, and highway commissioner for the Southern District of Mississippi. In thirty years of politics, he had never lost an election. Everyone anticipated a tough campaign.

Conventional wisdom held that Chip would prevail with a merged district drawn compactly to represent communities of interest (consistent with controlling federal case law). Legislators would have to gerrymander the district for Ronnie to have an advantage. The Mississippi legislature—under Democratic control since Reconstruction—was redrawing the lines. Chip had spoken to the Senate's presiding officer, Lieutenant Governor Amy Tuck, and Speaker of the House Tim Ford; both were Democrats.[3] They had agreed on a compromise plan, and Chip felt he could live with it. But when I arrived at Chip's office, I learned Tim Ford had told him the legislative compromise on redistricting had collapsed. Chip was facing a legislative battle over redistricting; a badly gerrymandered district could end his political career. The stakes for Chip were high. Moreover, I had just learned my nomination had drawn opposition. We both had our problems. Later, we would see these political battles merge in the form of a proffered Democratic deal.

It was not until ten o'clock that night that I learned for sure the hearing would go forward the next day. Rather than taking place in a large hearing room in the Hart Senate Office Building as originally scheduled, the Senate Judiciary Committee scheduled the hearing in a small but more ornate room, rich with history: the Senate Appropriations room inside the U.S. Capitol.

Confirmation hearings before the Senate Judiciary Committee for district and appellate judges normally attract only one or two committee members from each party. Home state senators usually appear and make statements on behalf of the nominee from their state. When I arrived for the hearing, I was surprised to see on the Democratic side not only Chairman Leahy, but also Senators Ted Kennedy of Massachusetts, Chuck Schumer from New York, and Dick Durbin from Illinois—all "blue state" senators. Senator Mike DeWine from Ohio represented the Republicans. Both Senator Lott and Senator Cochran testified on my behalf, and since Chip is a member of Congress, he took the opportunity to speak in support of my nomination as well.

My wife Margaret Ann, along with Chip's wife Leisha and their five boys, were there to support me. The other nominees also had family members present, and the room was crowded and cramped for space. The Democratic committee staff welcomed a group of observers and provided them with prime seating and coffee. I wondered why the families were not so welcomed. Later I learned those VIPs were actually members of the Far Left special-interest groups: my opposition and the masters of the Democrats on the committee.

After supportive statements for all of the nominees by home state senators, Democratic senators began asking pointed but polite questions. The senators directed the questions first to me, then the other nominees. Senator Schumer said he believed philosophy was an appropriate matter for consideration in the confirmation of judges, and everything should be out in the open. He said it was wrong to play "gotcha" politics. (Regardless of that statement, there would be plenty of "gotcha" politics played hardball; Schumer was one of the most active players.) Unfortunately, this was not to be my last hearing. John Nowacki, deputy director of the Free Congress Foundation's Judicial Selection Monitoring Project, recounted,

> Senator Charles Schumer took the unusual step of announcing that there would be a second nomination hearing for Judge Pickering. Second hearings are usually reserved for extremely controversial nominees whose answers at their initial hearing raise more questions. In Pickering's case, Senate Democrats and left-wing groups knew they would want a second shot at attacking the nominee, since they couldn't come up with any credible charges against him the first time around.[4]

Before I left the hearing, the Democratic senators and their staff requested I provide copies of unpublished opinions in additional areas: abortion, Voting Rights Act, Fair Housing Act, labor relations, Section 1983 (deprivation of rights under color of law), habeas corpus, equal protection, Prison Litigation Reform Act, and Anti-Terrorism Effective Death Penalty Act, as well as copies of cases where the Fifth Circuit had reversed me. The next day, I furnished copies of all the opinions in these subject areas that were in my chambers.

As soon as I responded to that request, Senator Leahy further requested copies of my unpublished opinions relative to violence against women, Fourth Amendment, and Eleventh Amendment cases. I again responded, providing copies of those cases. The next day I wrote Leahy and told him I had produced copies of all unpublished opinions in the subject areas requested that were available in my chambers. I noted the Fifth Circuit had reversed me only 25 times out of more than 4,000 cases[5] and told him I was "extremely proud of my record, including the high rate of affirmance."

A little more than three weeks after my initial hearing, Sheila Joy (my liaison at DoJ) called from the Justice Department to say the Democrats now wanted all of my unpublished opinions, not just those in the previously specified subject areas. They also asked for a list of all the criminal cases that had come before me including a list of all defendants. (I am still not sure why they wanted a list of the criminal defendants, unless they wanted to contact them to see if they were satisfied I sent them to the penitentiary. That answer should be obvious.) Sheila Joy told me to start copying the opinions, but not to send them until we received the formal faxed request from Senator Leahy. I had the opinions copied; no fax came.

Senator Trent Lott called on Monday, November 26, the first day back at work after Thanksgiving. Trent had worked closely with Senator Schumer on a bill to help New York City after 9/11, and before the Thanksgiving recess he had asked Schumer to help with my confirmation. The New York senator ran the traps and told Trent the Democratic staff on the committee had requested copies of material from me that I had not furnished. Schumer told him that if the Democrats had not made such a big deal over requesting the opinions, it would not have been necessary for me to provide them. Schumer said that once I provided them, he would help secure my confirmation before Christmas. Trent asked why I had not already sent the material, and I told him we had been awaiting a request from Senator Leahy, but that I would go ahead and send the material immediately.

As soon as I got off the phone with Trent, I sent the material to the committee by express mail. Later that same day, I received through the mail a hard copy of the letter from Senator Leahy dated some two weeks earlier. I thought it odd that this was the only time the committee did not deliver a request by fax. Afterward I learned, through leaked Democratic memorandums, that the purpose was delay. The special-interest groups wanted a second hearing, and they wanted it further removed from the unifying spirit that followed the September 11 attacks. For them, 2002 would be a better vintage for pure partisan politics.

A few days later, Chip saw Senator Schumer in the Capitol's House Dining Room having lunch with Congressman Tom Reynolds, a Republican from New York. Reynolds called Chip over to his table to chat, and Schumer told Chip he would help get me confirmed. He said he hoped it would not be necessary for me to come back for a second hearing, but if so, he would preside over the hearing and take care of me. When I heard this, I thought my confirmation was about to take place. But at that time, I had not yet learned that it was not Schumer or the other senators calling the shots. The Far Left secularist groups were the ones really in charge. Any good intentions Senator Schumer may have had could not escape the pressure of his Far Left base.

On December 6, the Far Left special-interest groups opposing me promised in a strategy conference call they could defeat me but it would be "nasty and contentious."[6] I thought they were bragging. They were not. I soon learned these organizations, not the elected senators, decided the course of action in the confirmation process.

There was a time when senators made the decisions on whom to support and whom to oppose, and they would call the special-interest groups to endorse those decisions before the public. The process had reversed. Now the special-interest groups made the decisions and used campaign contributions, grassroots activism, and political media savvy to keep the senators in line. These organizations, these culture warriors, determined who would be filibustered and who would receive a pass. The special-interest groups gave the orders; the Democratic senators voted and acted accordingly.

The left-wing special-interest groups leveled racial charges at my life and reputation, and although my supporters refuted them, I could see my nomination was going to get messy; but I never expected the fight that would develop over the coming years. The feminist groups and Senator Ted Kennedy increased their attacks against me due to abortion politics. It would not be a peaceful Christmas.

Later in December, the special-interest groups complained that Senator Trent Lott was putting unbelievable pressure on the Democratic leadership. Trent's only pressure was reminding the Democratic leadership that when one party leader told the other party leader a matter was personal to him, traditionally they had worked the issue out. My nomination, Trent advised the Democrats, was personal to him and he wanted to work with them to move my confirmation forward. They refused, perhaps reluctantly, but still they refused.

Senator Lott was always supportive of my nomination and he went to great efforts to secure my confirmation. However, I could tell his biggest disappointment was the rebuff from the Democratic Senate leadership with whom he had worked for years. They had turned him down flat. The kind of working relationship essential to the smooth operation of the Senate was deteriorating, another victim of the confirmation battles. While Trent was working Senate tradition, the special-interest groups held captive his Democratic colleagues. This paradigm shift eroded relationships, transformed debate into hyperbolic rhetoric, and escalated the downward spiral of lost comity, collegiality, and civility in the Senate.

In Senate Democratic press releases and statements, in newspapers articles and editorials, and in interest group action alerts and e-mails, my nomination grew in controversy and the rhetoric intensified in rancor. During the few months between my October hearing and my second

N O M I N A T E D : 2 0 0 1 | 13

hearing scheduled for February, the Bush Administration and I realized the assault on me was the test case, model, and rehearsal for future left-wing attacks on other nominees, and for potential Supreme Court candidates.

From time to time fellow judges would call and tell me that staff of opposition senators appeared embarrassed over obstructing my confirmation and regretted the attack but did not know how to retreat from the confrontation. The special-interest groups had backed the Democrats into a corner, and though some knew the opposition was not right, they could find no political escape.

On one occasion, I was having lunch in Washington with judges on the Judicial Branch Committee and the staff of Senate Judiciary Committee members when an aide to Senator Durbin—one of my most vocal opponents—approached, spoke, and gave me his card. He told me if he could ever be of any help to give him a call. The exchange struck me as odd. Sometimes even in politics, there are pangs of conscience.

At home, I enjoyed widespread support from Mississippi Democrats, some of whom had contact with senators opposing me. They would repeatedly report with messages to this effect: "Tell Judge Pickering not to worry, this is not about him." Maybe it was not about me. Maybe I was just a vehicle for the special-interest groups to send a message to President Bush regarding Supreme Court nominees, but it was my nomination they were rejecting and my reputation they were trashing.

The days slowly passed and it was Christmas 2001, almost a year since that Louisiana hunting trip when I learned my name was going to the White House for a Fifth Circuit nomination. Politics may stop or stall, but life moves on. My only brother Gene and I were sitting with our mother, now in the final stages of Alzheimer's. My father had died before my appointment, but I was pleased my mother was able to attend my investiture as a district judge. Gene and I were spending our final evening with her. At four o'clock the next morning, she quietly passed away.

A little after four-thirty that afternoon, Senator Leahy faxed my office noting I had forwarded approximately 600 copies of unpublished opinions, but he wanted those remaining of my estimated rendering of about 1,000. Leahy wrote,

> Please indicate whether or not any additional unpublished opinions, copies of which you have not been [sic] produced, exist in any form, including in paper files, in other court files, in archives, in clerk's files or elsewhere. . . .We appreciate your help in tracking down these several hundred missing opinions.

Senator Leahy had no way of knowing that his request came to me in a time a grief, but it couldn't have escaped his attention that his office sent it to me Friday afternoon, twenty minutes before the Christmas holiday was to begin. Likely, it was one of the last things his staff did in Washington before leaving on their own vacations. While the senators and their staff were taking a break, my staff and I would be working to meet their requests.

It became increasingly difficult for me to respond to all of the requests by the Democratic senators and keep up with my judicial duties. I'm sure the same is true of other judges who go through this process. Nevertheless, that was of no concern to the Democratic senators. They were on a political mission. The ends justified the means. And Democrats on the committee seemed to welcome the opportunity to accommodate the special-interest groups, to the inconvenience of nominees like myself.

(Some may say that I am overly critical of Democratic senators and that Republicans in the past have acted improperly as well. I believe these tactics are unfair and harmful to the process, whether committed by Democrats or by Republicans. It just so happens that the experiences I am writing about came at the hands of Democratic senators.)

In a court proceeding, discovery that is "unduly burdensome, harassing, or vexatious" can be quashed with the offending parties subject to sanctions. The sheer magnitude of requesting all unpublished opinions with so little basis for the request was unduly burdensome and harassing, and had the Democrats been before a conscientious judge in a court proceeding, they would have been sanctioned for discovery abuse.

During his first year in office, President George W. Bush nominated "sixty-four District and Circuit Court judges." By year's end, the Senate had confirmed twenty-one. That is a 33 percent confirmation rate compared to the 57 percent first-year rate for President Bill Clinton, 63 percent for Mr. Bush's father, and 91 percent for President Ronald Reagan.[7]

I was among the 67 percent of unconfirmed nominees in President Bush's first year. Despite Senator Schumer's promise, Christmas had come and gone; I was not confirmed. Nevertheless, I remained optimistic. I still thought the Senate would confirm me. But in just a few days, everything in my life would be put under a microscope. The left-wing special-interest groups would use stereotypes and innuendo to mischaracterize my record and ignore the life I had lived, a record and life in which I take pride.

Long before there was a culture war in America, there was another struggle that would shape Southern and national politics for decades. It was a battle for equal rights, justice, and the rule of law. It was a fight against oppression, inequality, and racial demagoguery. I lived through that struggle and it was during that time that I had to choose sides.

Choosing Sides: 1960s

I CAME OF age during the 1950s in segregated Mississippi, and for that matter in a nation largely segregated. The South was in denial—both in conscience and in reality—regarding matters of racial equality.

My parents married during the 1920s and purchased a small twenty-seven-acre farm. In 1937, I was born in the Hebron Community of western Jones County near the Leaf River. This was during the turbulent financial times of the Great Depression when many farmers lost their homes and farms. As our nation entered World War II, unable to pay the mortgage on our farm, my dad bought a dump truck. He used this truck to help build Camp Shelby near Hattiesburg, Mississippi, and the arsenal at Milan, Tennessee. My parents used the income from that dump truck to save the farm. My dad taught me when life is hard, work harder.

I grew up plowing, chopping, and picking cotton; breaking corn; cutting turnip greens; planting and digging sweet potatoes; and milking cows. I followed two mules—Kate and Ada—pulling a one-row cultivator. When I was fourteen, I traded the cultivator for a milking stool as we converted from row cropping to dairying. My dad bought more land and expanded the farm.

Like many folks in those days, my parents did not have much formal education. My father finished the ninth grade and my mother the eighth, but they continued to seek knowledge their whole lives and gained wisdom by experience. They were committed to education and made sure their children had the opportunity for schooling. My dad served as a trustee for the three-room school where I graduated from the eighth grade in 1951.

In addition to the school, my dad was also a leader in our church where he served as a deacon and Sunday school teacher. He served as scout master, trustee for the community cemetery, and was active in farm groups.

My mother was a gracious hostess and the best cook in the community. Everyone who ate with us talked about her yeast rolls, and my wife and daughters still use her recipe. Strangers were welcomed to her table and we frequently had preachers and schoolteachers in our home for meals. As long as Mother was able, my siblings and our families looked forward to occasions when we could gather around her table and enjoy food and fellowship.

My parents encouraged me to be all I could in the community, church, and beyond. They fully supported my involvement in 4-H, a civic, education, and training program sponsored by the Cooperative Extension Service of the Department of Agriculture. 4-H (Head, Heart, Hands, and Health) was more than agricultural education; it promoted national and international ideas and experiences and encouraged community and public service. I was elected state 4-H president, won the state 4-H public speaking contest, and was selected as national 4-H leadership winner. I joined five other 4-H-ers from across our country to present the 4-H *Report to the Nation* to President Dwight D. Eisenhower.

My son Chip meets with 4-H groups from Mississippi when they visit Washington D.C. He tells them that were it not for 4-H, he likely would not be a congressman today because his passion for public service followed mine, and my first taste of politics came from 4-H. It was quite a big deal for me as a young man to meet the soldier, general, statesman, and president—to meet Ike. But the commitment to public service that 4-H nurtured had been planted by my parents.

My father and mother demanded a strong work ethic, a commitment to faith and family, and a respect for my fellow man—regardless of race. I still remember my father's strong feelings that our black neighbors should be able to vote and his hope that one day they could. My parents provided me with guidance that produced a strong faith and instilled in me a keen sense of right and wrong.

There was never a question as to whether I would get a college education. My parents expected it. The thought that I might not go to college never entered my mind, even though there were no government grants or loans and few scholarships during those years. I had a good record and excellent grades, but a transferee from junior college was not eligible for the scarce scholarships available.

I went to high school at Jones County Agricultural High School and spent my first two years of college at Jones County Junior College (JCJC), both in Ellisville, Mississippi. During my senior year in high school and two years in junior college, I drove a school bus making $35 a month—money that paid for my first two years of higher education.

My high school principal was W. C. Thomas, and he had a daughter named Margaret Ann who treated everyone with respect, whether from town or the rural areas, and regardless of station in life. She had grace and caught my attention; I knew I could find no more supportive and loving wife or a better mother for my children. The best day of my life was on June 19, 1959, when I married Margaret Ann. She has always been a truly compassionate, supportive, and unselfish partner.

A college football trip to the Junior Rose Bowl in Pasadena, California, illustrates the culture of the times in which Margaret Ann and I grew up. In 1955, she was a cheerleader at JCJC where we were both freshmen. The JCJC Bobcats were the undefeated state football champions that year and had been invited to play the Compton California Junior College football team in the 10th Anniversary Junior Rose Bowl. There was one hitch: the Compton team was integrated and this would be the first time any public college in Mississippi would field an athletic team against an integrated team. Detractors from across the state leveled an avalanche of criticism against JCJC for accepting the invitation. But the administration of JCJC stood firm. Some of the parents would not let their children go, and as a result, the head cheerleader stayed home. Margaret Ann's parents had no such reservations. Margaret Ann traveled to Pasadena—a long way from home in 1955— and was head cheerleader for the game before a crowd of more than

57,000. That does not seem like much today, but it was a small step forward for Mississippi in the struggle to improve race relations and promote equal opportunities, and it was a number of years before the civil rights movement began in earnest.

During the summers of 1957 and 1958, I worked in the offshore oilfields of south Louisiana to help pay for my last two years of undergraduate schooling at the University of Mississippi—Ole Miss. My senior year in undergraduate school doubled as my first year in law school.

After we married, Margaret Ann taught school and I delivered newspapers, took a job in construction, and worked for men's housing to cover expenses of my additional two years of law school, also at Ole Miss. We did not have much, but we were happy, and we still are.

My parents supplemented my earnings and made sacrifices for my education, not the least of which was furnishing Margaret Ann and me, each year, a freezer full of vegetables and meat. I will always be grateful for their sacrifice, encouragement, and support. Most of all, I appreciate the positive outlook on life they fostered and the faith in God, confidence in myself, and respect for others they instilled in me.

In 1961, after graduating from law school, I hung out my shingle and started practicing law in Laurel, Mississippi, a picturesque Southern community. Great live oaks, cultivated like a painting in an artist's rendition of small-town America, shaded residential streets. These oaks stood firm and tall, a symbol of strength for generations until Hurricane Katrina's 110-mile-per-hour winds ripped through the area in 2005—more than 100 miles north of the Mississippi Gulf Coast.

Laurel is one of two county seats of Jones County, the other being Ellisville. Several counties in Mississippi have dual county seats, a civic anomaly remaining from times when inclement weather or poor roads could prevent citizens from easily reaching their local seat of government, or because of rivalry between competing towns.

Jones County took its name from John Paul Jones, the Revolutionary War hero often quoted as saying, "I have not yet begun to fight." From the time of the Civil War until the present, people have known Jones County by the moniker "Free State of Jones." The name is based on the story that this predominantly non-slaveholding county "seceded" from the Confederacy to form its own separate country. There is little evidence to support formal secession, but a number of Rebel deserters and Union sympathizers led by Newton Knight did fight Confederate soldiers in the Piney Woods of Jones County. These men owned no slaves and had little stomach for the war.

Today, most Jones Countians dismiss Newt Knight's army as simply a band of deserters, and most were, but a number were without question loyal to the Union. Historical records reveal that state and Confederate authorities viewed Jones County as a place where a lawless element exercised considerable power and control. Margaret Ann and I now live on the back forty of the old home place where I grew up within a half mile of where deserters were hanged by Confederate forces. Newt Knight's band had a hideout between old oxbow-cypress lakes in the swamps of the Leaf River that borders my farm. People still call that area "Deserters Den."

After the war, Confederate sympathizers in the Mississippi legislature changed the county name to "Davis County" for Jefferson Davis and the county seat of Ellisville to "Leesburg" for Robert E. Lee. The names were changed back during Reconstruction.[1]

Jones County saw acute division during the Civil War, and the same would be true during the civil rights movement a century later. Jones Countians have always had a spirited streak of independence and some tendency to resist authority. Some channeled this maverick spirit for good, others for bad.

Forty years ago, Jones County was a far different world from today. Whites and blacks lived in a culture of segregation drifting slowly toward integration partially through a natural progression, but mostly due to the actions of brave men and women. Cowards in white sheets terrorized, fire bombed, and murdered people simply for wanting to exercise rights enjoyed by their fellow Americans. White Mississippians made choices: most did not engage and remained silent; some became Klan sympathizers; others stood against the Klan.

The year of 1963 changed lives around the nation as well as in the Pickering family in Jones County. In April, Birmingham police arrested and jailed Martin Luther King Jr.; the following month in Birmingham, Alabama commissioner of public safety Eugene "Bull" Connor used firehoses and police dogs on black demonstrators: images broadcast around the world. In June, Byron de la Beckwith assassinated Mississippi NAACP field secretary Medgar Evers outside his home in Jackson. Two months later in August, King delivered his "I have a dream" speech in Washington D.C., and just fewer than three weeks later, four young black girls were killed while at Sunday school when the Sixteenth Street Baptist Church was bombed in Birmingham. In the midst of these momentous events in the civil rights struggle, we saw increasing Ku Klux Klan violence and intimidation in Laurel and Jones County. I won election for prosecuting attorney of Jones County in November of that year at the age of twenty-six; I served until 1968.

Before the civil rights movement, the Klan had dwindled in numbers and strength. During the civil rights movement, the Ku Klux Klan made a dramatic and violent comeback. The strength of and fear from this violent minority flowed from their radical ferociousness: a terrorism of hate. The Klan did not respect African Americans and their white supporters as ordinary human beings; they viewed blacks and anti-Kluckers as a subspecies.

The Klansmen were in a minority, but a larger number of sympathizers increased their power. The vast majority of white Mississippians were opposed to the violence of the Ku Klux Klan. However, most remained silent, some feeling it was not their fight, others out of fear or indifference.

During this time in Mississippi—and across the South—the question of statewide political leaders was not who supported segregation and who did not, because all viable candidates supported segregation. The question was who reluctantly supported segregation out of political necessity and who was a racial demagogue.

From Reconstruction until the closing 1960s, no candidate in Mississippi was elected to statewide office who did not pledge to support segregation. That was true throughout the South and included progressive political leaders like Senator William J. Fulbright of Arkansas; Senator John Stennis; Governors J. P. Coleman and William Winter;

and Lieutenant Governor Carroll Gartin—all of Mississippi; and likewise Georgia governor—later president of the United States—Jimmy Carter.

The overriding theme in any governor's race in Mississippi during the late 1950s and the 1960s centered on who was the staunchest segregationist. Progressive candidates like J. P. Coleman, Carroll Gartin, and William Winter—although pledged to support segregation—were defeated by more vocal segregationist candidates. Governor Winter and President Carter would later express their deep regrets for having campaigned as segregationist candidates, but at the time their choices were to run on a platform of moderate segregation and work within the system for progress, or they could have stayed out of politics. They would not have been viable candidates if they had not supported segregation. Both Governor Winter and President Carter became strong advocates for equal rights and racial reconciliation, and they remain important voices in this movement still today.

Mississippi did not elect a governor when race or segregation was not the main issue until 1971, when African Americans started voting in significant numbers and changed the political landscape of the South. But during the 1960s, blacks did not have voting strength, and those dedicated to maintaining segregation cast their interests aside. As the movement for civil rights pressed forward, the Ku Klux Klan pushed back with increased intimidation and violence.

My first year in public office saw numerous civil rights efforts, including large numbers of students and activists coming to Mississippi for Freedom Summer: an attempt to register blacks to vote and to integrate bus stations and lunch counters. Throughout the South, those committed to maintaining segregation at all costs met these activists known as Freedom Riders with fierce and violent opposition. Jones County was no exception. Violence erupted and segregationists attacked and beat Freedom Riders.

That summer, the nation's eyes turned to Philadelphia, Neshoba County, Mississippi, when three civil rights workers disppeared; they were eventually found murdered and buried in an earthen dam. The order for the murders originated in Jones County from the Imperial

Wizard of the White Knights of the Ku Klux Klan, a man named Sam Bowers. Bowers was "suspected in the orchestration of three hundred bombings, assaults, and arsons."[2]

ABC's *Nightline* reported,

> The regular Ku Klux Klan was not extreme enough for [Bowers's] purposes. He led a breakaway group called the White Knights, with . . . himself as their Imperial Wizard. Burnings, bombings, and beatings, they were all attributed to the White Knights. So were murders. The FBI blamed them for ten killings in Mississippi in the 1960s.[3]

Time Magazine noted, "Klan experts describe 'Sam Bowers' as the most dangerous man ever to don a white hood."[4] Leonard Zeskind, research director for the Atlanta-based Center for Democratic Renewal, told the Baton Rouge *Advocate* that Bowers is "considered by all authorities as America's most violent living racist . . . . He presided over what the FBI has called the most vicious reign of terror during the Civil Rights era." Jerry Himelstein, regional director for the Anti-Defamation League of B'Nai B'rith, told the *Advocate* that Bowers "led an organization that once boasted ten thousand members."[5] Bowers's White Knights of the Ku Klux Klan were headquartered in my hometown of Laurel. This Klan group was the most vicious of all the Klan cells.

As prosecuting attorney during this period, I saw in my own community the results of unchecked racial animosity. I saw the face of raw hatred as zealots determined to preserve segregation by force and violence wielded blackjacks and baseball bats against young blacks as they attempted to integrate lunch counters. They burned, bombed, and shot into homes and churches to intimidate, threaten, and injure those who dared to work for equality. District Attorney W. O. Dillard recalled, "Klansmen were 'throwing sticks of dynamite like they were firecrackers.'"[6]

Ku Klux Klan violence escalated and I faced three choices: (1) stand against the Klan and its violence and stand up for the rule of law; (2) side with the vocal and violent minority to oppress the rights of African Americans; or (3) do as many did, remain silent and do nothing. This was a life decision, a moral crossroads, a choice that would determine who I was. I had to choose sides. I took a stand against the Ku Klux Klan and its violence. I really didn't consider any other option. It was the right thing to do; it was what my faith told me I ought to do; it was what my parents had taught me to do. But at that time in our history, it was not the easy thing to do.

The district attorney and I filed criminal charges and took Klansmen to court, but evidence and convictions were hard to come by when most juries included one or two Klan members or sympathizers, and Klan intimidation reached into the jury room and into the homes of jurors.

Local, state, and federal law enforcement officers organized to fight these white-sheeted terrorists of the night. I still clearly remember riding to Jackson late at night with Chief Deputy Sheriff R. W. McMinn to deliver a Klan suspect to the Mississippi Highway Patrol to administer a lie detector test. On other occasions, McMinn and I rode south on Highway 59 for meetings at the University of Southern Mississippi in Hattiesburg to coordinate with fifty or more law enforcement officers— about half of whom were federal, a good number who were state, and the rest local law enforcement officers who could be trusted—in efforts to break the back of the Ku Klux Klan. Some local officers were in the Klan or were Klan sympathizers; a majority was not. Some tried to avoid the issue, but most local officers took their oaths of office seriously and joined in our resistance against the Klan.

This struggle reached into our communities and our friendships. One Saturday morning a friend and I were fishing in a boat on my farm pond. I had been concerned to see him hanging out with Klan members and sympathizers. He arranged to fish with me on this particular morning so he could tell me he had infiltrated the Klan as an FBI informant. He told me of attending Klan meetings and hearing Klan leaders whip their members into frenzy as they crossed a pistol and a sword on top of an open Bible. They would exhort their fellow Klansmen to protect the rights of "white Christian Americans" and to burn "N" houses. He told me of coming by my house late at night to make sure the Klan zealots did not try to burn down my home while my family slept. I was pleased to learn my friend had not taken the road of hate, but now I was concerned for his safety. He told me someone had to stop the Klan. He endangered his own life to help bring down the Klan, and I had great respect for what he was doing and prayed that God would guard his life.

During our fight against the Klan, I earned the confidence of the FBI and worked closely with Agent Bob Lee. One day, Bob came to my office and warned me to be careful as I exited my law offices through the adjacent alley—especially at night. He had learned the Klan had issued a "Number 2" on me, which meant they had authorized a plan for members to attack and physically assault me. I had previously prosecuted a Klansman for beating a local businessman with a chain made into a blackjack as the businessman was walking out of the back of his store. So I knew the Klan was capable of such a crime. Fortunately for my family and me, the Klan never carried out its plan to attack me. I made it through this time of terror without an attack against me or my family. Many African Americans and civil rights workers were not so fortunate.

Bob Lee was a reliable source of intelligence against the Klan. He provided a list of all the Klan atrocities committed in Jones County— numbering in excess of 100—which I used to draft a statement condemning Klan violence. District Attorney W. O. "Chet" Dillard and I persuaded Laurel's mayor, chief of police, and the sheriff of Jones County to join us in condemning Klan violence. Law enforcement had seriously deteriorated. Like those days of the Free State of Jones, we were again approaching a point of lawlessness in our county. We asked fellow citizens to sign petitions supporting "law and order" and opposing Klan violence. We needed people to take a stand against the Klan atrocities and stand up for the rule of law to restore order in our county. Some constituents ridiculed the idea of signing a petition, stating they were for law and order; but that was just their way to avoid taking a stand.

Dillard would later recount these times in his book *Clear Burning*:

> Shortly after I was elected, I was contacted by an elected official about whether I would be interested in joining the Klan. He said I could be assured of winning every case in court, both civil and criminal, to come before a jury . . . also the Klan could keep me in office through

their control of politics. They did have a stronghold in Jones County .
. . and the Imperial Wizard of the White Knights, Samuel Bowers, was
seen at most political events.

I chose not to accept the offer, rather to do my duty as best I
could, but I'm sure that the FBI, through resident agent Robert Lee,
felt like I was at least a Klan sympathizer because all of the contacts
with the Bureau were arms-length transactions. Any message from
them to me would come through a third party source, generally the
county attorney, Charles Pickering. Charles was a long-standing Jones
Countian with deep roots in the Hebron community, and Bob Lee
had known him for many years before I arrived in Laurel . . . .

The relationship between Charles and me was somewhat strained
at first because of the situation in which it appeared the federal people
had more confidence in his loyalty to the law enforcement cause while
the state forces seemed to place more confidence in me . . . . Yet, it
would not take long before we realized we both would have to join
forces because, with the evil elements of criminal activity, Klan,
strikes, and politics, it would be necessary that we sink or swim
together . . . .[7]

One night I was over at Chet's home working on a case related to a
Klan murder. A Klansman called my home and told my wife he had
some information, but he only wanted to share it with one person. She
told him to call me at Chet's house. When he called, Chet answered the
phone and the Klansman talked to him instead. He wanted to meet the
district attorney in a parking lot next to a funeral home.

Chet was concerned it might be a Klan setup and said later he "was
deathly afraid." I agreed to cover him. I went to the home of a law
enforcement officer and borrowed a pistol. Back then, funeral homes
stayed open all night so friends and family could sit with their deceased
loved ones. I slipped through the back entrance, went into the funeral
home chapel, and peered through the window with gun at ready. The
Klansman drove up. He turned off his car, stepped out, looked around,
and got into Chet's car. They drove off into the night where the reform-
ing Klansman shared his secrets with local law enforcement. Relieved it
was not a setup, I carried the firearm back to its owner and drove home.
This was not an action movie and, though proficient with a shotgun, I

was not as confident with a pistol. Had things gone awry, I am not sure who would have been in the greatest danger: the Klansman, Chet, or me.

I recently attended a ceremony unveiling Chet's portrait in the chancery courtroom where he presided over cases before retiring as a state chancery judge. Chet made remarks about this chilling period in our lives. He spoke of an FBI agent warning that a Klan member had threatened to kill him. Chet shared how he used to put tape on the hood of his car so he could tell if anyone had placed a bomb under the hood. This is the kind of story one would expect to see unfold in a movie about the Mafia, but not in Laurel, Mississippi.

Chet reminded me of a Ku Klux Klan member who asked to meet with us in the parking lot at the First Baptist Church where my family and I worshipped. In the shade of our church building, this Klan member told us he made a mistake joining the Klan, that he disagreed with what they were doing, and he wanted out. He wanted to meet with Chet and me because he wanted protection; he was afraid that if he quit, the Klan would kill him. Now, more than a generation later, many find it hard to imagine that kind of fear, but it was all too real back then.

We encountered daily the Klan's violence and terror against black Mississippians and their white allies, violence that in several instances turned to murder. There is no way you can vividly recreate the atmosphere of those years for individuals who did not live though those days or who lived through those days in a safer place. It is difficult for one generation to sit in judgment of what another generation did or did not do. Can we criticize the black father who swallowed his pride and bowed his head so as not to call the terror of the Klan onto his family? Can we criticize the white father who chose neither to support nor to fight the Klan because he didn't want their violence in his living room?

Those were dark days. But they were overcome with the help of brave young men and women who came to assist African Americans in asserting their rights. Federal law enforcement officials came in force, and were essential; but they would not have succeeded without the support of local law enforcement officers willing to take a stand. More importantly, change would not have happened without brave African

Americans who lived in Mississippi and who, like our patriot founders in 1776, risked everything to win their right to vote and to achieve equal rights.

One of these courageous Mississippians was Vernon Dahmer, a farmer in Forrest County, a county adjacent to Jones County. He encouraged his friends and neighbors to vote. He allowed black people to pay poll taxes in his grocery store. Just like terrorists in the Middle East today, the Klan killed him for asserting his rights as an American citizen.

On the night of January 10, 1966, Vernon Dahmer's wife and children awoke to an inferno, their house filled with smoke and fire engulfing their modest home. Vernon was defending his family, shooting from his front door and window at the Klansmen who had firebombed his home. While keeping the Klan at bay, he handed his children one by one to his wife through a back window. They fled into the woods. The smoke and fumes scorched Vernon's lungs, killing him the next day at the same hospital where his ten-year-old daughter Bettie was being treated for severe burns.

Years later, Bettie recounted her story to Voices of Civil Rights:

> The people who killed my father could have done so anytime, just like they did Medgar Evers, because he was a working man. My father was out cutting timber, buying a cow, running a farm, and doing all kinds of work on top of civil rights. I had a hard time coming to grips with the fact that these people were trying to kill a whole family like us to send a message.[8]

The fanatical person who ordered this murder was also Sam Bowers.

While defending his family, Vernon Dahmer shot out a tire on one of the Klan vehicles. Law enforcement officials quickly found the abandoned vehicle and traced it to the culprits. Jimmy Finch and Jim Dukes, prosecutors for Forrest County, brought Sam Bowers to trial for the death of Vernon Dahmer. They called and asked if I would testify that Sam Bowers had a bad reputation for violence. I told them I would. Under well-established legal precedents, my testimony could only be to the point and brief. The prosecutors asked if I knew Sam Bowers's reputation for "peace and violence" in the community in which he lived. I testified that I did. They asked me if it was good or bad. I testified that Sam Bowers's reputation for "peace and violence" was bad. That was all to which I could legally testify and the prosecutors asked me nothing further.

The Klan's power was still strong and people were afraid to stand against them. The trial ended in a hung jury—no decision. Sam Bowers walked free for the fire bombing death of Vernon Dahmer in the late 1960s, but changes were coming, and Sam Bowers, many years later, would again face the consequences of his wicked deed.

In 1967, the Klan distributed a newsletter in Jones County titled "The Citizen-Patriot" proclaiming it was dedicated to "the truth of the Christian civilization." The newsletter condemned District Attorney Chet Dillard and me for cooperating with the FBI. The rag sheet read,

> The honest citizens of Jones County have recently been defrauded by certain officials . . . of the form and letter of legality by the clever manipulations of Chet Dillard and Charles Pickering . . . [U]nderstandably, weaklings such as Dillard and Pickering are afraid of the FBI, we respectively invite the loyal citizens of Jones County to return to the polls on August, 8, 1967, and have then and there this Writ.

Chet Dillard was defeated for reelection in that August 8 primary, and I was defeated in the November general election while running for the state House of Representatives.

That same year, Sam Bowers was convicted in federal court for violating the civil rights of Andrew Goodman, Michael Schwerner, and James Chaney, the three civil rights workers who were murdered in Neshoba County. In 1967, he received a ten-year sentence at the federal penitentiary in Washington state but served no more than six years before he was back in Mississippi.

In 1998, the state of Mississippi retried Sam Bowers for the fire-bombing death of Vernon Dahmer. State prosecutor Bob Helfrich again brought to light his vicious deeds.

Another former Klansman and FBI informant, Billy Roy Pitts, testified that Bowers ordered the murder at a 1965 meeting at a Mississippi farmhouse . . . . Pitts described the KKK's code for referring to different kinds of attacks: a No. 1 was a cross burning; a No. 2, a whipping; a No. 3, a fire-bombing; and a No. 4, a killing. Pitts claimed that Bowers was the only man in the Mississippi KKK at the time of the crime who had the authority to order No. 3 and No. 4 attacks.[9]

The prosecution argued Bowers ordered the attack on Vernon Dahmer.

Times had changed in Mississippi. The Klan's grip of fear was long since gone, their ideology repudiated, their very existence almost eradicated. To a new generation of Mississippians, the Klan was a relic of a forgotten past, legendary bogey men, or even—as would later be portrayed in the Cohen Brothers' movie *O Brother Where Art Thou?*—a comical and ignorant band of miscreant dunces. However, they were in fact American terrorists: real, dangerous, and evil. That the truth could be so quickly forgotten shows how dramatic was their fall from power. The facts of the case were still clear through the fog of years. and the jury found Sam Bowers guilty beyond a reasonable doubt. He was sentenced to life in prison. No appeal was taken, so Sam Bowers would spend the rest of his life in a Mississippi penitentiary. On November 6, 2006, Sam Bowers died while confined to the Mississippi penitentiary. The state prepared to send his body to a pauper's grave, until a relative anonymously claimed the body.

Some issues never seem to go away. While I was presiding on the federal district court in Hattiesburg—and during my confirmation battle for the Fifth Circuit Court of Appeals—a petition was filed challenging the conviction of Sam Bowers. It was alleged that Mississippi's Constitution had never been adopted; therefore, the court that convicted him was illegally constituted and his conviction unconstitutional. The case came before me. I was requested to recuse myself because it was alleged that Sam Bowers had ordered the Ku Klux Klan to use its power to defeat me in two statewide elections.[10] It is difficult to say whether my loss of those two elections had anything to do with Klan opposition. But it is clear that after I prosecuted the Klan and testified against Sam Bowers, Klansmen and Klan sympathizers opposed me in every election in which I was a candidate. Since a judge must avoid even an appearance of bias or prejudice, I recused myself. The judge who considered the petition dismissed it as without merit.

After I lost my election for the Mississippi House of Representatives in 1967, I immersed myself in my law practice and farming but continued to be active in community affairs. Toward the end of that decade and into the early 1970s, when public schools integrated in Mississippi, many whites around the state incorporated new private schools to provide an alternative to what would soon, in many cases, become black-majority schools. When school integration came to Laurel, my wife and I counseled our friends and neighbors against creating a new private school. The community largely stood together and created no new private school in Laurel or Jones County.

Margaret Ann and I kept our children in public school, even though it meant our children were bused across town at a time when there was a long-established private school one block from our home. All four of our children attended integrated schools, some 70 percent black. Our children benefited from having friends of different races. We thought it important to support public education and provide a quality school environment for children of all races.

In 1971, I ran for the state Senate from Jones County. Activists in the African American community circulated a marked sample ballot with Democrats marked in all but two slots. For governor, the mark was for an independent: civil rights activist Charles Evers, brother of slain NAACP field secretary Medgar Evers. For state senator—in response to my fight against the Klan and my interaction with the black community—a mark was placed by my name, a Republican. I was elected to the state Senate with two-thirds of the black vote and two-thirds of the white vote. It was the first time Jones County had ever elected a Republican to the state Senate. It happened not through racial polarization, but through racial cooperation—working together. (Today, my nephew Stacey Pickering represents our county in that same Senate seat.)

Through the years, I continued to work to improve race relations—not because of any political advantage, because most African Americans identified themselves as Democrats. But rather, I think it weakens our country and makes it more difficult to make progress when we are divided on the basis of race. Therefore, I continued to reach out and build bridges between the races: in politics, in private practice, in my community, in my church, in Mississippi's universities, and around the state.

In 1976, as chairman of the Mississippian Republican Party, I made a concerted effort to broaden our party's base. Like most of the South, Mississippi had long been solidly Democratic. We settled most of our elections in the Democratic Primary, with the winner of that election coasting—often unopposed—to victory in the general election. But the Republican Party was growing in Mississippi as conservative whites saw their former national party drifting more and more to the Left. I believed we needed to attract conservative blacks into our party as well, so I hired James King as the first African American field man for the Mississippi Republican Party. James was not just the Republican Party's face for the black community; he also advanced our work in the white community. I also reached out to and addressed annual meetings of the Mississippi NAACP, previously an unheard of action for a Republican leader. The Republican Party is a party of principles and ideas; these values and beliefs hold no color, and race should not separate men and women of like minds from working together for common goals.

In my private law practice, I primarily represented the proverbial "little man"—plaintiffs who had been injured or wronged. But I also represented business clients: an oil refinery, a local bank, a cable television company, and briefly a major insurance company. After my stint as prosecutor, I sometimes engaged in limited criminal defense work.

Over the years, I had both black and white clients. I didn't always prevail, but I won far more than I lost and made a decent living for my growing family. In a community like ours, you usually know folks on both sides of any given legal controversy. Sometimes this can lead to discomfort and sometimes even to ill will.

In 1981, a sixteen-year-old white girl was operating a grocery store and a young African American man was charged with using a knife to rob her. I was a friend to the girl's family, but I believed the young man was innocent. I took his case—not a popular decision with many in the white community. Through the course of the proceedings, we proved his innocence and the jury found him not guilty. I believe the law provides justice and protection to blacks and whites alike. I attempted to live that out in my law practice, as in the rest of my life.

In order to create better race relations and understanding, I organized and chaired a bipartisan, biracial committee in Jones County in 1988 and 1989. We built on that model in 2000 when I convened a biracial group to address the needs of primarily African American children at risk in Laurel.

The Christian faith teaches that God is no respecter of persons. He loves all of his children equally, regardless of race. Scripture teaches that all who believe find salvation. In Mississippi, we are moving toward better race relations through our common faith. While serving as president of the Mississippi Baptist Convention in 1985, I presided over the session of the convention addressed by the pastor of the first African American church to affiliate with our convention.

Our shared faith has to be one of the most effective vehicles for advancing racial understanding and reconciliation. That is why for several years I have supported Mission Mississippi, a group seeking to promote racial reconciliation through Christian faith. I joined their board of directors after retiring from the bench. The efforts of Mission Mississippi are helping to bring the races together across Mississippi and heal old wounds on all sides.

Mississippi's universities also are contributing to racial reconciliation. In the early 1990s, my son Chip, son-in-law Jerry Montgomery, and I helped integrate our fraternity at the University of Mississippi. In 1997, I wrote a friend and suggested he help create an entity at the University of Mississippi to promote better racial understanding and reconciliation. Later, I wrote to the chancellor of the university and made the same suggestion. Former Democratic governor William Winter—one of our nation's most outstanding leaders in promoting racial reconciliation, and a strong supporter of my confirmation—had already encouraged the establishment of such an institute. I assisted Ole Miss chancellor Robert Khayat and Governor Winter in creating the William Winter Institute for Racial Reconciliation and served on its initial board of directors.

Jackson State University—Mississippi's largest traditionally black university—launched 1-Mississippi in 2005, an organization commemorating James Meredith's integration of Ole Miss and his 1966 civil rights march down Interstate 55. They requested I serve on the leadership team and I accepted. At one of the meetings of the group, James Meredith and I both spoke. I later joked with him that in matters of promoting racial reconciliation, he sounded more like the conservative and I sounded more like the liberal. But racial harmony is neither conservative nor liberal—Republican nor Democrat. For example, in September 2005, the International Black Broadcasters Association gave me its Civil Rights Award at their annual banquet held in Memphis, Tennessee. The keynote speaker was comedian and activist Dick Gregory. Without question, he and I disagree on most ideological and political issues, but even with such differences, there is common ground in our common humanity.

In May 2006, we found more common ground in Mississippi. In 1959, Korean War veteran Clyde Kennard attempted several times to become the first African American to enroll at what is now the University of Southern Mississippi. He was arrested for allegedly receiving $25 worth of chicken feed on the testimony of a nineteen-year-old named Johnny Lee Roberts. He was convicted and sentenced to the state penitentiary. Recently, Roberts recanted his testimony and admitted he lied, saying Kennard "wasn't guilty of nothing." Jerry Mitchell, the award-winning civil rights investigative reporter for the Jackson *Clarion Ledger*, wrote numerous articles bringing attention to the injustice done to Kennard.

It was clear to many of us who lived through that era that Clyde Kennard was innocent and his conviction was simply the result of his attempt to integrate one of our institutions of higher learning. Clyde Kennard's conviction was a gross miscarriage of justice.

Many Mississippians wanted Governor Haley Barbour to grant a posthumous pardon of Kennard, who died of colon cancer in 1963. But Governor Barbour believed a pardon, the restoration of rights, was not the appropriate remedy for someone already deceased.

Barry Bradford, a high school history teacher at Adlai E. Stevenson High School in Lincolnshire, Illinois, called me to see if I thought we could file a petition in federal court to clear Clyde Kennard's name. Bradford had previously worked with my son Chip and Mississippi's African American congressman Bennie Thompson to pass a resolution in the House of Representatives to honor the lives and accomplishments of Medgar Evers and his widow Myrlie Evers-Williams, who served as president of the NAACP.

Bradford's high school history class had now made it a project to correct the injustice done to Clyde Kennard. While talking to Bradford, it dawned on me that the place to go to correct this injustice was the court that convicted Clyde Kennard—the Circuit Court of Forrest County—the same court where I testified against Sam Bowers. Bob Helfrich, who successfully prosecuted Sam Bowers in 1998, was now circuit judge for Forrest County. I knew him to be a judge committed to justice. I knew the district attorney there, Jon Mark Weathers, was a fair prosecutor and a man of integrity.

I called former governor William Winter to enlist his support. We decided to file a petition of exoneration to clear Kennard. I also contacted Justice Reuben Anderson (now an attorney in private practice who was the first African American to serve on the Mississippi Supreme Court and the first African American to be elected president of the Mississippi Bar) and Judge Barry Ford (a law partner with me at Baker Donelson Bearman Caldwell Berkowitz Law Firm who was the first African American elected judge to the First Circuit Court District of Mississippi—a predominately white district) to join us. I enlisted the support of the current president of the University of Southern Mississippi, Dr. Shelby Thames; and the immediate past president and president emeritus, Dr. Aubrey Lucas. Mrs. Effie Dahmer, widow of Vernon Dahmer, and their son Vernon Dahmer Jr. also joined us along with numerous other prominent African Americans and whites. It was a bipartisan, biracial group. District Attorney Jon Mark Weathers and Governor Haley Barbour joined our petition. One poignant moment was when ninety-one-year-old Dr. Glen Pearson, a white physician who treated Clyde Kennard, laboriously made his way to the courtroom to sign the petition.

Judge Bob Helfrich noted that his upstairs courtroom is where it all started and that this courtroom is where it should all end. He observed it was not an issue of black and white but it was an issue of right and wrong. Judge Helfrich declared Clyde Kennard innocent and declared his conviction null and void. Nearly fifty years later, the vindication could not give Kennard his life back or enroll him in the University of Southern Mississippi, but the correction is symbolic of the many steps Mississippi is taking today toward better race relations.

Republicans and Democrats, blacks and whites working together, exonerated Clyde Kennard's name. Mississippi has made tremendous progress since the 1960s with individuals effectively working together from all parties and all races to seek justice.

Governor Haley Barbour has appointed a commission to establish a world-class National Civil Rights Museum in Mississippi. I have the honor of co-chairing this commission with Reuben Anderson, the first African American elected to the Mississippi Supreme Court, as well as the first African American chosen to serve as president of the Mississippi Bar. We are joined in this endeavor of unity by more than three dozen others: black and white, Republican and Democrat, liberal and conservative.

Unfortunately, those who seek political advantage through division in Washington D.C. are not interested in this type of unity.

Based on my record of more than forty years (a record of which I am proud), never in my wildest imagination would I have dreamed I would be accused of being a racist—or even that subtle and nefarious euphemism "racially insensitive"—until leftist radicals used a false conservative, white, Southern stereotype to smear my reputation in their effort to send a message to President Bush.

Unfortunately, during these entire proceedings, my record was not contrasted with the senators who were voting against me. Which ones personally fought the Klan in the 1960s and put their families and homes in jeopardy? Did they take a stand in their home states when there was racial violence or when there were busing boycotts? Had they had hands-on experience promoting racial reconciliation in the local community where it is most essential? How many of them sent their children to majority-black public schools? Have they been guests in the homes, the churches, the funerals of their black neighbors? Do they have black neighbors? I hope they have had similar experiences because America needs all of us working together to achieve racial reconciliation. However, I suspect few of them participated in the civil rights struggle in the South during the 1960s, and I suspect most of them sent their children to exclusive private schools and live far away from black neighborhoods.

During his failed 2004 campaign for president of the United States, Senator John Kerry of Massachusetts criticized President Bush for nominating me. But when asked what he did during the civil rights era, Kerry responded that while he did help raise funds for the freedom rides, he himself did not go south. Kerry said, "I went from a very difficult personal choice about going or not going. I was on one of the athletic teams at the time. I did not go."[11]

I also read a fundraising letter Senator Dick Durbin sent to Democratic supporters. He bragged about standing against my nomination as evidence of his support for civil rights. He went on to say he wished he had come south to participate in the civil rights movement, but a part-time job and looming exams forced him "to cancel an all-night drive to march in Selma with [his] fellow students from Georgetown."[12] I could not help believing that somehow his letter was a salve for his own conscience. Still, as I mentioned, who can criticize the past? We all had our own priorities, and Senators Kerry and Durbin had theirs.

It was wrong for conservative southern politicians to demagogue the race issue in the 1950s and 1960s to maintain political power. It is wrong for liberal northern politicians to demagogue the race issue today to keep us divided to gain political power.

Although the opposition painted me as a racist and attacked me as being "insensitive to civil rights," the issue that powered the conflict against my nomination was abortion. If they, in fact, had been interested in civil rights and had looked at my record, they would have supported my nomination, not attacked me. Yet, their concern was abortion, and my personal beliefs on that subject were clear, and public since 1976, just three years after *Roe v. Wade*.

Abortion:
The Engine of Opposition

THE ABORTION ISSUE drove the engine of opposition to my nomination and to those of other Bush nominees who were attacked by Far Left secularist groups.

A memo detailing a December 6, 2001, conference call among liberal and feminist groups discussed their strategy for fighting our nominations. The participants predicted "a major fight in January over Charles Pickering." They said the "Courts of Appeal are where we should all be focused . . . . They are the farm team for the Supreme Court. 14-15 nominees are really problematic, awful record on choice and reproductive rights." They wanted to let the Democratic senators know "these issues are non-negotiable." They plainly stated their fear: "We have lots to lose because right to abortion isn't in Constitution. Only in Roe. Boils down to judicial interpretation."

My record on this issue reveals why they opposed me. In 1976, I was chairman of the Mississippi Republican Party, a delegate to the Republican National Convention in Kansas City, and a member of the Platform Committee. It had been three years since the divisive *Roe v. Wade* decision, and it was the first opportunity for either party to make a statement on the issue in their national platforms. On the Platform Committee, I chaired the Human Rights and Responsibilities Subcommittee that recommended a plank opposing *Roe v. Wade* and advocating a constitutional amendment to overturn it. The convention adopted the plank and the GOP was on its way to being identified as the "pro-life party."

While serving in the Mississippi State Senate (1972–1980), I voted for a resolution calling for a constitutional convention to propose an amendment to overturn *Roe v. Wade*. I also served two years (1983–1985) as president of the Mississippi Baptist Convention. During that time, the convention passed a resolution calling for the outlawing of abortion except to protect the life of the mother.

Personally, as a political leader, as a legislator, and as a church leader, I opposed abortion. However, in 1990 I was nominated and unanimously approved by the Senate to hold the position of a federal district court judge. I took an oath. I took off my partisan political hat when I put on my judicial robe.

As a judge, I was no longer in a position to advocate a political or personal philosophy; my principles dictated I follow the rule of law: the Constitution of the United States, federal statutes, and controlling precedent—decisions of the U.S. Supreme Court. For ten years on the federal district court, I followed controlling precedent and had pledged to continue that action on the circuit court of appeals. Although the Supreme Court can—if a majority wishes—overturn *Roe v. Wade*, the circuit courts cannot. Circuit judges must follow Supreme Court precedent.

Sometimes people ask me, "But wouldn't you want to follow your pro-life beliefs?" The answer is most certainly yes. But my pro-life beliefs are consistent with all my beliefs. Those beliefs dictate that my role as a lower court judge is to follow Supreme Court precedents. I believe the abortion issue is a matter for legislative debate, or constitutional amendment, and would not have been at my personal judicial discretion.

If you look back at my involvement in the abortion issue before becoming a judge, you will see the consistency. I advocated change through the proper democratic process, not through judicial activism. My record on both the district and appellate courts confirms I followed the rule of law; I followed precedent. In looking at my ten years on the district court, the ABA would not have given me its highest rating had I acted otherwise.

Let me be clear: I oppose abortion. I believe it is the unjustified taking of innocent human life. But that did not give me the right as a district court judge—or even a circuit court judge—to go against controlling precedent, any more than liberal judges' beliefs should give them the right to create new rights not found in the Constitution. These issues should be decided by legislative bodies or by the people themselves, not by the courts.

It is not enough for the left-wing special-interest groups that a nominee subscribes to the rule of law. Despite their claims that they oppose judicial activism, they do want activist judges—liberal activist judges. They want judges to create new rights and expand those rights. Boyden Gray explained this on National Public Radio, saying,

> Nan Aron who is one of Ralph Neas' colleagues, on the left if you will, she's chairman of the Alliance for Justice, once said at a Federalist Society debate[1] . . . "because the Republicans now control the House, the Senate, and the White House for the first time in basically a hundred years, there is obviously no way we're going to get any new rights created by the congress, so now we have to look to the courts to create new rights that we won't be able to get from the legislature." Now that's her talking, those are her words almost verbatim.[2]

What new rights do Nan Aron and her groups want the judiciary to create? These Far Left groups want abortion rights expanded. They support abortion on demand in its most extreme forms: partial birth abortion (which would be murder if a teenage girl and her boyfriend did the same thing without the aid of an abortionist), teenage abortion without parental consent or even parental notification, as well as abortion without spousal notification or consent.

These groups want to expand or reinterpret the Constitution and to redefine marriage to include same-sex couples. Conversely, they want to diminish or reinterpret the Constitution to limit the rights of people of faith. They want to exclude any reference to God from the public square, from the public arena, from public discourse. They seek not separation of church and state; they want the elimination of God from our country.

It was not sufficient for them that I would follow controlling precedent as the law of the land; they wanted a judge to expand *Roe v. Wade*. They are unable to expand *Roe v. Wade* through the proper mechanisms: legislative or the amendment process. Therefore, they seek judges to do it for them. But I was not the kind of judge they were looking for.

Their litmus test is abortion. The fact that a judge is both qualified and committed to the rule of law is not sufficient. They want judges who think like they think and feel like they feel. Because I did not believe as they did, because my personal, religious, and political values differed from their beliefs and values—and because I honored the rule of law—they opposed me.

While abortion drove the engine of opposition and the passion of these activists, it was not a politically sufficient reason to defeat a nominee. Not only did they want to keep conservative jurists off the appellate bench, they also wanted to send a message to the White House: if you make nominations like these to the Supreme Court, this is but a taste of what you can expect. To send this message, they would use any means necessary. To win this battle in the culture war, they launched their attacks.

The Attack

FOR ME 2002 began the same way 2001 ended: Democrats on the Judiciary Committee requesting my answers to their various inquiries and seeking copies of all my unpublished opinions. My staff and I used reams of paper responding to their requests as we pulled the documents from the clerk's office and from the federal court archives in Atlanta. People for the American Way requested from my court reporter copies of sentencing transcripts as to various criminal defendants. The Democrats' questions and requests for documents throughout the month of January paralyzed my ability to take care of court work. My staff and I spent virtually all our time responding to Judiciary Committee Democrats.

Meanwhile, some of my African American supporters told me that Congressman Bennie Thompson of Mississippi was terribly offended I had not made a courtesy visit to him before my nomination went to the Senate. This, they told me, was why he and the state NAACP were opposing my nomination.

At the time, Mississippi had three Democrats in its House congressional delegation and none in the Senate. Gene Taylor, a maverick conservative Democrat from the Mississippi Gulf Coast, was the most senior of the delegation. Bennie Thompson, the only African American in the Mississippi delegation, was second in seniority. Mississippi's third Democratic congressman was Ronnie Shows, who due to redistricting was about to be locked into an incumbent-against-incumbent race with my son, Chip.

Because the House of Representatives has no constitutional responsibilities involving the confirmation of judges, I had not thought to visit with any of the congressmen from Mississippi, Democrat or Republican, about supporting my confirmation. Since Congressman Thompson was Mississippi's highest ranking African American in Washington, apparently he felt I should have given him the courtesy of coming by to seek his support. There was no slight intended on my part; I would have been happy to have called on him. I sought to rectify this perceived oversight.

Although I knew no administration likes for its nominees to meet with anyone opposing their nomination, I have always felt that people who disagree should sit down and attempt to resolve differences. I thought it would be constructive if I met with Congressman Thompson. After all, I had a good record regarding race relations and civil rights. I didn't see anything to lose. So, my African American friends arranged for me to meet with Congressman Thompson on an upcoming trip he was making to Hattiesburg.

We met at the Covington House, a restaurant on Highway 49 near Collins, about twelve miles from my home. Around ten-thirty that Saturday morning, Jack King—one of the owners of the Covington House—led us into a private room. The congressman had a cup of coffee and I had a glass of tea. Both being hunters, we discussed this common hobby and had a pleasant visit.

I gave Congressman Thompson a memorandum outlining my work to protect civil rights and to promote better racial understanding and reconciliation, beginning with my fight against the Ku Klux Klan in the 1960s and my testimony against Sam Bowers. He seemed to appreciate the material but told me he felt there should be an African American appointed to the federal district court in Mississippi, or to the Fifth Circuit Court of Appeals. I agreed that African Americans should be appointed and stated that I personally knew African American judges and attorneys well qualified to serve on the federal bench. (At the time, the only African American on the federal bench in Mississippi was Judge Henry Wingate, appointed by President Ronald Reagan in 1985.) But choosing nominees was a political decision in which I was neither able by position, nor allowed by judicial ethics, to participate in making. The president and Mississippi's senators make those decisions.

When we had finished our conversation, the congressman told me, "I can go back and tell them that you are a good man, but we need something." (By "them," I assumed he was talking about the Congressional Black Caucus and/or the NAACP.) He stated three times, "I can go back and tell them that you are a good man, but we need something." I understood Congressman Thompson wanted to be the kingmaker for a judicial appointment. He would run interference for my nomination and help move it through the Senate in exchange for being able to choose a federal judge, or at least have significant input on the choice of an African American to the federal bench for whom he could claim credit. I was in no position to listen to, consider, or accept such a deal. He wanted something that was not mine to give.

I walked with Congressman Thompson out to his car, met his wife, and we said our good-byes. As he left, I still did not know what he would or would not do in regard to my nomination. Later, one of Congressman Thompson's friends told me that he did not intend to withdraw his opposition, but he also did not plan to actively do anything further to fight my confirmation.

Back in Washington, it was mid-January and the Bush Administration had realized the Far Left special-interest groups and Democrats intended to make my nomination the big fight in a political war over judicial confirmations. Viet Dinh, assistant attorney general and head of the Office of Legal Policy in the Justice Department, and Noel Francisco on the staff of the White House Counsel's Office, called and requested that I come to Washington to prepare for my upcoming hearing. They told me I would be the test case for other nominees, and they were concerned that the Democratic Judiciary Committee chairman, Patrick Leahy, would schedule my second hearing on short notice and we would be unprepared. At the time, I was confident of confirmation and reluctant to make the trip, but they stressed the importance of the fight. I agreed to come.

About this time, Senator Trent Lott told the Associated Press he had "Commitments of support" for my confirmation from Judiciary

Committee Chairman Leahy, and Senate Majority Leader Tom Daschle. Trent said, "I have been assured they are going to vote on him in early February and he will be confirmed overwhelmingly."[1]

As noted, Senate tradition called for professional courtesy between party leaders to support nominees personally supported by their counterparts. Helen Dewar of the *Washington Post* wrote, "It is unusual for senators to reject a home-state friend of one of their leaders, regardless of party."[2] *Human Events* quoted a GOP Senate leadership aide as saying, "It's been a tradition that a leader does not oppose a leader's nominee . . . . You just don't do that."[3] Regardless of tradition or the support Senators Leahy and Daschle promised Senator Lott, the influence of the Far Left special-interest groups was too strong when the time came for a vote, and the Democratic leaders backed down.

On January 24, just one week before Senator Leahy would schedule my second hearing, Far Left groups held a press conference at the National Press Club denouncing my nomination. They aimed all their guns at me in a barrage choreographed by People for the American Way (PFAW). They launched the attack. PFAW's twenty-four-page attack became the textbook for Democratic senators during their questioning of me before the Senate Judiciary Committee. They used it as the authority for their talking points and the background for their press releases and e-mails.

These Far Left groups criticized me—in their words—because of my "career and record on civil rights"; "hostility to reproductive rights"; "hostility to civil and constitutional rights"; "failure to publish" more of my opinions; and my "troubling record of reversals."[4]

The truth of my record reveals I was never reversed in any voting rights case or employment discrimination case. I never handled an abortion case. Of the thousands of cases I presided over, 99.5 percent were affirmed or not appealed.

As to my "failure to publish more of my opinions," district courts do not set precedent, so the Judicial Conference of the United States strongly discourages district judges from publishing opinions. I followed this policy and as a general rule published only when I thought an opinion would be helpful, mostly in situations where there was no

THE ATTACK | 49

controlling precedent or the controlling precedent was not clear. I
published almost 10 percent of the opinions I rendered, about average
for district judges and more than some confirmed Clinton nominees
had published.[5] (The legal community and fellow judges view district
judges who publish excessively in areas clearly established as wanting to
see their name in print.) PFAW lacked credible material to criticize me,
so they complained that there were too few published cases to distort.

PFAW found no "smoking gun" to support their accusations. So
they took quotations out of context, omitted factual background, and
distorted what I had said or done. These mischaracterizations were
woven together to fit their depiction of me. PFAW followed what would
be their standard practice for all targeted Bush judicial picks: dehuman-
ize the nominee and turn him or her into a political issue devoid of
human traits. It is easier to attack an issue than a person. On a personal
level, it is difficult to treat an individual other than with decency. While
in Washington that week, I rode up on the elevator with Democratic
senator Chris Dodd of Connecticut. We were face to face, so I extended
my hand and introduced myself. As we shook hands, Senator Dodd
responded, "I know who you are. What they are doing to you is wrong."
But in the end, when the vote came over filibustering my nomination,
Senator Dodd's vote was not there.

I felt the most disturbing accusation made by People for the
American Way was their attack on my faith. They devoted four pages in
an attempt to paint me as a "dangerous theocrat." Their first criticism
had nothing to do with my judicial duties and involved a statement I
made six years before my unanimous confirmation to the federal district
bench. As president of the Mississippi Baptist Convention in the 1980s,
I told Mississippi Baptists the Bible is "the absolute authority by which
all conduct of man is judged." I challenged Mississippi Baptists to live
according to the teachings of the Bible. PFAW attacked me not for an
action or even my words as a judge, but for this statement made as a
private citizen and a lay leader of a religious organization supporting one
of the most basic tenants of Christianity: the authority of Scripture.

Roger Clegg, vice president and general counsel of the Center for
Equal Opportunity, responded in a law journal article:

PFAW apparently considers [the above quote made to Mississippi Baptists] a damning quote. . . . But there are millions of Americans who believe that; indeed, those who believe the Bible is scripture could hardly believe otherwise. . . . If, as H. L. Mencken declared, Puritanism is the fear that someone, somewhere is happy, then surely the PFAW report betrays its own fear, that someone, somewhere believes in God.[6]

Republican senator Mitch McConnell of Kentucky, speaking at my confirmation hearing, said,

Frankly, as a Southern Baptist myself, I don't know what else you would say at an annual meeting of the Southern Baptist Convention, particularly when you are the president. Given that you were speaking on a purely theological matter, in your personal, private capacity. I thought the only thing disturbing about this was that people would seek to hold it against you.[7]

Next, PFAW criticized me for quoting Scripture in an opinion where I wrote, "One of the oldest recorded codes of laws provides: 'The innocent and the just you shall not put to death, nor shall you acquit the guilty' (Exodus 23:7)." But Supreme Court decisions cite the book of Exodus fifteen times, and liberal Supreme Court justices like Earl Warren, Thurgood Marshall, and William Brennan quoted passages from the Old Testament. Considering I was a district judge required to follow Supreme Court precedent, it hardly seems a just criticism that I did as the Supreme Court has done on a number of occasions.

PFAW further criticized me for responding in kind to comments made by a defendant during sentencing. The presiding judge in any criminal case must offer the defendant an opportunity for allocution— the chance for the defendant to speak before sentence is imposed. This particular defendant told me that Christianity played an important role in his life: he attended mass, he sponsored Latin masses in the confer- ence room of his office, and he abstained from meat on Fridays all as a part of his religious practice. In response, I told him, "It is not too late for you to form a new beginning. For yourself and others, I hope you will do that. You have a lot to offer. You can become involved in Chuck Colson's prison fellowship or some other such ministry, and be a benefit to your fellow inmates and to others and to their families." I did not coerce or force religion on this defendant in any manner; I responded to his statements and encouraged him in the future to make a positive contribution in a manner consistent with the beliefs he espoused.

PFAW disapproved of remarks I made at the sentencing of another defendant with a long and extensive background of crime. The defendant brought a nun and priest to court to testify on his behalf, and nuns and priests frequently attended his six-week trial. I told the defendant that after his discharge from prison and while under supervised release, "You will involve yourself in some type of systematic program whereby you will be involved in the study and consideration of effects and consequences of crime and/or appropriate behavior in a civilized society. This may be a program through your church or some other such agency or organization so long as it is approved in advance by the probation service." I gave him the freedom to choose his church or some other organization; I did not impose his church on him, and this choice in no way violated the Constitution.

Roger Clegg summarized the accusations against me relating to religion by saying, "The PFAW report concludes from these snippets that Judge Pickering is a dangerous theocrat. This is absurd."[8] Senator McConnell found the accusations "evidence of a hostility toward religion by your accusers" and to be "quite incredulous and completely inappropriate."[9]

PFAW's accusations clearly indicate they are so hostile to religious beliefs they would rather hardened criminals never be rehabilitated than to be exposed to religious thought. They criticized my faith that day at the press conference, but they knew that would be a difficult criticism to sell to the American people. They would wait until later to unveil the assault they would use as the centerpiece of their effort to derail my nomination—a Southern judge and a cross-burning case.

A few days after their press conference, People for the American Way requested from my court reporter a transcript of the sentencing of

Daniel Swan in a cross-burning case that came before me. After reading this transcript and seeing it accurately reflected what I had told Swan, I was not overly concerned. At that time, I had no idea how my opponents would distort and misrepresent that case with its symbolism. It turned out that all my opposition had to do was bring up the specter of a burning cross to close the minds of many people.

On Monday, January 28, I traveled to Washington to work with the staff of the Justice Department and the White House for three days in preparation for my confirmation hearing. Tuesday night, I joined Chip for the president's State of the Union address. On our walk to the Capitol, Chip asked me what I would do if I were not confirmed. I could not answer the question. Despite the previous week's attack on my nomination, the thought had never crossed my mind.

After the president's address, we walked out of the Capitol and saw a national media correspondent interviewing Senator Orrin Hatch. We walked over to speak to Hatch, and when he finished the interview, he turned and said, "Judge, we are going to do all we can to get you confirmed. I think we can." Then he paused, hesitated, and said, "But I'm not sure." That was the second indication that evening that my confirmation could be in trouble. That week in meetings with Senators Thad Cochran and Trent Lott, I began to realize the nature of the coming storm over judicial nominees. Cochran told me since he had been in Washington he had never seen anything like the opposition that had snowballed against my nomination and doubted I would get much support at all from the Democrats. Lott, though concerned, still thought I would be confirmed.

Thursday, one week after the PFAW-led attack at the National Press Club, the NAACP held a press conference in Jackson opposing my nomination. Regrettably, in recent years the NAACP has become more of a political organization than a civil rights organization. It has morphed into an extended arm of the Democratic Party closely aligned with the Far Left special-interest groups that are equating sexual preference and abortion rights with race. (Two years later during a *60 Minutes* investigation, a local NAACP official admitted to civil rights activist Charles Evers that they opposed my nomination because of a request from the national organization, not because of my record in Mississippi.)

But at this press conference, the NAACP told the media they had in their possession an audiotape that would blow my nomination out of the water and guarantee I would not be confirmed. The political intrigue of a mysterious audiotape made the headlines, but a look at the record showed—just as with all the left-wing attacks—the charge was more fiction than fact.

Britton Mosely came before me as a plaintiff in an employment discrimination case. He said he wanted to offer the tape as evidence to support his claim, but that I had prevented this and sabotaged his case. In reality, transcripts of the case show I clearly and specifically offered the plaintiff's counsel an opportunity to introduce the tape, but Mosely's own lawyer had stated on the record that the tape was unintelligible and they were not going to offer it. Furthermore, despite the scarcity of evidence offered by Mosely, I did not give a directed verdict, which would have dismissed his case. Instead, I let the case go to the jury. Mosely lost his case before the jury, not because of any ruling I made.

Not only were the grounds of this NAACP press conference totally bogus, but Mosely's own attorney later wrote a letter in support of my confirmation:

Very frankly, I was somewhat apprehensive about trying a case before Judge Pickering. I knew his political ideology was Republican and he was very conservative. I have been a "yellow dog" Democrat all of my life. Notwithstanding our difference in political philosophies, I was pleasantly surprised with the manner, professionalism, and fairness with which Judge Pickering conducted the trial of this lawsuit . . . .

My client made numerous allegations against the Mississippi Department of Corrections, but simply was unable to substantiate same with appropriate witnesses. I felt that Judge Pickering allowed the case to go to the jury when, in fact, there was really not enough proof to avoid a judgment as a matter of law. Even though Judge Pickering did allow the case to go to the jury, they found for the Defendant . . . . I was treated professionally, courteously, fairly and I feel my client was treated the same.

I received a call from the NAACP in Washington. I gave them
the same set of facts that I am relating to you.[10]

The NAACP knew the truth, but they attacked regardless.

As I continued preparation for my hearing, Chip was facing his own
political battle. As previously mentioned, the 2000 census revealed that
under the decennial reapportionment of Congress, Mississippi would
lose a seat in the House of Representatives, leaving five incumbent
congressmen but only four congressional seats. Chip was engaged in a
redistricting fight to determine the fate of his campaign for a fourth
term in Congress.

While redistricting was a legislative responsibility, the fight quickly
moved to the courts. Mississippi's Joint House-Senate Legislative
Committee on Congressional Redistricting had conducted hearings
around the state and drafted a plan, but the chair of the committee,
Representative Tommy Reynolds, stuck the plan in his hip pocket and
went home without making the plan available to the public until the
special session of the legislature convened. He had hoped to keep the
plan secret until that time so no one would have time to develop
meaningful opposition. Fortunately, someone provided a copy of the
plan to Chip, and he and the Republican Party were able to counter the
unfairness of the plan with their own draft plans.

The House rejected a compromise plan that would have combined
the two districts to give Chip and Ronnie Shows both a fair shot in a
campaign. Instead, the House determined to create a safe Democratic
district and to put the two Republican congressmen against each other
by putting Chip's central Mississippi Republican strongholds into fellow
Republican Roger Wicker's north Mississippi district. To do so, they
drew a district from the Tennessee border down into central Mississippi's
Jackson suburbs, creating a distorted funnel-shaped district that gave
birth to its name, the "tornado plan."

One of the biggest losers under this plan would be east Mississippi
and the city of Meridian. Meridian was the home of Chip's predecessor,
Congressman G. V. Sonny Montgomery, who represented Mississippi in
Washington for thirty years. As in any state, distinct regions require

different priorities and develop competitions with other areas of the state. So it was with Meridian and east Mississippi that faced combination with the Mississippi Gulf Coast.

A former state senator from Meridian who had served as president pro tem of the Senate, Glen DeWeese, was dying of cancer. The night before he died, DeWeese called the Senate leadership to his hospital room and had them promise not to gerrymander away the influence of Meridian and east Mississippi. Though controlled by Democrats, the Senate leadership pledged to honor his request, which was a rejection of the House of Representatives' tornado plan.

The Senate supported DeWeese's request of compact districts that would represent the various communities of interest and ensure each major military base and state university would be in separate congressional districts. The Senate would have compromised to achieve a higher BVAP (black voting age population) in the district—which was the objective of House Democrats in order to protect Ronnie Shows—yet still maintaining compact districts. But the House wanted more and would not compromise; they chose court instead.

Democratic leaders, hedging their bets if they did not win in the legislative process, filed a lawsuit in a chancery court perceived to be friendly to Shows and the Democrats. They neither announced the filing of the suit nor served process to other interested parties. In Mississippi, if the legislature fails to discharge its responsibility to redistrict, circuit courts and not chancery courts have jurisdiction. The Democrats filed in the wrong court.

When the Republican Party learned this suit had been filed but not served, they filed a protective lawsuit in federal court. The federal court deferred to the state court, but said that if Mississippi did not have a finally approved redistricting plan in sufficient time for the elections to go forward, then the federal court would draw a plan. Under the Voting Rights Act, any change in election procedures in Mississippi, including the redrawing of congressional district lines, must be pre-cleared by the U.S. Department of Justice.

The chancery judge adopted without change the plan advocated by the Democrats and supported by the House, but the Republicans appealed the decision. The state Supreme Court took no action, which meant the state had no final plan. The failure of the state Supreme Court to act on the chancery court ruling killed the Democratic plan. Under the Voting Rights Act, the Justice Department can only clear a final plan. The Justice Department could not consider the plan adopted by the chancery court, which was still awaiting Supreme Court action. It was not a final plan. With no final state plan, the federal court stepped in and handed down a redistricting plan that was similar, but not identical to, the Senate plan. While the chancery court and House plan was favorable to Democratic congressman Ronnie Shows, the federal court and Senate shaped plans were favorable to Chip.

The *Greenwood Commonwealth* in the Mississippi Delta editorialized,

> From a purely aesthetic point of view, the Congressional redistricting plan approved Monday by a federal panel is superior to the one adopted six weeks earlier by a state judge. . . . their version produces four relatively compact districts, as opposed to the plan approved by Hinds County Chancellor Patricia Wise, which takes the predominately north Mississippi first district and stretches it out all the way to the Jackson suburbs. . . . one point in the Federal judges favor is that they drew their own plan, whereas, Wise adopted wholesale a version recommended by a clearly self-interested group of Democratic plaintiffs.[11]

Sam Hall, then editor of the newspaper in Natchez, Mississippi, but later communications director for the Mississippi Democratic Party, wrote,

> the truth behind redistricting is that the Fed's plan is better for the state. The black voting age population (BVAP) is higher in more districts, it maintains some semblance of regionalism, military bases are all divided into separate districts, and the four major research universities—Mississippi State, Jackson State, Southern, and Ole Miss—are all in separate districts. . . . the Federal panel didn't gerrymander from the Tennessee state line down to Central Mississippi to achieve a district that dilutes the third. Democrats have been shame-

less in admitting that they were dissecting the state for their own political gain. Now they want to act shocked and accuse Republicans of playing partisan games.[12]

Publicly, Congressman Thompson had said little or nothing about my nomination since our meeting in Collins. After the federal court panel announced its redistricting plan, Thompson went ballistic and came down against my confirmation with renewed fervor.

Congressman Thompson attacked not only my nomination, but also those supporting me. Referring to those who supported my confirmation in the African American community, he stated, "Jesus had twelve disciples; one of them betrayed him. I'm sure there is a Judas who will come up and support him."[13] Thompson was obviously referring to the support I had from federal district judge Henry Wingate, a former member of the NAACP; civil rights activist Charles Evers, brother of slain civil rights leader Medgar Evers; various African American judges and attorneys; and the leadership in the African American communities in Laurel and Hattiesburg.

Congressman Thompson said any African American who did not follow his lead was a "Judas." This tactic, frequently used by Democrats, portrays any black who does not hue to the party line as not being truly black. Charles Evers immediately challenged Bennie Thompson as to who had been most active and involved longer in the civil rights movement. The African Americans who knew me best, with whom I had lived and worked with my lifetime, continued to be supportive. Early Gray, father of the young black man I defended in 1981, responded to Thompson, "I didn't betray anybody. I just told the truth."[14]

The day of the NAACP attack in Jackson, Senator Leahy scheduled my second hearing for the following week. Leahy's office then sent a fax to the Justice Department asking for responses from me about the Daniel Swan case. Although my court reporter had received a request regarding this case a few days earlier, this was the first time this case had been raised with me.

If they could not defeat me on my record, they would use symbolism to block my nomination. They wanted to create an image of a person unworthy of confirmation, so they turned my life and reputation on its head and painted me as "racially insensitive." They used a false stereotype of a conservative, religious, white Southern judge, painting me as an unreconstructed racist. They did not care that their mischaracterizations hurt race relations, were untrue, and grossly distorted my record. They wanted to block my confirmation by any means necessary. They raised the specter of the most hated symbol of racial oppression: a burning cross.

A Burning Cross

THOSE OPPOSED TO my nomination asked me about hundreds of cases, fishing for an expression, some assertion, any statement that might give basis for a challenge to my nomination (in addition to abortion). They lay low and waited in ambush with the case they would rely on most heavily. They wanted me to have little time to prepare for their attack as to that case.

The case started on a cold January night in 1994 in southwest Mississippi. A group of young people gathered around a fire built in a fifty-five-gallon drum near a country store. As they drank whiskey, a seventeen-year-old named Jason Branch[1] bragged that he had fired a shot from his pistol into the home of an interracial couple living down the road. He swore he was going to run the couple out of town. Soon, Branch's talk turned to cross-burning. Around midnight, the group dispersed, but three young men remained and decided they would burn a cross in the front yard of the interracial couple.

Branch; Mickey Thomas, a twenty-five-year-old with a lower IQ; and twenty-year-old Daniel Swan left the country store in Swan's truck. They got lumber and built an eight-foot cross, which they doused with gasoline. They leaned the cross against a tree in the front yard of the interracial couple and lit it with a cigarette lighter. They had poured gasoline on the cross but had not soaked it, so the fire went out shortly. The family slept inside unaware of the activity outside until the husband discovered the scorched cross the next morning.

Branch could not help boasting of their exploits, and as word got around the small town, all three young men were arrested for violating the couple's civil rights by burning the cross in front of their house. Additionally, they were charged with using fire to commit a felony, which carried a minimum five-year sentence. Branch received a third charge for shooting into the home a few weeks previous; the bullet was found in the wall of the room where the wife and the couple's baby had been sleeping.

Because Branch was a juvenile and Thomas was of low intelligence, the Civil Rights Division of the Clinton Administration's Justice Department—headed by Attorney General Janet Reno—offered both men plea bargains with home confinement and no jail time. Both accepted their deals.

The Justice Department also offered Swan a plea deal: they would drop the charge of using fire to commit a felony if he would plead guilty to the cross-burning charge and be sentenced to the penitentiary for eighteen months. Because Swan was smarter than Thomas and older than Branch, the Justice Department wanted him to serve a year and a half in prison for committing the same crime, while the other defendants served no jail time.

The cross-burning charge is a hate crime that requires racial animus, that is, racial animosity. Swan denied that he had racial animus; he claimed that he was just drunk. He felt it was unfair for the other two to get off with home confinement and no jail time when he would have to go to the penitentiary for eighteen months. He rejected the plea bargain and went to trial.

I presided over Swan's trial where he was convicted both as to the cross-burning charge and the charge of using fire to commit a felony. As the evidence of that night's activities came out and those involved testified, it became clear that the government had bungled the case.

The ringleader that night was Branch. In addition to his previous acts of intimidation against the family (shooting into their home), his young life was long on racial animosity. He riddled his speech with racial epithets; his own family admitted that he hated black people; he had been suspended from school for fighting with African Americans. Branch wanted to drive the interracial couple out of their neighborhood, and burning the cross was just the latest move in that attempt. For all that, the Clinton Justice Department gave him a plea deal with zero jail time.

On the other hand, Swan had no previous criminal history, no previous history of racial animosity, and before this event a decent reputation in the community. But following his conviction of the same crime committed by Branch, the government recommended seven and a half years in the penitentiary.[2] The government exacerbated this disparity when it dismissed the charge against Branch for shooting into the room where the mother and baby were asleep.

Federal law requires judges to consider proportionality in sentencing: "The court, in determining the particular sentence to be imposed, shall consider the need to avoid unwarranted sentence disparities among defendants with similar records who have been found guilty of similar conduct."[3] The Fourth Circuit Court of Appeals recently reaffirmed the importance of avoiding disparate sentences in federal courts, finding that a disproportionate sentence was unreasonable and remanding a case for resentencing.[4] The sentences recommended by the Clinton Justice Department in the Swan case—zero jail time for the ringleader versus seven and a half years for a less culpable defendant—was far more disproportionate than the sentence rejected by the Fourth Circuit.

I told the government attorneys this was the worst case of disproportionate sentencing that had ever been recommended to me, a factor I was compelled by law to consider. If courts do not sentence people who commit the same crime to proportionate sentences, it destroys respect for the judicial system and attacks the very foundation of our notions of fairness and equality. Our most basic sense of justice is frustrated when two people who commit the same crime, at the same time, at the same place receive vastly different punishments. We feel that injustice even more when a ringleader escapes punishment while the court drops the hammer on a less culpable co-defendant.

During my confirmation process, I met with the Mississippi Legislative Black Caucus, and one African American legislator, prominent trial attorney Ed Blackmon, reminded me of an occasion when he appeared before me as counsel for the ringleader of a drug conspiracy who had pled guilty. The government prosecutors had recommended the ringleader receive less time than another defendant who was "the mule"—the drug transporter. I refused to accept the plea and required the government to go back and renegotiate the plea agreements with both defendants so that the sentences were proportionate. I refused to sentence "the mule" to more time than the ringleader. I encountered the same dilemma with Branch and Swan.

I sought to uphold and maintain the principle of proportionate and fair sentencing in my courtroom. I consistently required sentencing reports of probation officers to include charts and graphs of the sentences I imposed on jointly indicted defendants so that I could make sure I maintained proportionality in the sentences. The probation officers who regularly appeared before me attested that I was more concerned about proportionality, and required more work from them in that area, than any other judge they worked with.

So with the Swan case, three times I instructed the prosecuting attorneys to discuss the great disparity in the sentences they were recommending with their superiors in the Justice Department in Washington and to ascertain if the Justice Department was being consistent nationwide. Assistant United States Attorney Jack Lacey, who was assisting the Civil Rights Division with the Swan case, wrote to Linda Davis, Criminal Section Chief of the Department of Justice, saying he "personally agreed with [me] that the sentence" recommended by the Justice Department was "draconian."

When the government attorneys failed to respond to my inquiry for four months, I ordered the attorneys representing the Justice Department to confer with Attorney General Janet Reno to find out if this was the consistent policy of the Department of Justice nationwide. Rather than comply, they entered into a plea agreement with Daniel Swan in which the government dropped the charge of using fire in the commission of a felony, just as they had done with Branch and Thomas. In return, Swan agreed not to appeal his conviction or his sentence. He would have to serve his time.

I sentenced Swan to twenty-seven months in the penitentiary: the appropriate sentence imposed by Congress under federal guidelines for cross-burning as to a defendant who went to trial. If he had pled guilty, his sentence would have been about eighteen months.

Swan argued during his trail that his actions were more that of a drunken prank than an act of intimidation, but I remember the fear created by a burning cross. Before I sentenced him, I told Swan, "This is conduct that . . . will not be tolerated." I told him he committed a "heinous crime," engaged in a "despicable act," a "dastardly deed," and that he had "to pay a debt to society for a reprehensible crime" he had committed.

I admonished Swan,

> I don't have any feeling that what you did should be swept under the rug or what you did, that you are an innocent person. . . . You are going to the penitentiary because of what you did. And it is an area that we have got to stamp out; that we have got to live races among each other. And the type of conduct that you exhibited cannot and will not be tolerated. So I don't want you to think that you are going to the penitentiary for something somebody else did. . . . I would suggest that during the time that you are in prison that you do some reading on race relations and maintaining good relations and how that can be done.[5]

The twenty-seven-month sentence I imposed on Swan was 50 percent more time than the Clinton Justice Department under Attorney General Reno had originally offered Swan if he would plea bargain.[6] The sentence imposed was the sentence agreed to by both the Civil Rights Division of the Justice Department and Daniel Swan; it was the precise punishment prescribed by Congress for cross-burning.

Those opposing my nomination paraded the Swan case with its powerful imagery of a burning cross in an attempt to exploit the stereotype of someone soft on cross-burners. It makes no sense. Why would I stand up against bigotry when it was acceptable in the 1960s only to go soft when it is despised today? Why would I stand against cross-burners when it was dangerous only to go soft when the power of the state now protects minority rights? Even politically, why would I stand against those who burned crosses when they were politically powerful only to change sides when those of us seeking reconciliation are finally winning?

No one has accused the Justice Department under President Bill Clinton and Attorney General Janet Reno of being soft on cross-burners because they offered Swan an eighteen-month jail sentence or agreed to the twenty-seven-month sentence I imposed. No one accused Congress of being soft on cross-burners when they mandated an eighteen- or twenty-seven-month sentence for cross-burning under the sentencing guidelines. But that did not keep my opponents from labeling me soft on a cross-burner.

Because the Senate Democrats asked me about the Swan case so near the time for my hearing while I was reviewing dozens of other cases, I reviewed only the transcript of the Swan sentencing and not the entire file. Although it had taken place seven years earlier, I felt comfortable with the facts and law of the case. I failed to appreciate that the attack against me would be based more on symbolism than substance. By the end of my hearing, I would know all too well that the Democrats were more interested in politics than my actual record.

Senator Ted Kennedy suggested my desire for proportionate sentencing stemmed from concern for leniency toward white defendants and not African Americans. His statement was totally untrue. Senator Kennedy had no knowledge whatsoever of my record in that regard. But by assuming the worst and making such accusations, he received press and praise from Far Left groups. I was amazed how judgmental Senator Kennedy can be of others without any evidence, knowledge, or basis for his harsh judgment.

Byron York wrote about Kennedy's attack in *National Review*.

On March 14, 2002, at the Judiciary Committee meeting in which Democrats killed the Pickering nomination, Sen. Edward Kennedy suggested that Pickering practiced a selective form of leniency—that he went easy on a racist cross-burner and tough on everybody else, including blacks convicted of crimes in his court. One week later, on March 21, Pickering sent Hatch a letter in which he said, "I have consistently sought to keep from imposing unduly harsh penalties on young people whom I did not feel were hardened criminals." . . .

Pickering went on to describe several cases in which he "departed downward. . . . Pickering sent Hatch the names of the cases, the case numbers, letters from the defense lawyers involved, and the phone numbers of people to call to check his account of his sentencing practices."[7]

The several cases which I discussed all involved African American defendants.

During the more than thirteen years I was on the district court bench, I departed downward far more times than I departed upward. I can only remember departing upward three or four times, and those instances involved defendants who committed extremely egregious crimes or had an odious criminal history not adequately reflected by the guideline calculations. I departed downward at least eighteen or twenty times, perhaps more. Of my downward departures, more than three-fourths involved African American defendants.

Usually when I departed downward, I would call counsel for the prosecution and counsel for the defendant and the probation officer to the side bar and explain my concerns. These cases typically involved first-time offenders with no previous criminal history, or women who would leave vulnerable children at home. Without exception, the prosecution agreed with the downward departures—that is, until the Swan case.

One case in which I departed downward involved an interracial couple charged with drug crimes. Both husband and wife would have received sixty-month sentences under the guidelines without a downward departure. But the family had extraordinary medical problems: the wife had been hospitalized "several times for a total of approximately ten weeks, due to . . . Crohn's disease" with complications; and one son had had four brain surgeries due to tuberous sclerosis. I concluded the couple's two children would suffer severely with both parents sentenced to the penitentiary. With agreement by all parties, I sentenced the husband to sixty months in prison and departed downward so that I sentenced the wife to home confinement under strict supervision, but no jail time. This is one of those cases that ended well. The wife obtained an unusually good job where she succeeded so well her company wanted to send her temporarily to Alaska. She and her probation officer contacted me for permission and I agreed. Later she sent me a thank-you note with a stamp on the outside that read "God's love never fails" and an inscription inside reading, "Words alone could never thank you for what you have done. We appreciate it and we are working to prove you right." There are few times that a judge comes away from a criminal case with a positive feeling—a sense of having helped a person, a family, and society. This was one of those rare cases.

Another case involved an African American male who stood before me for sentence some seven years after he had committed a drug crime. I departed downward and sentenced this defendant to probation with no jail time. His attorney's letter of support for my nomination best tells the story:

> There is one case in particular that I believe highlights Judge Pickering's fairness regardless of race or status of the defendant. I represented William S. Moody . . . a 32 year old black male who pled guilty to possession with intent to distribute cocaine. . . . Mr. Moody was unaware of any charges against him and had moved with his family to New York City. . . . he showed himself to be a good father and provider for his family. The way he lived his life demonstrated that he had, in fact, changed and became a good and productive member of society. When Judge Pickering was made aware of this marked change in Mr. Moody's life, he made a heartland exception and went outside the sentencing guidelines, which allowed Mr. Moody to go home to his family and allowed Mr. Moody to be monitored for a year. At the end of this year, we appeared in front of Judge Pickering once more. It was shown that William Moody had thrived due to the Judge's compassionate decision. I believe that I speak for my client, Mr. Moody, when I state that Judge Pickering is a fair and compassionate man, which translates into being an excellent judge.[8]

New York Senator Chuck Schumer and Senator Dick Durbin joined Senator Kennedy in his racial demagoguery. But Schumer could have learned the truth of my record if he had just inquired of William Moody, his own constituent.

Other attorneys who represented African American defendants before me also wrote letters of support. Carol Ann Estes Bustin wrote to Senator Patrick Leahy regarding a downward departure I made:

> Most recently, I represented an African American twenty-year-old male brought before the Court for sentencing on a possession with intent to distribute drug charge. My client, a first-offender, did not have a high school degree and admitted to drug use since age 8. Judge Pickering expressed concern for the future of my client and a desire to assist him with improving his life. Judge Pickering granted a reduction in the sentencing guidelines . . . thus enabling my client to qualify for several rehabilitative opportunities while incarcerated . . . . I believe my client's sentencing experience with Judge Pickering may have been a positive life-changing experience for the defendant.[9]

Attorney Scott Swartz related another example to Senator Leahy:

> Recently I represented a young African American gentleman who was charged in a crack cocaine operation. . . . Based on the assistance provided by my client, the government moved for a downward departure in his sentence. Judge Pickering followed that recommendation and reduced my client's sentence by some ten (10) years. Judge Pickering has always given careful consideration to the sentences he has imposed in the cases which I have handled. I have personally observed Judge Pickering take a true interest in trying to make criminal defendants turn their lives around to become productive citizens.[10]

Senators Kennedy, Schumer, and Durbin were more concerned with creating a caricature of me as a racist soft on a cross-burner as demanded by Far Left special-interest groups than with my actual record. They were not interested in the letters from attorneys who actually appeared before me in court and knew the truth. My desire in the Swan case for proportionate and fair sentencing was consistent with my career on the bench for not just white defendants, but African Americans as well.

When the *Atlanta Journal Constitution* sent reporters to Mississippi to do an in-depth analysis of my record, their headlines revealed their findings: "Evidence doesn't support charges of racism against Charles

Pickering" and "The Cross-Burning Trial—AJC review shows fairness, not bias, at the root of ruling."[11]

Steve Henderson, reporter for Knight Ridder newspapers, wrote, "The State Legislature was . . . where Pickering began his crusade to keep first-time offenders out of prison. He sponsored several bills to create separate jails to focus on rehabilitating, rather than punishing, those who might be redeemable."[12] Henderson's report showed a consistency in my concern for first-time offenders both while I was in the legislature and while I was on the bench.

But symbols are more powerful than words, and a burning cross is the most terrifying of all; it is the symbol of racial oppression. I know how terrible it is: I fought it in the 1960s before many of my detractors were born and while others were sitting on the sidelines.

My opponents believed their cause of protecting a "woman's right to choose" justified smearing a nominee's reputation, besmirching a nominee's record, and engaging in racial demagoguery. In their style of politics, the end justifies the means. My second hearing made this all too clear. My opponents attacked on other issues, but misrepresenting the Swan case was their central assault to block my confirmation. They understood that to succeed in defeating my nomination, they would have to make my next hearing "nasty and contentious." They did. It was.

As Promised: A "Nasty and Contentious" Hearing

AS THE YEAR 2002 came into focus, the special-interest groups' strategy of derailing the nominations of conservative judges in order to protect (in their minds) abortion rights, as well as send a message to the White House on potential nominations to the Supreme Court, gained steam. We better understand the organizations' and the Democrats' agenda now thanks to the leak of Democratic strategy memos detailing secret meetings held in Senator Kennedy's office. Manuel A. Miranda obtained and leaked the memos to the *Wall Street Journal* in November 2003. Miranda is the former counsel to Senate Majority Leader Bill Frist and former senior counsel to Senator Orrin Hatch when he was chairman of the Judiciary Committee. Democrats claimed Miranda hacked their computers to get these memos; Miranda claimed the memos were on an open server accessible to both Republicans and Democrats, and he did nothing wrong by looking at files on an open computer. Nevertheless, Miranda lost his job over the incident. Regardless, the memos make the coordinated effort between the leaders of the Far Left special-interest groups and the Democratic senators and their staff very clear.[1]

I could not figure out why I had no opposition for five months only to suddenly develop it just two days before my hearing. These memos—released months later—explain the reason. The "nasty and contentious" hearing promised by the special-interest groups back in December was just around the corner. Confirmation proceedings were going to spiral to a new low.

A memo addressed to Illinois senator Dick Durbin from his staff dated October 15, 2001 (just three days before my first hearing and one day before the groups announced their opposition to my nomination), provides the background and a list of the culture warriors lining up against conservative judicial nominees:

> You are scheduled to meet with leaders of several civil rights organizations to discuss their serious concerns with the judicial nomination process. The leaders will include: Ralph Neas (People for the American Way), Kate Michelman (NARAL), Nan Aron (Alliance for Justice), Wade Henderson (Leadership Conference on Civil Rights), Leslie Proll (NAACP Legal Defense & Education Fund), Nancy Zirkin (American Association of University Women), Marcia Greenberger (National Women's Law Center), Judy Lichtman (National Partnership), and a representative from the AFL-CIO. The meeting will take place in 317 Russell, with Senators Kennedy and (possibly) Schumer also present.

A second memo described the meeting:

> The immediate catalyst for Tuesday's meeting was the announcement last Thursday that the Judiciary Committee would hold a hearing in one week on district court judge Charles W. Pickering, Sr., a highly controversial nominee for the Fifth Circuit. The interest groups have two objections: (1) in light of the terrorist attacks, it was their understanding that no controversial judicial nominees would be moved this fall; and (2) they were given assurances that they would receive plenty of notice to prepare for any controversial nominee . . . .
>
> Recognizing that Thursday's hearing is likely to go forward, the groups are asking that the Committee hold a second hearing on Pickering in a few weeks when they will have had adequate time to research him fully. The decision to schedule Pickering's hearing was made by Senator Leahy himself, not his staff, so the groups are likely to ask you to intercede personally. They will also seek assurances that they will receive adequate warning of future controversial nominees.

(The left-wing special-interest groups had already determined I was controversial, though they claimed they needed time to research me fully. Obviously, they did not base their belief that I was controversial on my record, as they had yet to research it.)

Another memo to Senator Durbin, dated November 6, 2001, reiterated the groups' desire for delay: "The groups would like to postpone action on these nominees until next year, when (presumably) the public will be more tolerant of partisan dissent." So soon after the September 11 terrorist attacks, the voters were in no mood for extreme partisan politics, and the groups knew it and sought a delay to remove the hearing from the national feelings of unity.

On November 7, 2001, Senator Durbin's staffer wrote another memo summarizing a meeting Durbin had missed the previous afternoon:

> You missed a meeting with Senator Kennedy and representatives of various civil rights groups. This was intended to follow up a meeting in Senator Kennedy's office in mid October, when the groups expressed serious concern with a quick hearing for Charles Pickering and the pace of judicial nominations generally.

The groups wanted to slow down the confirmation process that was already moving at a snail's pace. The memorandum continued, "Yesterday's meeting accomplished two objectives. First, the groups advocated for some procedural ground rules." The groups wanted "a commitment that nominees voted down in the Committee will not get a floor vote." The memo continued,

> Second, yesterday's meeting focused on identifying the most controversial and/or vulnerable judicial nominees, and a strategy for targeting them. The groups singled out three—Jeffrey Sutton (6th Circuit); Priscilla Owen (5th Circuit); and Caroline Kuhl (9th Circuit)—as a potential nominee for a contentious hearing early next year with a eye to voting him or her down in Committee.

The groups were looking for nominees who were either vulnerable or controversial, or both. At the time, I was not among those identified in their hit list. On information received from the left-wing special-interest groups, the staffer divided the Bush nominees into three categories: "the good," "the bad," and "the ugly":

> Based on input from the groups, I would place the appellate nominees in the categories below:

Good	Bad	Ugly
Clifton (9th Cir.)	Shedd (4th Cir.)	Boyle (4th Cir.)
Melloy (8th Cir.)	Roberts (D.C. Cir.)	Owen (5th Cir.)
O'Brian (10th Cir.)	L. Smith (8th Cir.)	Sutton (6th Cir.)
Howard (1st Cir.)	Pickering (5th Cir.)	Cook (6th Cir.)
B. Smith (3rd Cir.)	Tymkovich (10th Cir.)	McConnell (10th Cir.)
	Gibbons (6th Cir.)	Estrada (D.C. Cir.)
	Steele (11th Cir.)	Kuhl (9th Cir.)

The memo also noted the motivation of the special-interest groups to engage in this unprecedented confirmation battle. It said the groups wanted a "Big fight early next year. Three benefits: 1.) Sends message on Supreme Court; 2.) Forces WH to bargain; 3.) Encourages more moderate nominees. To work, need all 10 Dems on board and need commitment not to go to the floor."

They did not single me out among the three nominees originally targeted for a contentious hearing. They did not list me in the group's worst category, "the ugly"; they just categorized me as "bad." Yet eventually the groups blocked me in committee and, a year and a half later, filibustered me. The November 7 memo explains the reason: "Query: will it be possible to get all 10 Dems to commit before a hearing? Doubtful. There is a big risk. We must choose a nominee tailored to our weakest link, e.g., Pickering is bad, but is he bad enough? Probably not—finish him AFTER." The memo targeted Carolyn Kuhl, Jeffrey Sutton, and Priscilla Owen as the nominees "most controversial and/or vulnerable." The memo writer said Kuhl was a "bad idea" because

Senator Boxer would never return the blue slip, so "why waste that power." The writer continued,

> Sutton will be hard to beat—very strong paper record, impressive credentials . . . Sutton is personification of the threat the New Federalism poses to Civil Rights, but his defenders will muddle debate. Why not use someone else, show WH we mean business. . . . [Judge Priscilla Owen] is from Texas and appointed to [Texas Supreme Court] by Bush, so she will appear parochial and out of mainstream. She is definitively anti-abortion.

They had selected Priscilla Owen as their target. She was anti-abortion, and the groups thought her vulnerable. But my hearing came up before her hearing and the groups reacted to that change in plans. The memos explain why opposition against me erupted after I had drawn none for five months. The groups wanted to send a message to the White House—no conservative nominees to the Supreme Court—and they thought I was vulnerable, that they could use the specter of the burning cross in the Swan case to defeat me. My nomination was first over the hill, so they took aim and fired.

Stephen Henderson, writing for the Knight Ridder papers, laid it out: "The assault was so easy. Take a white, conservative, religious judicial nominee from Mississippi, pluck a few votes from his career in the state Senate, a handful of cases from his time on the Federal Bench, and use them to brand him as an enemy of racial progress."[2]

As my confirmation hearing neared, the news media announced the big fight over judicial nominations was approaching. *USA Today* reported that my confirmation hearing was "kicking off what likely will be a series of bruising fights over President Bush's judicial nominees."[3] *National Review* called the hearing "the first major judicial, confirmation battle of the Bush Administration."[4] A *New York Times* article by Neal Lewis called my hearing

> the beginning of a long expected war over judicial nominations . . . . Civil rights and abortion rights groups have selected Judge Pickering, now a Federal trial Judge, as their first major target for defeat. . . . Two

competing depictions of Charles Pickering have been put forward. His opponents describe him as a 'throw back to the old segregated South,' . . . His supporters have portrayed him almost as a kind of Atticus Finch, the heroic lawyer standing against bigotry in the novel "To Kill a Mockingbird." They say he has been a progressive figure on racial issues in Mississippi, and they praised him for testifying against a Ku Klux Klan leader at a murder trial in the 1960s.[5]

The *New York Times* article quoted James King, the first African American Republican field man in Mississippi, whom I had hired. King said he was "stunned that anyone would charge that Mr. Pickering was insensitive on the issue of race. . . . He has always been my mentor."

Elliot Mincberg of People for the American Way (PFAW) acknowledged to *Human Events* that despite the volumes and reams of paper they had required me to produce, they had found "no smoking gun":

No single accusation in the report is particularly damning in itself. . . . It is the Judge's record as a whole . . . that poses a problem for PFAW. In an interview with the *Legal Times*, Mincberg made his point more clearly. "There is not a single smoking gun. This is a mosaic." This "mosaic" pieced together by PFAW is meant to impress through the sheer number of its pieces—and through the many dubious inferences it contains . . . [but as the *Washington Post* opined] "None of these incidents, when examined closely, amounts to much. But opponents string them together, gloss over their complexities and self-righteously present a caricature of an unworthy candidate."[6]

The *National Review* noted that the PFAW report leveled dozens of accusations against my nomination, but

While the charges sound quite ominous, a close look at the case shows there is little, if any, evidence to support it. . . . Given the paucity of evidence against Pickering, one has to ask why PFAW, along with other liberal interest groups, is attacking him with such energy. Perhaps the urge to label a 64-year-old white man from Mississippi as a racist is just too strong to resist. More likely, though, it appears that PFAW is acting because activist organizations need to *act*. . . .

Democrats and their interest-group supporters have been wanting a fight, and now, in the unlikely case of Charles W. Pickering, they have one.[7]

The real objective, the ultimate target, was not my nomination to the Fifth Circuit Court of Appeals; it was the Supreme Court. Everyone knew this even without the Democratic strategy memos. Viet Dinh from the Bush Justice Department told *USA Today*, "The outside interest groups have made clear that the nomination of Judge Pickering and other lower court nominees is a warm-up practice for an eventual Supreme Court nominee."[8] Senator Trent Lott told *Fox News* Sunday, "This is really about the Supreme Court . . . this is a shot at the President saying, 'If you come up with a basically conservative Republican who is pro-life, we are going to take him down.'"[9] It was little consolation to me that the real motivator was not me or my record, but potential Supreme Court vacancies. It was my reputation they attacked; it was my nomination that would be voted on.

The Judiciary Committee scheduled my hearing for Thursday afternoon, February 7, at two o'clock. I returned to Washington on Tuesday before the hearing so I could finish preparing. Margaret Ann came with me. I have one brother, Gene, who is eight years younger than I am; he lives near our home in the western edge of Jones County. I also have one sister who is eight years older and who lives in Crosby, Texas. They both decided to come up the day before the hearing to be present and supportive.

While preparing for the hearing, an assistant to Viet Dinh came in and made a request so insignificant that I don't remember the nature of it. However, when I indicated a reluctance to comply, the assistant quickly responded, "Well, this is the president's nomination." I retorted, "Well, if the president wants his nomination back, he can have it. This process quit being fun a long time ago." The assistant backed down and we resolved the dispute. In truth, this really was the president's nomination and one I was honored to receive, but the process had turned ugly. The excessive demands by the Democrats and special-interest groups for information, which they then distorted to attack my record and character, disheartened me. But while aggravating, their attack had the opposite effect than what they intended. Rather than causing me to back down and withdraw—which they wanted—it emboldened me to defend my name and the process.

Another encounter was more foreboding. Late Thursday morning I was making final preparations for an opening statement to respond to the charges that the special-interest groups continued to levy against me. A justice department lawyer—one of Viet Dinh's assistants—walked into the room where I was working. She had internal memorandums from the Civil Rights Division of the Department of Justice written by the government attorneys who appeared before me during the Swan cross-burning case.

Viet Dinh was out of town at a retreat. Attorney General John Ashcroft was holding with the heads of the various divisions within the Justice Department. The assistant did not give me copies of the memos or allow me to review them, saying she thought these memos might be made available to me at some point, but not yet. Then, without telling me what was going on, she explained she did not agree with what was being considered and left me to finish my preparations puzzled and a little concerned. But at that moment, I needed to finish my statement. I didn't have time to analyze what she said or what was happening.

The White House Counsel's Office had decided at the last minute to reverse their previous decision not to deliver internal Justice Department memos to the Judiciary Committee. The White House sent the memos to the Judiciary Committee and the Democrats in control of the committee, although I myself had not been given an opportunity to review them. When I walked into the committee room, Senator John Edwards, with White House aspirations on his mind, was reviewing these documents and preparing to examine me in a way to make a name for himself among the left-wing special-interest groups so powerful in the Democratic primary.

How the White House could make such a strategic blunder on "the president's nomination" is beyond me. The memos contained nothing incriminating or destructive, but without reviewing them and refreshing myself as to the facts, the law, and the context of events transpiring seven years past, I was ill prepared to answer the type of questioning that awaited me.

At the Senate hearing room, Senators Trent Lott and Thad Cochran came by to visit before the hearing started. Chip was there with the rest of my family. Civil rights activist Charles Evers; Judge Johnny Williams, an African American friend and chancery judge from Hattiesburg; and James King, the man I had hired to work for the Mississippi Republican Party, were present in support of my nomination. Frank Montague, a defense lawyer from Hattiesburg who had served as president of both the Mississippi Bar and the Mississippi Defense Bar, as well as plaintiff lawyers Mike McMahan of Hattiesburg and Dickey Scruggs of Pascagoula, were also present. Several members of the Mississippi congressional delegation staff attended.

California Democratic Senator Diane Feinstein, not Senator Chuck Schumer who had presided at my first hearing and who had promised to protect me if it was necessary to have a second hearing, presided over the hearing. Perhaps having Feinstein preside was an attempt to put a softer face on the hearing; but, while she was gracious, she was a single-issue voter—abortion—and there was no way she was going to vote for me regardless of the hearing. Whatever the attempt, the hearing did not have a soft touch. Democrats were unable to camouflage their attacks.

Following Senator Feinstein's remarks attempting to justify the second hearing (which of course made no mention that the left-wing special-interest groups had demanded it), Republican senator Mitch McConnell of Kentucky made an opening statement on my behalf. He recounted my life story, with strong emphasis on my fight against the Klan. McConnell stated, "[a] twenty-seven-year-old Charles Pickering stared in the face his political future." He spoke about Margaret Ann and my children, how my children did not "understand hate and murder" that confronted us at that time during the civil rights movement. He imagined that when I was away from home at night, Margaret Ann would "lie awake in fear, hoping she would hear her husband's footsteps coming home." He described how "Charles Pickering reached down in his soul and embraced the only thing he [had], his religious faith." He shamed my opponents, saying, "while it is easy in Washington in 2002 to make a speech or sign a bill in favor of civil rights after decades of changed racial attitudes in schools and society and in the press, who among us would have had the courage of Charles Pickering in Laurel, Mississippi, in 1967? Who among us would have had the courage of his wife, Margaret, to stand with him?"[10] His graciousness stunned me and his words moved my family and my supporters.

Senator Patrick Leahy entered a statement into the record also seeking to justify my second hearing, as well as citing the failure of Republicans to approve many of President Bill Clinton's nominees. Leahy utilized this tactic at nearly every hearing. He would blame the Republicans for past failures to consider nominees. Republicans would argue back. Each party would attempt to blame the other for failures of the process and to justify their own actions. These discussions had nothing to do with the qualifications of nominees then before the committee. To nominees whose future hung in the balance, these exchanges were disconcerting and beneath the dignity of the Senate. The confirmation fight over the Bush nominees was not the Senate's finest hour.

Following my opening statement that addressed the charges raised against me by the groups opposing my nomination, Senator Orrin Hatch delivered a strong statement on my behalf:

> I am . . . troubled at what appears to be a national agenda by a coalition of leftist interest groups who have spent months hunting around for an excuse to use the Pickering nomination as a way to attempt to paint this administration's nominees as extreme. Although I am concerned by the underlying agenda, I believe they have picked the wrong nominee for that.[11]

Hatch outlined the support I had in Mississippi from all walks of life, including Democrats and African Americans.

At my first hearing in October 2001, questions from Democratic senators were pointed, but nonetheless civil. In my second hearing in February 2002, all pretext of civility was gone. The gloves were off; it was bare knuckles.

Senator Leahy led off by trying to paint me as incompetent because I had been reversed twenty-six times out of some 4,000-5,000 cases. I thought CNN captured our exchange well. Leahy opined, "You say you will follow the law, not your personal opinion. But I look at your record as a district judge and you have been reversed by the Fifth Circuit at least 26 times. Now, either that was because you followed your personal opinion or you didn't follow the law. It has got to be one or the other." I responded, "But 25 or 26 out of 4,000; that is slightly more than one-half of 1 percent of the cases that I have handled."[12] Leahy did not come off well in this exchange covered by CNN.

For any judge to be reversed no more than one-half of 1 percent of all cases handled is a good record. With my ABA rating and overwhelming support from the Mississippi Bar, the charge that I had a bad record concerning affirmances was difficult to sell. Only a partisan would make the accusation that such was a bad record. In fact, when my nomination was still pending before the Senate—one and a half years later—we compared my reversal rate with other judges. Not only was my reversal rate for all cases handled less than one-half of 1 percent, but also of those cases actually appealed, my reversal rate was only some 6 percent (26 cases out of 424 actual appeals).[13] My reversal rate was well below the median reversal rate of all judges in the Fifth Circuit, and furthermore it was one-third lower than the U.S. Department of Justice's nationwide average of 9.1 percent.[14]

Consider the contrast of my record with two Clinton nominees: Judge Wallace Tashima of the central district of California, nominated to the Ninth Circuit Court of Appeals; and Judge Diana Murphy of the eastern district of Minnesota, nominated to the Eight Circuit Court of Appeals. During his 15 years on the trial bench, Judge Tashima was reversed 96 times out of 7,792 cases for a reversal rate of 1.2 percent. During her 14 years on the trial bench, Judge Murphy had 84 reversals out of 6,705 cases, also a reversal rate of 1.2 percent. Of the 4,567 cases I had handled over some 11 years, I had 26 reversals for a reversal rate of one-half of 1 percent, less than half that of these two nominees. The Senate unanimously confirmed both those judges a few years earlier, and Senator Leahy expressed no concern of their reversal rate.[15] I do not suggest that Tashima and Murphy did not have a good rate of affirmance; but rather, this contrast demonstrates the hypocrisy and lack of merit of the Democratic charges that I had been frequently reversed, was incompetent, or unwilling to follow the law.

Next, Senator Ted Kennedy challenged me because he found only two or three cases in which I had ruled for the plaintiff in employment discrimination cases. I responded, "I had my staff go back and look . . . . I had 170 closed cases [employment]. I had 68 settled, 51 summary judgments granted, 11 voluntarily dismissed, and 3 tried to verdict. So more than half of the cases that came before me either settled . . . were voluntarily dismissed or they went to trial."

Kennedy knew I had never been reversed for failing to provide equal employment protection for any plaintiff. Furthermore, Mary Baltar—a plaintiff who had an employment discrimination case before me—had written a letter stating that I "treated her fairly," and when she found out I was going to be handling her case "she did not request a jury" because she trusted me to determine not only the law, but the facts as well. Jim Wade, a Democratic attorney who probably handles more employment cases than any other lawyer in Mississippi, wrote a letter to the editor expressing his strong support for my confirmation and attesting to my fairness in employment discrimination cases.

Kennedy's premise was even more fundamentally flawed. A judge cannot keep statistics to make sure that he rules for an equal number of plaintiffs and defendants. Each case has to be determined on its own merits, not to make sure that you rule for a plaintiff the same number of times that you rule for a defendant. If I had not properly handled employment discrimination cases, where was the case in which I had been reversed? Where was the evidence? There was none. Kennedy did not let the facts get in his way.

Senator Kennedy questioned me because I had described some employment cases as frivolous. The ones he cited indeed were frivolous, which I am sure is why he did not discuss the facts of the cases. Had he done so, he would have looked ridiculous. As it was, he still came across supporting frivolous lawsuits. I responded, "Whenever frivolous lawsuits are brought . . . that hinders the good lawsuits. . . . I think that is detrimental to African Americans who have good claims."[16] Again, CNN carried this exchange that was favorable to me. I believe without question judges must allow legitimate lawsuits to go forward but dismiss frivolous lawsuits as soon as it becomes obvious they are not legitimate.

Senator Dick Durbin's questioning crossed the line of decency. He tried to paint me as an unreconstructed racist because I practiced law with the late Carroll Gartin. While I was in law school in 1959, Carroll ran for governor of Mississippi. Ross Barnett, one of Mississippi's most vocal and rabid segregationist governors, defeated Carroll, who was the sitting lieutenant governor. The White Citizens Council supported Barnett because of his total commitment to segregation. In 1963, Carroll was once again elected lieutenant governor. He passed away in 1966.

Durbin was relentless in his accusations that Carroll Gartin ran as a segregationist. Not only was Durbin trying to paint me as a racist through guilt by association because I practiced law with Carroll—which by itself is reprehensible—but he was judging him through a twenty-first-century perspective and not that of the 1950s and 1960s in Mississippi. If Durbin wanted to be critical of my record, so be it. However, it was entirely inappropriate to make charges against a man who had been dead for almost forty years and to bring pain to his elderly widow and children just for the sake of making a partisan political point in a different time and era and for something that had nothing to do with him.

Besides his lack of decency in the attack on the late Carroll Gartin, Durbin was just plain wrong. Mississippi's *Clarion Ledger* editorialized,

[F]ormer Democratic Governor William Winter—a long time Democrat who serves on the board of directors of Ole Miss' Institute for Racial Reconciliation with Pickering—said that the Judges' association with Gartin is actually a positive. "Carroll Gartin was regarded as a progressive political figure at the time."[17]

Winter said that,

> such a relationship must be put into perspective of the times. "Carroll
> Gartin was no racist. . . . [H]e did, as did every political candidate in
> those days, give lip service to segregation." . . . Pickering "has been
> one of this State's most dedicated and effective voices for breaking
> down racial barriers." Winter also said that he and Pickering have
> worked closely together as members of the Institute for Racial
> Reconciliation at the University of Mississippi.[18]

Veteran political columnist Bill Minor has covered Mississippi
politics for six decades, including the turbulent years of the civil rights
movement and integration. He is perceived by many Mississippians as
very liberal, by some Mississippians as moderate, but considered by none
as conservative. Most agree he has been one of the most active journalis-
tic advocates for civil rights in the state. Minor wrote,

> Those who cite Federal District Judge Charles Pickering's having
> practiced law in Laurel during the 1960s with then Lt. Governor
> Carroll Gartin as indicative of Pickering's segregationist past are
> barking up the wrong tree.
>   This writer knew almost all of the players on the scene back in
> those days of racial extremism and Gartin, who died suddenly in
> 1966, was far from being one of the racists. Gartin, in fact, was
> defeated for Governor in 1959 after being branded as a "moderate" (a
> term implying being soft on segregation back then) by the segrega-
> tionist White Citizens Council . . . .
>   Certainly, if Pickering's association with the late Carroll Gartin is
> the best "evidence" foes have against his judgeship appointment, they
> don't have much of a case.[19]

Republican senator Jon Kyl of Arizona came into the hearing room
during Durbin's questioning. Kyl responded to the tenor of Durbin's
accusations:

> I do want to comment a little bit on the tone of what I perceive. I was
> here in the very beginning and then picking up recently, and I just

wonder what the public must think watching a hearing like this: a candidate who twelve years ago passed the Committee and the Floor unanimously when he became a Federal district judge, who served with distinction, and now is being cross-examined here as if he is almost a criminal. Very tough questioning on that side of the dais, very negative questioning against this nominee. . . . I think as a committee we have to be very, very careful because history will judge us.[20]

The inquisition by Senator John Edwards was the most vicious of all. He had reviewed copies of the memos from the Swan case that I had not been allowed to see. Earlier that morning, my wife Margaret Ann and Chip's wife Leisha had attended the National Prayer Breakfast where Edwards had been one of the co-chairmen. He had commented at the prayer breakfast that there was "a sweet, sweet spirit" in the room; but there was nothing sweet about his spirit that afternoon.

Early in January, supporters of my confirmation told me Senator Edwards was committed to vote for me. As opposition began to mount, these supporters started attempting to reach Edwards; he would not return their phone calls. One person who had close contact with Edwards advised me that since he was running for president, he was getting nervous that if he supported me, the liberal feminist groups would not support his national campaign.

He had not been present for any of the rest of the hearing. He came into the hearing room just in time to make his attack. Although I was somewhat doubtful of his support, I was still hopeful, and as he sat down, I looked up at him and smiled. Edwards responded to my smile by striking like an adder.

He had prepared an ambush with copies of the memos I had not seen. By the inflection of voice, he made it sound like I had said things that I had not said. He would cut me off before I could finish answering questions. He interrogated me relentlessly. If he had been a prosecutor and I a criminal, his approach would not have been different. He showed no deference, no respect to the Third Branch. He portrayed a call I made to Frank Hunger at the Justice Department during the Swan trial as unethical.[21] Although he was unable to find time to call his friends and my supporters before the hearing, after he had viciously questioned me, he immediately left the room and called one of them to tell him what he had done.

Months later on CNN's *Inside Politics*, Ted Kennedy told Judy Woodruff, "John Edwards's questioning of . . . Mr. Pickering, destroyed Mr. Pickering, as he should have been destroyed."[22] How uncivil and unbecoming a United States senator to think that a judicial nominee's reputation should be destroyed. Kennedy has a double standard for himself and others.

Professor Michael Krauss, professor of law at George Mason University and president of the Virginia Association of Scholars, reviewed the ethical issues raised by Edwards concerning the Swan case. Professor Krauss has taught legal ethics for a number of years and measured my conduct in the Swan case against the *Model Code of Judicial Conduct.* He concluded that what I did in the Swan case "merits praise, not criticism." He said he closely examined my actions and found "a determined effort by Judge Pickering to discharge, faithfully and competently, his judicial duties under our Constitution."[23]

The hearing adjourned a little after six-thirty that evening, four hours and thirty-five minutes after it began. I was exhausted. As I walked with family and friends from the hearing to Union Station to get a bite to eat, I learned from Chip that the Democrats had intertwined my confirmation battle and his redistricting fight.

A Democratic operative named Richard Buckman who had worked closely with congressmen Bennie Thompson and Ronnie Shows approached a lobbyist and former aide to Senator Trent Lott about a possible deal: my confirmation in exchange for Chip agreeing to the Democratic redistricting plan. When Chip told me about it, I retorted, "We quit child sacrifice a long time ago." Chip was a young man and I was approaching, and now am, a senior citizenship. There was no way I would let Chip give up his congressional seat in exchange for continuing my judicial career. Of course, the truth of the matter is that we don't know if Buckman made the offer with any authority from Shows or Thompson and even if he did, whether or not they could have delivered such.

However, Carl Cameron of *Fox News* reported discussions of the deal had surfaced among Senate Democrats:

> Sources with direct knowledge of the talks say some Judiciary Committee Democrats opposed to the nomination had discussed the exchange with other members of the Senate who had privately expressed support for the deal. They could not say, however, whether the proposed deal was concocted by lawmakers on Capitol Hill or the intermediaries themselves.[24]

Regardless, the proposal was a non-starter.

My day was over; the press's day was just getting started. An Associated Press story reported, "the grilling of U.S. District Judge Charles [Pickering] went on for more than four hours. . . . A Republican said Democrats treated the Judge like a criminal."[25]

The Capitol Hill newspaper *Roll Call* published a headline proclaiming "Edwards's Tactics Draw Ire" and described Edwards's actions as "blistering" and "relentless." The writer commented on Edwards's tactic of "frequently cutting Pickering off and forcing him into one-word and yes-or-no answers." The article quoted "lifelong Democrat" Dickey Scruggs as saying, "'[Pickering] is getting a bum rap.' . . . Scruggs said that he left the hearing disgusted with Edwards, who he felt was twisting the facts of the case and playing the role of 'the heavy' at the behest of other Democrats."[26]

Moderate columnist Mort Kondracke wrote a column titled "Pickering Fight Shows Liberals at Their Worst," noting,

> Democrats are . . . adept at character attack. . . . It's time for liberal groups such as People for the American Way and the NAACP to quit using character assassination to defeat conservative judicial nominees—and for Democratic Senators to show some independence from them. . . . In what ought to be a humiliating blow to the anti-Pickering assault brigade, The New York Times last Sunday reported that African American leaders in his hometown overwhelmingly vouch for him and dismiss charges that he's racially prejudiced. . . . People for the American Way Director Ralph Neas was reduced to

saying that those who have watched Pickering at close hand for decades know less about him than Washington activists. . . . I'd trust Mississippi civil rights leader Charles Evers, who backs Pickering, a lot sooner than the NAACP's Julian Bond and Kwesi Mfume. . . . Close examination by Jonathan Groner in Legal Times and Byron York in National Review pretty clearly discredit Neas' charges that Pickering has been biased in employment and voting-rights cases and was too lenient—and may have behaved unethically—in a cross-burning case. . . . York has demolished the basis for attacks on Pickering by Democratic presidential hopeful Sen. John Edwards (N.C.) in the 1994 cross-burning case.[27]

A *Washington Post* editorial took the Democrats to task for their mean-spirited attack:

> Opposing a nominee should not mean destroying him. And the attack on Judge Pickering has become an ugly affair. His critics have focused for the most part not on his qualifications, temperament, approach to judging or on the quality of his judicial work. The judge's opponents, rather, have tried to paint him as a barely reconstructed segregationist. To do so, they have plucked a number of unconnected incidents from a long career. . . . The portrayal is particularly unfair. . . . The need on the part of liberal groups and Democratic senators to portray him as a Neanderthal—all the while denying they are doing so—in order to justify voting him down is the latest example of the degradation of the confirmation process.[28]

The conservative *Human Events* praised the *Washington Post* and *New York Times* for condemning the approach taken by Democrats: "Last week, the character assassination reached such a nasty and dishonest pitch, that even two liberal newspapers, *The New York Times* and *The Washington Post*, felt compelled to weigh in—in defense of the President's man."[29] When the liberal press is appalled at how liberal Democrats treat a conservative nominee of a Republican president, Democrats must have crossed a line.

One headline proclaimed "Democrats Bork Pickering as Test Run for Bush Supreme Court Nominations."[30] "To Bork" has been defined as a "relentless effort by interest groups . . . creating a grotesque image of the person in order to build public pressure by alarmed constituents."[31] Judge Robert Bork, looking back on the fight over the Bush nominees, said, "I think it's nastier than it's ever been probably."[32] A law professor at George Washington University, Jonathan Turley, said, "These people have entered the dangerous realm of symbolism . . . some of these nominees appear almost to have been selected at random."[33] An Associated Press reporter concluded, "Somewhere, behind all the labels . . . there are . . . people."[34]

Jerry Mitchell, Klan expert and civil rights award-winning newspaper investigative reporter, has written numerous articles that helped bring about the prosecution in recent years of Klansmen charged with civil rights violations from the 1960s. He wrote, "Criticism of how he stood on civil rights is nothing new for U. S. District Judge Charles Pickering of Laurel. He got plenty of flack from the Ku Klux Klan in the 1960s when he prosecuted members for violence."[35] Jay Nordlinger wrote in the *National Review*, "The most delicious line uttered in this whole business came from Medgar Evers's brother, who said, 'The NAACP and the Klan are the only two organizations [in Mississippi] that are against him.'"[36]

Neither Judge Robert Bork nor the Reagan Administration was prepared for the onslaught against his nomination to the Supreme Court. Justice Clarence Thomas was likewise not prepared for the unprecedented attack on his confirmation. When it became evident that Justice Thomas was not going to be confirmed unless he came out swinging, he convinced the White House Staff to unleash him and let him defend himself. He did so aggressively and accused his opponents of a "high tech lynching." I can still vividly remember watching it on television. He gave an impassioned defense. He was superb. He was masterful. But he was not prepared for the hearing. Neither was I.

Byron York wrote,

As improbable as it might seem to veterans of confirmation wars, some in the GOP were surprised by the ferocity of Democratic attacks on Pickering. Some Republicans were apparently lulled into a sense of confidence by Pickering's lack of any obvious vulnerabilities; after all,

Pickering had been unanimously confirmed to the U.S. District Court ten years before, with the votes of Democratic senators who now oppose him. Also, the American Bar Association, assessing his decade of work on the bench, gave Pickering its "well qualified" rating. And he had the support of many community leaders, both black and white, in his home state of Mississippi, as well as the support of both home state senators. . . . Yet the Democratic attack came, and some Republicans were not ready for it. . . . even some of the Senate's less confrontational Republicans have realized that the Pickering fight was just the first of many to come.[37]

My second hearing was history. Just as the left-wing special-interest groups promised, it had been "nasty and contentious." I had the support of all Republicans on the Judiciary Committee, but that was only nine out of nineteen, not enough to get out of committee. There were ten Democrats on the committee, and if I could not get the vote of one of them, my nomination could not move forward. Whether one of the Democrats would exercise a profile in courage and stand against the left-wing special-interest groups remained to be seen. But of one thing I was now certain: I wanted to fight to the last breath. The Senate Judiciary Committee would (after delays) reconvene for a vote on my nomination on March 7. I had one month to find one vote.

Looking for One Vote

DUE TO THE switch of Senator Jim Jeffords, Democrats controlled the Judiciary Committee the entire time my nomination had been under consideration. Prior to his switch, the math on the Judiciary Committee was on the side of the Bush nominees. There had been ten Republicans and nine Democrats, so on a straight party-line vote, all of us could have been—and I am convinced would have been—reported to the Senate floor. When Jeffords switched, the math reversed and a straight party-line vote could bottle any nominee up in committee and deny any of us an up or down vote before the full Senate. To make it out of the Judiciary Committee, a nominee needed all the Republicans and at least one vote from the Democrats.

What if Jeffords had not switched parties? Marty Wiseman, head of the Stennis Institute at Mississippi State University, said,

> Pickering would not have had a problem if the Senate had not changed hands in the summer when Sen. Jim Jeffords, I-Vt., bolted from the GOP, throwing the majority to the Democrats. If the GOP had retained control, it's likely it would have swiftly approved the 64-year-old federal judge.[1]

Speculating on what might have happened does not change reality.

Immediately after my second hearing, several Democratic senators forwarded me numerous questions and requests for follow-up answers. I doubt most of them cared what I had to say because they had already made up their minds. In most cases, the senators were probably not even involved; it was likely their staffs requesting information at the behest of the left-wing special-interest groups who were trying to build their case against me and appeal to their activist grassroots and fundraising donor base. Regardless, I had to respond. So when I returned to Mississippi from my second hearing, I was doing the same thing I did before I left—forwarding reams of paper to Washington.

Now I and those supporting my nomination had an additional task. We were looking for one Democratic vote. I needed at least one Democrat to allow my nomination to go to the floor. In the end, this Democrat did not have to support my nomination, did not have to vote to confirm me. The Democrat could even oppose me, but support the principle that every nominee deserves an up or down vote, and so vote with the Republicans to move me out of committee. We were told Senator John Edwards was going to be that vote—that is, until the hearing. Now we had to look elsewhere for that one essential vote.

Three days after my hearing, Senator Trent Lott appeared on *Fox News Sunday*. He was not as confident as he had been before the hearing when he predicted my overwhelming confirmation. He was asked if he thought I would win confirmation. He responded, "I think it is going to be close . . . but I certainly hope he does. He deserves it. This is a very unfair besmirching of a good man's record."[2]

One week after my hearing, the Associated Press reported,

> Republicans have delayed the vote on Pickering for two weeks as they [seek] to find a Democrat on the Committee to vote for Pickering . . . . White House officials, including Counsel Alberto Gonzales, have been calling Democrats and visiting Capitol Hill in search of that elusive vote. . . . [President Bush said,] "We are seeing a disturbing pattern where too often judicial confirmations are turned into ideological battles. . . . Democrats seek to undermine the nominations of candidates who agree with my philosophy that judges should interpret the law and not try to make law from the bench."[3]

We were picking up signals that Senator Joe Biden might be the Democrat on the Judiciary Committee who would vote to bring my nomination to the floor. When Chip served on Senator Lott's staff years before, he had developed a working relationship with Senator Biden. A person close to the situation suggested that Chip might find Biden responsive to a heartfelt personal letter from Chip asking him to support me. Chip wrote the letter.

Meanwhile, Senator Biden had a number of Democratic trial lawyer friends and supporters from Mississippi who backed my nomination. They, along with former Mississippi governor William Winter, planned to visit with Biden; but Biden sent word it was not necessary for Governor Winter to come up. I hoped this meant that Biden was going to support me and just had to figure out how, and that the visit by Governor Winter was unnecessary. Word came back to Senator Lott that if Chip would back off on congressional redistricting in Mississippi and concede to a plan more favorable to the incumbent Democrat Ronnie Shows, that it would be easier for Biden to vote for me. To sweeten the deal, there was mention of guaranteeing an African American as my replacement on the district bench. We had heard both offers before; Biden was looking for cover.

Senator Lott scoffed at the suggestion Chip should roll over in redistricting: "Chip is a young man. I had rather have Chip in Congress for many years than Charles on the Fifth Circuit for a few years." I agreed. There was no consideration of Chip caving on redistricting.

There was no opposition to an African American as my replacement. I believe the Mississippi federal bench needs more diversity. But no one dictates to U.S. senators who they will recommend for the judiciary to the White House; the president makes the final decision. There was a willingness for this to happen, but unwillingness to do a "quid pro quo." Such a guarantee was not possible.

Senator Biden remained a possibility until about a week before the vote. At that time, the White House released a quote Biden had made during the Clinton Administration that every judicial nominee was entitled to an up or down vote. Claiming the White House could not coerce him, Biden immediately announced his opposition to my nomination. However, there were real reasons he never came through. First, he wanted to preserve his option to run for president, and after Senator Edwards's vigorous interrogation, he didn't want to be the only potential Democratic candidate for president to alienate the Far Left groups by helping get me to the floor. Second, he and his trial lawyer friends from Mississippi had a falling out, removing their influence in his decision-making.

Three weeks after my hearing, I was working late in my chambers on responses for the Democrats on the Judiciary Committee. I received a call from Ana Radelat, a Gannett reporter and Washington correspondent for the *Jackson Clarion Ledger*. She asked a few preliminary questions and then said, "I hate to be the one to break bad news." She paused and asked if I had heard about Senator Lott's comments earlier that day. I had not. She quoted Senator Trent Lott as saying, "I am not advocating this, but [Judge Pickering] has got to decide whether he wants to go forward with the vote if the votes aren't there, whether he wants to terminate the process." I responded, "I have no thought of withdrawing."

After Ana Radelat's call, I quickly called Chip to find out what was going on. He had already checked with Trent, who told him that he was not trying to suggest that I should withdraw in any manner whatsoever, that someone had asked him the question and he had simply responded that such a decision was for me to make. Chip issued a statement confirming what I had already told Ana Radelat: "My father has no intent of withdrawing."[4] Trent also moved to quash any thought he was trying to signal that I should withdraw: "In an interview, Lott said that he never suggested that Pickering withdraw his name. 'My recommendation would be that he stick with it,' Lott said."[5] I have no feeling at all that Trent was suggesting I not go the distance. Some people in Washington D.C. would use an opportunity like that to send a signal, but that is not Trent's style. If he wanted to encourage me to withdraw, he would have called and told me personally, not send a message through the media. Many Washington reporters don't understand that type of straight shooting.

My committee vote was scheduled for March 7. Chip and Karl Rove discussed whether it would be helpful if some of my Mississippi supporters joined President Bush and me at a press event. The White House liked the idea. Joining President Bush and myself at the White

House were Mississippi Democratic Attorney General Mike Moore; civil rights activist Charles Evers; former Democratic congressman G. V. (Sonny) Montgomery; Judge Johnny Williams, the first African American to be elected to a chancery judge position in Hattiesburg; and Jones County Supervisor Melvin Mack. Laurel Democratic mayor Susan Vincent, African American pastors, and other prominent whites and blacks, most of whom were Democrats, also joined us in Washington.

As President Bush and I sat in front of the fireplace in the Oval Office, he said, "I believe this man should be confirmed. . . . I know him. I have known him for a long time. But more importantly, people from Mississippi have known him. Democrats and Republicans know a good, good, honorable citizen, and they are playing politics with him up here."[6]

The *Wall Street Journal* reported,

President Bush had an Oval Office meeting with Mr. Pickering, a rare moment in which he shared some of his own precious political capital. . . . Mr. Bush and his nominee sat before the cameras, flanking the Oval Office fireplace in the same seats used to publicize visits from foreign heads of state, and the President called on the Committee to send the nomination to the full Senate.[7]

I walked with the president and the dozen Mississippi supporters who came with me to the Oval Office out into the Rose Garden. Dr. Condoleezza Rice, Karl Rove, Chief of Staff Andy Card, and Chip joined us. My supporters were excited to have their picture made with President Bush and Dr. Rice. In fact, I recently visited with Melvin Mack, who has since become the first African American mayor of Laurel. He proudly displays the photos from our White House visit on the walls in his office.

The *Wall Street Journal* correctly analyzed the reason behind my opposition: "Abortion-rights advocates chose Mr. Pickering for their first big push against a Bush judicial nominee because of his record in state politics," where he opposed abortion while in the Mississippi State Senate and backed a plank in the GOP platform calling for the reversal of *Roe v. Wade.* "For both sides, the Pickering clash is seen as a warm-up to battles over Supreme Court nominations. . . ."[8] But this warm-up loss before the Supreme Court battles started, according to Jim Backland, a lobbyist for the Christian Coalition, would "galvanize" and motivate conservative groups.[9]

When we left the Rose Garden, the twelve Mississippians who came with me to the Oval Office went to an area designated as the "sticks," so named because members of the press stick out their microphones and interview people who have visited with the president. Attorney General Moore told the press that attorneys from his office were in my court frequently and that I was concerned about the rights of indigents and prisoners, and if there were any sign of discrimination or hostility to civil rights, he would know about it. He asked the press if they knew Charles Evers. He told them, "Charles Evers's brother was slain in the civil rights movement and Charles Evers would not be here supporting Judge Pickering's nomination if there was anything wrong with Judge Pickering." He continued, "Who knows more about the Judge, the people of Mississippi or the people in Washington who live in a logic-free zone?"[10]

Charles Evers's support for my nomination was consistent and positive throughout the process. He wrote,

> In recent days, I have been saddened and appalled to read many of the allegations that have been put forth about Judge Charles Pickering . . . . . As someone who has spent all my adult life fighting for equal treatment of African Americans, I can tell you with certainty that Charles Pickering has an admirable record on civil rights issues. He has taken tough stands at tough times in the past, and the treatment he and his record are receiving at the hands of certain interest groups is shameful.[11]

After visiting with the president, I met Margaret Ann and other supporters of my confirmation in the Indian Treaty Room in the Old Executive Office Building adjacent to the White House. When those who went to the "sticks" finished their interviews, they joined us there for an update and briefing by Judge Gonzales, the president's counsel; and Viet Dinh, head of the Office of Legal Policy in the Department of

Justice. Afterward, Chip and Leisha took the group to the Capitol for lunch in a room outside the office of the Speaker of the House. Following lunch, these Mississippi supporters fanned out across the Senate office buildings trying to convince at least one Democrat on the Judiciary Committee to support my nomination.

I went to visit with Senators Trent Lott and Thad Cochran. We had hoped that Thad's rapport with Senator Herb Kohl of Wisconsin would provide the needed vote. Alternatively, perhaps Senator Russ Feingold, also of Wisconsin, would be a possibility as Cochran co-sponsored the Campaign Finance Reform Bill with him and Senator John McCain. Thad tried both of these men, and Trent worked tirelessly throughout the process; but they could not budge any of the members of the Judiciary Committee.

Trent told me that Senator Orrin Hatch thought if we did not get a commitment from at least one Democrat by the end of the day, we should go ahead and let the committee vote the next day, effectively killing my nomination. Hatch felt that if the Democrats blocked my nomination, other Bush nominees would be confirmed because they could not fight more than two or three nominees. He was mistaken. None of us expected the Democrats to obstruct as many nominees as they did.

I told Trent I understood that if any member of the committee requests the vote be set over for a week, under the rules, the vote is automatically postponed. Trent told me that was true and I said, "We have fought this far, and if we don't have the commitment of at least one Democrat by tomorrow, I would like for the vote to be put off for another week. I want to fight to the last breath."

I had come a long way from having reservations about whether or not I wanted a nomination to the Fifth Circuit to wanting to fight to the very end. If I buckled, if I caved in, I thought it would make it harder for other nominees to be confirmed, embolden the left-wing groups seeking to block conservatives from the bench, and give some semblance of credibility to the charges against me. I have never liked to give in to a wrong; I have never liked to lose a fight. Trent quickly replied, "If that is what you want, I'm with you. I'm sure Senator Hatch will agree."

As I walked into Senator Hatch's office, he gave me a big bear hug and we visited for almost an hour. He told me the same thing he told Trent: if they defeated my nomination, it would make it easier for future nominees to be confirmed. I told Senator Hatch, "If tomorrow when the committee meets we haven't secured the commitment of at least one Democrat, I would like for the vote to be postponed. I want to fight for that vote until the last breath." Hatch was supportive and said if I wanted to fight another week he would do everything he could to help, saying, "I'll personally request the vote be set over."

Senator Patrick Leahy was not pleased the vote on my nomination was postponed. He had wanted to defeat my nomination that day and bickered with Senator Hatch over the matter. Still, the committee followed the rules and my vote was set over for one week. My nomination was still alive, but barely.

Family life continues in the midst of political fights. Paige, my oldest daughter, told me she had to stop letting her children watch newscasts of my nomination fight. Her four-year-old daughter Emily woke up several nights in a row crying from bad nightmares. Emily told her, "I'm scared that the woman I saw on television shouting at Uncle Chip and saying bad things about Papa is coming to get me." You know the opposition is shrill when it gives children nightmares. Judicial confirmation should not be so dramatic or vitriolic.

Another of our daughters, Christie Chapman, delivered our nineteenth grandchild the day after my visit to the Oval Office. She and her husband Clint named her Lucy after my mother who had died in December. On the way back from Washington, Margaret Ann and I decided to drive over to Opelika, Alabama, to visit our newest grandchild. Afterward we drove to Callaway Gardens in Georgia for a couple of nights to rest and recharge. It turned out that doctors who volunteer to do medical-mission work with Southern Baptists around the globe were there having a weekend conference, and at breakfast we met a minister of music with this group. He inquired as to what I did, and I told him, "Well, right now I am sort of fighting for survival. President Bush nominated me for an Appellate Court." He said, "Oh, they're doing to you what they are doing to that fellow, Pickering." I responded,

"You're right. I am Pickering." We had a good visit and received considerable encouragement from him and others in the dining room. New friends and family provided some necessary encouragement and rejuvenation, but the battle continued.

During the weeklong delay on my committee vote, former Mississippi governor William Winter came to Washington and joined with Chip and Frank Hunger (former Clinton assistant attorney general and brother-in-law of Al Gore) to seek that elusive Democratic vote. The three of them visited with Democrats outside their weekly caucus asking for support on my nomination.

Governor Winter argued, "You are not going to get a better nominee from this administration than Judge Pickering. If you block him, you'll get someone more ideologically to the Right." He and Frank both pointed out that opposition to my nomination would hurt Democratic candidates in the South. Governor Winter and Frank did everything they could to get at least one vote for my confirmation, and Chip was working tirelessly alongside.

Frank Hunger had written a letter of support for my nomination but had requested that Chip not release it until Frank was sure that the Democrats had it. Frank delivered his letter to the Judiciary Committee and requested the Democratic staff to sign a receipt. After three days, he authorized Chip to release his letter of support.

Senator Leahy denied the committee had ever received Frank's letter. Frank told the press that what Leahy said was not true—that he had a signed receipt to prove it.

Leahy came by in a huff and chastised Frank for contradicting him to the press. After Leahy went into the caucus room, Frank grew incensed that he should be rebuked for telling the truth. When Connecticut senator Joe Lieberman walked by, Frank flagged him down and asked him to deliver a colorful message to Leahy. After hearing what had happened, Lieberman smiled as he walked into the caucus room and quipped, "There is a Yiddish word that might fit better."

The day before the vote, President Bush issued another statement in support of my nomination:

Judge Pickering is a respected and well-qualified nominee who was unanimously confirmed twelve years ago to the District bench. . . . I strongly urged his confirmation. . . . While tomorrow's vote is about one man, a much larger principal is also at stake. . . . Unfortunately, we are seeing a disturbing pattern, where too often judicial confirmations are being turned into ideological battles that delay justice and hurt our democracy. The American people deserve better.[12]

The verdict was at hand; we had done all we could do; there would be no more continuances. Either the committee would vote me onto the Senate floor where I had majority support for confirmation, or they would bury my nomination in committee. The prospects did not encourage me.

Confirmation Limbo:
Bottled Up in Committee

ON MARCH 14, 2002, the Senate Judiciary Committee was poised to
vote on my nomination to the Fifth Circuit Court of Appeals.
Washington D.C. was divided over my nomination: Republicans and
conservatives on one side, Democrats and liberals on the other side. But
back in Mississippi, I had widespread support from Democrats (some of
whom were liberal), lawyers, African Americans, Republicans, conservatives, and even the press.[1]

The support I had from those who knew me best—both Democrat
and Republican, both black and white—was no match for those who
opposed my nomination but did not know me. These special-interest
groups had more influence over the members of the Senate Judiciary
Committee than did all the statewide elected Democrats in Mississippi.
That the Democratic members of the Senate Judiciary Committee were
among the party's most liberal senators compounded the problem.

Margaret Ann and I decided to watch the committee debate on C-
SPAN in my chambers in Hattiesburg. We went to lunch with our
friends Judy King and Wesley and Lillian Breland, and then the five of
us went back to my chambers with my staff to watch the debate and
vote.

The debate over voting me out of the Judiciary Committee went
along the same lines as the questioning had gone five weeks earlier. The
Democrats attacked my nomination. The Republicans strongly
defended my record.

Senator Ted Kennedy opened the debate:

> Judge Pickering has demonstrated in his appearances before the Committee and in other circumstances that he's certainly a decent and generally kind individual. But we are . . . talking in this case about the qualifications for the Circuit . . . and it seems to me, Mr. Chairman, that this nominee just fails to meet the kind of criteria in his core commitment to these fundamental values that warrant and justify an affirmative vote. So I intend at the appropriate time to vote in the negative.[2]

Senator Orrin Hatch responded for the Republicans and addressed the excessive requests for the production of documents:

> I cannot recall another nominee who has been subjected to document production of this scope . . . . [T]his Committee never allowed outside groups to dictate Committee procedure in this way . . . . I have grave concerns about the public perception of calculated fishing expeditions that these requests have created.

Senator Jon Kyl of Arizona observed, "I really believe that some of the opposition to Judge Pickering . . . boils down to a real desire to keep conservatives off the court as much as possible." He warned against allowing ideology to become a litmus test because "that would be the beginning of the end of an independent judiciary. We should not do it. We have to stay away from politicizing our confirmation process."

Senator Jeff Sessions of Alabama recounted hearing Mississippi Democrat Hodding Carter in the Reagan years say, "We liberals have gotten to the point we want the Judiciary to do that for us which we can no longer win at the ballot box."

The Democratic senators followed Kennedy's cue and distanced themselves from charging me as a racist. Senator Russ Feingold said,

> I think it can be said that this may be an extraordinarily fine man. I don't debate that. As an appointment to the Fifth Circuit Court of Appeals, it is a very polarizing and divisive appointment . . . . Mr.

> Chairman, I think that members of the Committee know me well
> enough to believe that I do not think that Judge Pickering is a racist,
> nor do I think he's a bad person. . . . I do wish him well in his contin-
> ued work, however, on the District Court.

A few months later on the Senate floor, Feingold had changed his mind regarding my position on race. He said, "I am not convinced that [Judge Pickering] will give all who come before him a fair hearing, especially on racial justice matters."[3] Feingold wanted to criticize me as a racist, but when challenged on it, wanted to deny he was making that false accusation.

Senator Chuck Schumer concurred with Feingold: "There are some out there who have gone too far in characterizing Judge Pickering personally. He has been unjustly branded by some as a racist. That's not fair. I don't believe Judge Pickering is a racist. I believe he is a decent and honorable man."

Schumer also shared Feingold's short-term memory loss because he too changed his mind in January, saying I showed "glaring racial insensi-tivity"[4] and that my nomination showed "Richard Nixon's Southern strategy is still alive and well in the White House"[5]—a subtle attempt to connect me with a perceived race-baiting strategy.

Senator Dick Durbin said,

> I agree completely with those who have said Judge Pickering is not a
> racist. That is an unfair characterization of this man . . . and there
> were times in his past where he showed real courage on the issue of
> civil rights. And I'm sure it was a much more difficult task for him in
> the state of Mississippi than for many of us who lived in other parts of
> this nation. . . . I am sincerely sorry for Judge Pickering and his family,
> some of whom are here today.

Less than a month later, Durbin sent a fundraising letter to his supporters bragging about standing up against my nomination, writing, "Back in Illinois one of Pickering's critics in Chicago said to me: 'He can change the sheets but he can't change who he is.'"[6] If Durbin were truly sorry about the slander thrown against me, he would not have compared me to a malevolent and reprehensible Klansman in an attempt to raise campaign funds. Durbin also joined his colleagues in attacking me the following January saying that with my re-nomination "the White House called into question all of its promises to demonstrate that the party of Abraham Lincoln was truly committed to civil rights."[7] He claimed at the hearing that I showed "real courage on the issue of civil rights" when there were those to challenge him. When he spoke without fear of rebuttal, he said my nomination questioned Republicans' commitment to civil rights.

Democratic senators' statements that they were not accusing me of being a racist were incredulous. They might not have used the word "racist," but by using the specter of a burning cross and other synonyms and symbols, they clearly conveyed the message that I was an unreconstructed racist. They constantly used me as a scapegoat, used me for fundraising and grassroots development purposes, and told their constituents that they were blocking extremist candidates who wanted to turn the clock back on civil rights.

These Democrats never missed an opportunity to do all in their power to caricature me as a racist, soft on cross-burners, insensitive to civil rights, and to use this scarecrow to alienate black voters from Republicans and President Bush. They shamelessly demagogued the race issue. I guess I shouldn't have been surprised because human nature doesn't change, and I had seen racial demagoguery long before these senators attacked me.

While I did not attend the committee vote, Chip decided that if the Democrats were going to say bad things about me, they were going to say them to his face. He sat on the front row in the hearing room. The Associated Press reported "Pickering was not present, but his son, Rep. Charles Pickering, R-MS, had a seat in the front row of the spectators section. 'What is happening to your father today is a great injustice,' said Sen. Mitch McConnell, R-KY, addressing his remarks to the young Congressman."[8]

During a recess, Chip stood up to stretch and chat, and representatives of the special-interest groups took his chair. When the committee came back in session, Chip had to find another seat and wound up sitting right behind Senator Schumer. Schumer stated that I had no African American support in Mississippi, and Chip could not refrain from audibly saying, "That's not true," which seemed to visibly shake Schumer. Rather than endure correction from Chip throughout the hearing, Democratic staff members asked the special-interest emissaries to vacate Chip's chair so he would not be so close to the senators.

When everything to be said had been said by both sides, nothing had changed. Senator Leahy called for the vote on the motion to report my nomination favorably to the Senate floor. On a straight party-line vote, ten Democrats voting "no" and nine Republicans voting "yes," the motion failed.

Denis Rutkus, a specialist in American government for the Congressional Research Service, has written extensively about the confirmation process. He observes,

> When judicial nominations have failed to be reported favorably, it usually has been the case that they received no committee vote at all, and were kept in committee until the final adjournment of Congress, when they were returned to the President (unless withdrawn by the President before then). . . . On rare occasions, however, the Judiciary Committee has voted on judicial nominations in a way other than approving motions to report favorably.

Nominees in the past have been confirmed who were reported out of the committee with a neutral or negative recommendation, thus allowing the full Senate the opportunity for advice and consent despite the lack of support from a majority of the committee.[9]

Earlier that week, Chip had spoken with Senator Hatch about that strategy. Chip suggested Senator Arlen Specter, a moderate Republican from Pennsylvania who had helped Democrats bring Clinton nominees out of committee, make a motion that I be reported out with no recommendation, or with a negative recommendation.

So when the first vote failed, Senator Specter made a motion that my nomination be submitted for a full vote by the Senate without a recommendation. That vote, likewise, failed on a straight party-line vote, ten to nine. He then moved that my nomination be reported with an unfavorable recommendation. For the third time, the committee voted on a straight party-line vote not to report me to the Senate floor.

The Democrats on the committee knew that if I were voted out of committee I would likely be confirmed, so they switched from opposition to obstruction. They were too beholden to their groups to let my nomination move forward. The groups had gotten the commitment they wanted from the Democratic senators. A nominee without support of a majority on the committee would not go to the floor, not with a favorable recommendation, not with a neutral recommendation, not with an unfavorable recommendation, not at all. The obstruction of the Democrats was now a matter of record.

Those who supported my nomination at the hearing wore buttons: "Stop the Bickering Confirm Pickering." After the vote, the conservative groups supporting my nomination had buttons printed: "Remember Pickering." At this point, I hoped Senator Hatch was correct and my defeat would mean victory for other Bush nominees. Ultimately, this would be true; but we were three years and many fights away, and my confirmation struggle would be over before that would happen. In the short term, there would only be more escalation.

I did not fax my concession statement to the White House or the Justice Department for review until after the committee started debating my nomination. I did not want to give any indication that I was backing down, nor did I want to do anything to discourage the White House from trying to get that last vote. After I faxed my proposed statement to the Department of Justice and to the White House, Viet Dinh called and advised that the White House wanted me to put in a sentence that "I will not withdraw" and further "I hope the Senate will find a way to confirm my nomination." I told him I would add to the statement "I will not withdraw," but that is all that I wanted to add. A couple of weeks later, I would have added both statements, but at that moment, I was exhausted from the fight and I didn't want to say any more.

A CNN crew was in Hattiesburg doing a story on my confirmation, and they inquired if they could come to my chambers and if I would make a statement after the vote. I told them they were welcome to come to my Chambers, but that my wife, friends, and I were watching the vote in my private library. After the vote, I told the reporter I would issue a brief statement, but it was not going to be lengthy; it might not be worth his time to wait. The CNN reporter and a reporter for local television station WDAM stuck around in my chambers just outside my library where we listened to the debate and vote.

When the vote concluded, Margaret and I went outside the courthouse where a CNN reporter, a reporter from the local NBC affiliate WDAM, and a reporter for Gannett Newspaper's *Hattiesburg American* were waiting. I issued the following statement:

> I am disappointed that the Judiciary Committee has failed to forward my nomination to the full Senate. Although I am disappointed, I am in good spirits. I will not let what has happened to me during this process embitter me, or shape the balance of my life. Life is too precious. My faith has not been weakened. I will not withdraw my name.
>
> I am extremely disturbed that judicial confirmation has degenerated into such a bitter and mean-spirited process. I sincerely hope that no other nominee has to go through what has happened to me. The price of public service should not be so high.
>
> I am grateful to President Bush for his strong support. I likewise am appreciative of the consistent and unswerving support of Senators Lott and Cochran. I am touched, and humbled that those who know me best, my friends and neighbors in Mississippi, both African American and white, both Democrat and Republican, have defended my record in such a gracious and magnanimous way.

President Bush called me "a distinguished judge unfairly denied a chance to serve his country." He further stated,

> Judge Pickering has earned the praise and support of those who know him and know him to be a fair and measured judge, an advocate of civil rights and a dedicated member of his community. . . . He has served with distinction and deserves better than to be blocked by a party-line vote of ten senators on one committee.[10]

Senator Lott immediately went to the Senate floor and said, "I take it personally. [It is a] slap at Mississippi. This action may very well elect a Republican governor in Mississippi."[11] (The following year, the incumbent conservative Democratic governor, Ronnie Musgrove, was defeated by Republican Haley Barbour.)

Senator Hatch declared, "Mr. President, today is the Ides of March. I would call on my Senate colleagues to 'Beware.' The fight they started with Judge Pickering is one that others may end. I hope, however, to quote Shakespeare further, that they have not crossed the Rubicon, that the die is not cast."[12]

Senator John Breaux, a conservative Louisiana Democrat, said of the vote, "I am fearful that the Senate is going to look like the Israelis and the PLO. . . . It's a real recipe for stalemate and for Congress becoming more irrelevant when it can't get anything done, even simple things."[13]

Senator Lott went to work. He immediately blocked Majority Leader Tom Daschle's nominee for the Federal Communication Commission, he blocked a one-and-one-half-million-dollar request for funds by the Judiciary Committee, and he "added an amendment to the Energy Bill that would force action on judicial nominees."[14] "Lott tacked his amendment on to Sen. Dianne Feinstein's (D-Calif.) amendment on energy derivatives, tying up her provisions in procedural knots."[15] The *Washington Post* reported that "[u]sing a variety of retaliatory strikes, Lott succeeded in needling the Democrats almost daily with surprise moves aimed at making them pay for rejecting Pickering."[16]

Various newspapers around the world covered the reaction. The *Chattanooga Times Free Press* said, "U.S. District Judge Charles W. Pickering . . . was the first warrior to fall in a struggle that could prove long, painful, and fascinating."[17] The *New York Times* commented, "People on both sides of the issue were keenly aware that they were testing the battle lines for future confrontations over the ideological shape of the federal courts. The hearing also exposed a whiff of retribution."[18] The *Times* article continued, "Virginia Thomas [wife of Justice Clarence Thomas] published an open letter to Judge Pickering in the *Wall Street Journal* today and said he was being opposed 'because you will not rule in favor of the hard left's political agenda.' Mrs.

Thomas . . . said 'the Democrats on the Committee and the outside groups that egg them on don't think of you as a human right now.'"[19]

The *Daily Telegraph* in London, England, reported,

> White House officials have accused Democrats of "Borking" Judge Charles Pickering. . . . It has also laid bare the fault lines through American politics separating the conservative constructionists who believe in strict interpretation of the 1787 Constitution and liberals who see it as a "living" document to be viewed in the context of modern times.

The London newspaper also referenced Virginia Thomas's article in the *Wall Street Journal*: "'You are but a pawn in a much larger battle over whether an independent judiciary will prevail, or whether a liberal judicial litmus test will transform our courts into another political branch with a Liberal bent.'"[20]

In Senator Leahy's own backyard, the *Burlington Free Press* editorialized that in 1998 Leahy said, "Partisan and narrow ideological efforts to impose political litmus test on judicial nominees and to shut down the Judiciary must stop." The editorial continued,

> Unfortunately, Leahy has not always heeded his warning. . . . This year, Leahy and other Judiciary Committee Democrats refused to allow Bush Appeals Court nominee, Charles Pickering, a full Senate vote. A white, male Mississippian, Pickering was portrayed by some opponents as a racist, an anti-feminist and a homophobe with extreme political and social views. Pickering's actual record gave a different impression.

By week's end, Senator Schumer admitted the fight was not as much about me as it was about sending a message to President Bush:

> Sen. Charles E Schumer, a New York Democrat and member of the Judiciary Committee, said on Thursday, that his principle reason for opposing Judge Pickering was to signal to the White House that it could not hope to send up legions of conservative judicial nominees and expect the Democrats to accept them willingly.[2]

Back home, the Bar Associations in both Hattiesburg and Laurel hosted receptions for Margaret Ann and me. It gave me an opportunity to express my sincere appreciation for the support of the home folks. I told them, "There has never been a time in our lives when Margaret Ann and I have felt a more overwhelming sense of gratitude, or a deeper sense of appreciation, than we have felt for our friends and neighbors at home during these past several months."

I pointed out that many African Americans who had supported me in Forrest and Jones Counties had been pressured to turn against me, but "stood strongly in support of my nomination. . . . I hope that this will be another step forward . . . demonstrating to the world, and to those of us who live in this area, that African Americans and whites can talk and communicate with one another and can work together for common goals."[22]

Even though I did not withdraw, I was at peace with the result and determined to go on with life. My nomination was blocked in committee—in confirmation limbo—and I thought the battle was behind me; but the election of 2002 lay just ahead.

Election of 2002

TWO DAYS AFTER the Democrats on the Judiciary Committee blocked my nomination from going to the Senate floor, I was back on the farm enjoying the things I usually do on Saturdays. I checked on the cows and calves and strolled through the greening pastures and fields to check the fences. I drove around the farm to examine the timber, the roads, and the food plots planted for wildlife. I scouted for wild turkey and prepared for spring turkey season opening in just one week. (That season I called in and took three long beards, a successful season and the limit in Mississippi. Fortunately for me, the old gobblers were more responsive than the Democrat senators, or I would have done my turkey hunting at the grocery store.)

On the following Monday, I began thanking those who supported my confirmation: senators who had spoken for me as well as Mississippians who wrote letters of support, sent letters to the editor, and traveled to Washington on my behalf. I ramped up overtime work on my judicial duties in an attempt to bring my court docket current.

Though the Democrat-controlled committee refused to allow my nomination to go to the full Senate for consideration, I had not withdrawn my nomination and it was still pending. But I did not anticipate confirmation. I thought the chances of my nomination resurfacing were remote; I thought my fight was likely finished. I put confirmation out of my mind and buried myself in my judicial responsibilities as district judge.

It is difficult for the party of a sitting president to pick up seats in Congress in mid-term elections—just ask Bill Clinton about 1994.

Besides, the deck was stacked against the Republicans in 2002. The Democrats had only fourteen Senate seats up for election while the Republicans were defending twenty seats and were certain to lose one or two.

Of course, I was interested in my son's election and I kept up with his progress even though I could not participate. As a judge, I could not attend his campaign speeches or events; but Margaret Ann could and did. The Mississippi Republican Party had prevailed in its redistricting battle with the Democrats, and Chip was running in a safer district than Republicans had offered the Democrats in the failed compromise earlier in the redistricting battle. Chip's campaign appeared to be going well, and rather than an impediment, the fight over my nomination had energized Mississippi conservatives. I have always appreciated the support Mississippians have given my family and me. However, I was somewhat surprised that the attack on me became a campaign issue outside of Mississippi in Senate and House races across the nation.

One week after Democrats voted down my nomination in committee, the Capitol Hill newspaper *Roll Call* reported,

> Rep. Lindsey Graham (R-S.C.) is already rehearsing a portion of his speech for when President Bush comes to visit, possibly next week, to pump up his bid for a Senate seat. "Mr. President," Graham expects to say, "I look forward to working to confirm your judicial nominations. I will be an ally in your cause." As the Senate continues to deal with the reverberations from the Judiciary Committee's party-line rejection of U.S. District Judge Charles Pickering's bid for a circuit court seat, Graham and other House Republicans gunning for Senate seats are already using the fight as a rallying cry for their own campaigns. . . . Graham and Rep. Greg Ganske (R-Iowa), who is seeking to oust Iowa Sen. Tom Harkin (D), said they believe they can specifically use the Pickering case to score points with voters. . . . Graham and Ganske . . . said . . . the Pickering case . . . has fired up voters, at least the conservative base voters who will be key to turn out in a mid-term election. Two weekends ago, Ganske said, he had eight county GOP conventions and found that Pickering's nomination was "a hot issue," and was met with great applause when he railed against Senate Democrats for the way they treated him. "I really didn't have to

explain who Judge Pickering was" . . . . Graham [echoed] a theme
some GOP aides have hinted at, namely that Southerners will be
particularly put off by the Democrats' racially tinged rejection of
Pickering, one that seems to imply that an older white man from that
part of the country can't belong to the "new South." . . . Sen. Zell
Miller (D-GA) concurred that southern voters would abandon
Democrats just as they did in the 2000 election . . . . "The political
repercussions are too obvious to ignore. Politically, this action may
very well elect a Republican governor in Mississippi . . . make it even
more difficult for Democratic candidates to be successful in the
South," Miller said . . . . Miller, who has made re-electing
[Democratic Senator Max] Cleland his top political priority this year,
said Tuesday that he spent a good deal of time over the weekend
reading letters to the editor in local papers, and that it is obvious
where sentiment lies in Georgia over the Pickering nomination. "It
does not go unnoticed," he said.[1]

A week later, MSNBC weighed in on the question of judicial confirmations becoming a campaign issue.

Still smarting from the Senate's rejection of his appeals court nominee
Charles Pickering, President Bush is using his battle with Democrats
over judicial nominations to gin up campaign money for Republican
candidates. . . . "We're going to have more fights when it comes to the
judiciary," Bush told GOP donors in Atlanta Wednesday at a fundraising dinner for Rep. Saxby Chambliss, the Republican who is
seeking to topple Sen. Max Cleland, a first-term Democrat . . . . Bush
assailed Cleland for not supporting his choice of Pickering. . . . "I put
up a good man from Mississippi the other day, and I don't remember
the senior senator from Georgia defending this man's honor . . . .
We've got to get good, conservative judges appointed to the bench and
approved by the United States Senate."[2]

On April 15, the *Washington Post* reported the White House's effort
to make confirmation of judges front and center in the off-year senatorial elections.

President Bush, Vice President Cheney and the White House's top political adviser, Karl Rove, have each sought to convert the failed judicial nomination into a useful political theme, saying that Pickering's defeat illustrates why voters this fall should tip the Senate back into GOP control. . . . Two days in a row last month, Bush broached Pickering's defeat at political events he attended in Georgia and Texas. . . . At least one prominent GOP candidate has picked up the theme. Two weeks after Lamar Alexander decided to run for the Senate from Tennessee, he chose the defeat of Pickering, whom he had known for years, as the topic for his first radio spot. . . . "President Bush was right about Judge Pickering . . . and I'm running for the Senate to support him [President Bush]."[3]

A May 13 article in *Roll Call* reported how Democrats and Republicans had diametrically opposite views on how the judicial confirmation issue was playing in heartland America.

Senate Democrats say they expect no long-term political damage on the issue. Democrats . . . say . . . it garners virtually no interest among voters, leading them to conclude they won't pay a political price for fighting President Bush's nominees. "This is not a high-priority issue for most Americans," said Sen. Dick Durbin (D-Ill.), a member of the Judiciary Committee. "It's just not an issue at home. It's just a nonissue," said Sen. Mary Landrieu (D-La.), who faces re-election this fall.

The article reported that Democratic pollster Mark Mellman had assured Democrats "this is the flattest issue there is." Republicans saw the issue just the opposite.

Since the party-line rejection in early March of Judge Charles Pickering's nomination to an appellate court seat, Republicans have sought to mount a convincing public-relations offensive linking judicial nominations to other GOP accusations of Democratic obstructionism, a strategy focused on winning Southern votes. . . . The Bush White House has been very reluctant to highlight any polling that it has done, but it's become clear to GOP Senators and their aides that the White House has

seen data that shows the issue is resonating. . . . Heeding the
pleas from the White House to step up the attack, more than
two dozen GOP Senators attended a press conference and rally
to decry Democratic handling of judicial nominees. . . . Sen.
Susan Collins (Maine), one of the GOP's leading moderates,
was on hand, wearing a "Remember Pickering" sticker.[4]

Senator Bill Frist, then chairman of the National Republican
Senatorial Committee, predicted that

> when the votes are counted in November, "I think it will be a one-seat
> net gain up or down for either the Republicans or the Democrats"
> that will decide which party dictates the Senate's agenda for the next
> two years. . . . Frist also said the Republicans will be focusing their
> attacks on [the Democratic] strategy of blocking most of Mr. Bush's
> second-year agenda, especially the Democrats' stalling tactics on most
> of the president's judicial nominees. . . . The Democrats' defeat of
> Mississippi's U.S. District Judge Charles W. Pickering . . . would be a
> major campaign issue against the Democrats, he said . . . . "this
> obstruction . . . is catching hold. It is the applause line at town
> meetings. It has become real to people as we look at the obstruction of
> judicial nominees, and Pickering has come to symbolize that. He has
> become the embodiment of that," he said. "And it's not just in the
> South. It has been elevated to a national stature."[5]

Although my nomination was blocked, the issue of my confirmation had become a rallying cry for Republicans, a tangible example of
Democratic obstruction. The enormous power Far Left secularist groups
exerted over the Democrats was too obvious to deny. Republican
activists and voters alike were ready to respond.

In July, C. Boyden Gray, a former White House counsel to President
George H. W. Bush and the current President Bush's nominee as ambas-
sador to the European Union, joined with several Republican leaders
and conservative activists to form the Committee for Justice. This
conservative organization, which would challenge the liberal special-
interest groups and defend President Bush's judicial nominees, grew out
of the defeat of my nomination.[6] The Committee for Justice began to

bring unity and effectiveness to the conservatives' defense of the left-wing attacks on the Bush judicial nominees. The *Weekly Standard* reported,

> Most prominent of the new conservative groups is the Committee for Justice, whose formation in July 2002 was prompted by the defeat of the Pickering nomination. C. Boyden Gray . . . serves as chairman, while Sean Rushton is the group's executive director. Rushton pings out daily e-mails to around 200 Washington "conservative types" (mainly activists and Hill staff) and 800-1,000 journalists. These frequently offer . . . rebuttals of PFAW's latest mischief.[7]

I regret that my nomination had to be blocked in order to generate support to defend others, but I am glad that because of my battle more people and groups became engaged in a concerted effort to confirm conservative nominees.

In August, President Bush came to Madison Central High School in Mississippi to discuss medical liability reform and worker pension protection. Chip flew into Jackson on Air Force One with the president. After the school event, President Bush attended a fundraiser for Chip's congressional campaign. It was a political event and I could not attend, but Margaret Ann, the proud mother, was there, and President Bush had kind words to say:

> I want to say something as clearly as I can about why we need to control the United States Senate. I put a good man up named Judge Pickering for a higher court—and the people who control the Senate maligned this good man's character. They didn't treat him right. It's not good for America to have this kind of politics—take a good person and not treat him well. . . . We need to change the United States Senate, so that we end this kind of politics on the judiciary and allow good people, good, honorable judges to serve our nation. The Senate did wrong by Judge Pickering. I did right by naming him to the bench.

Two days later, Margaret Ann and I were talking with Chip by phone on his birthday. I was upstairs in my office on the phone and Margaret Ann was downstairs on another phone when she told us she was having chest pains. Within twenty minutes, I had her at the emergency room in Laurel, some sixteen miles from our home. The emergency room doctor quickly analyzed the situation and gave her a high-powered shot that provided immediate relief from intense pain. She had suffered a heart attack, but fortunately sustained no heart damage. We transferred to the hospital in Hattiesburg, and a few days later, she had heart surgery: a quadruple bypass.

The day before Margaret Ann's surgery, I sat with our oldest daughter Paige Dunkerton and her husband Rick as she delivered our twentieth grandchild, another beautiful little girl named Joanna Christine. Meanwhile, our youngest daughter Christie's two-year-old daughter Emma had "scalded skin syndrome" with blisters all over her body. "Scalded skin syndrome" could have affected her kidneys and could have been very serious, but thankfully, it was not. But when Margaret Ann had her surgery, little Emma was still under quarantine.

With my wife in one hospital, a recently born grandchild in another hospital, and a second grandchild in yet a third hospital, my concerns for Chip's campaign took a back seat; the confirmation struggle was out of my mind.

Margaret Ann recovered, little Emma healed, and Joanna Christine and her mother did fine. With the family stable again, my attention to the state of the nation's government returned as the nightly news intensified over the approaching election.

On September 5, 2002, two months before the mid-term elections, Democrats decided to do to nominee Priscilla Owen, justice on the Texas Supreme Court, what they had done to me. Three times, on a straight party-line vote, Democrats on the Senate Judiciary Committee rejected motions to report her to the Senate floor. President Bush called the action "shameful . . . they have distorted her record and misconstrued her opinions. They have determined that a nominee's experience, academic credentials, and character are inconsequential."[8] But the special-interest groups had not pressured Democrats to go after Owen

because of her qualifications; they disagreed with her judicial philosophy—her personal beliefs. As in my case, they wanted a judge who
thinks as they think and feels as they feel on abortion and other cultural
issues, and who will rule accordingly despite the law and Constitution.

The questioning of Owen, like my own questioning at the hands of
the Democratic senators, was intense: "strident grilling."[9] Just as my
defeat appeared to be aiding Republican Senate candidates around the
country, so did Owen's—especially for her fellow Texan John Cornyn.

Cornyn, himself a former Texas Supreme Court judge, was the
state's Republican attorney general. He was engaged in a hotly contested
open Senate race with Democratic nominee Ron Kirk, the mayor of
Dallas. When Democrats shot down Owen's nomination, shockwaves
rippled throughout Texas: "A top White House official who asked not to
be named, responding to Owen's defeat, told reporters that 'Ron Kirk
just lost the Senate race.'"[10] When Cornyn won his Senate seat, he
appropriately took a position on the Senate Judiciary Committee.

District of Columbia Circuit Court of Appeals nominee Miguel
Estrada had a committee hearing in September, but no vote. Fearing
they could not hold their coalition together to block a Hispanic
nominee right before the election, one can surmise the groups
"requested" Chairman Patrick Leahy not to bring his nomination up for
a vote.

As shown by leaked strategy memos, the groups had already
instructed Democrats in regard to Estrada. A November 7, 2001, memo
prepared for Senator Dick Durbin read,

> The groups . . . identified Miguel Estrada (D.C. Circuit) as especially
> dangerous, because he has a minimal paper trail, he is Latino, and the
> White House seems to be grooming him for a Supreme Court
> appointment. They want to hold Estrada off as long as possible.[11]

The groups assured Senator Ted Kennedy they could handle the
Hispanic demographic through a media campaign and prevent a
backlash:

Ralph Neas called to let us know that he had lunch with Andy Stern of SEIU [Service Employees International Union]. Andy wants to be helpful as we move forward on judges, and he has great contacts with Latino media outlets—Univision and others. Ralph told Andy that you are anxious to develop a strategy for the Supreme Court and a strategy for dealing with conservative Latino Circuit Court nominees. . . .[12]

Republicans had been appealing to Hispanics—who share the cultural conservatism of the GOP—and Democrats did not want to see this demographic group voting with Republicans. Despite Ralph Neas's assurance, they postponed Estrada's vote until a time when the political fallout for rejecting a Hispanic nominee might be less. In fact, he did not receive a committee vote until twenty months after he was nominated, and even then only after the 2002 election when Republicans regained control of the Judiciary Committee.

The Democrats pursued Miguel Estrada, Priscilla Owen, and me as high-profile targets, obstructing our nominations in committee and burning their political capital on us instead of their Republican opponents. But other Bush nominees were languishing as well without even having had hearings. One writer later noted that, after two years, only fourteen Bush circuit judges had been confirmed and twenty-three were pending. By comparison, "[i]n his first two years in office, President Clinton nominated twenty-two Circuit judges, with nineteen confirmed . . . the elder President Bush nominated twenty-three Circuit judges with twenty-two confirmed. . . . President Reagan nominated twenty Circuit judges with nineteen confirmed."[13]

The disparity and obstruction resonated with voters. Three weeks before the election, an article in the *New York Times* carried the headline "Bush Places Senate's Delays on His Judicial Appointees at the Core of Campaigning" and quoted the president: "One of the reasons to change the United States Senate is to make sure the good judges I nominate get a fair hearing, a swift vote and approval."[14]

On election night 2002, Chip won a resounding victory, receiving 64 percent of the vote and carrying twenty-one counties in a district comprised of all or part of twenty-eight counties. Any time you win two-to-one, you've had a great victory. I was proud of Chip; he deserved to win. He would have won under the compromised redistricting plan; but it would have been closer. And he would have had a solid win without my confirmation fight, but my battle boosted his margin of victory. Chip's political storm was over; mine would soon renew.

Conservatives carried the day across most of the nation with Republicans claiming the contested elections: Lindsey Graham in South Carolina; Elizabeth Dole in North Carolina; Lamar Alexander in Tennessee; Saxby Chambliss in Georgia; John Cornyn in Texas; Jim Talent in Missouri; John Sununu in New Hampshire; and Norm Coleman defeated former Vice President Walter Mondale in Minnesota. Democratic victories included a win in Arkansas by Democratic attorney general Mark Pryor, the son of a former Arkansas governor and U.S. senator, and a squeaker in South Dakota by incumbent Tim Johnson over challenger John Thune. Thune would go on to defeat Democrat leader Tom Daschle in 2004. The Republicans gained a net of two Senate seats and retook control of the Senate.

The Republicans also increased their margin in the House of Representatives. All in all, it was a good night for Republicans, for President Bush, and a political vindication for the Bush judicial nominees who, while caricatured and maligned, had been successfully defended—and even promoted—as a campaign issue. This was the first time that a sitting president had gained seats in both the Senate and the House during mid-term elections since Harry Truman, fifty-two years earlier.

The morning after the elections, Senator Trent Lott's adrenaline was flowing. Under the headline "Pickering to get second chance," the *Hattiesburg American* quoted him as saying, "'Charles Pickering will be one of the first, if not the first, judge confirmed next year' . . . . Lott said part of the reason Republicans swept into power in the Senate after Tuesday's elections was because of the 'abuse and mistreatment' of the president's judicial nominations."[15] In Washington, Lott's spokesman reiterated, "With the Senate in Republican hands, we will move decisively to confirm Judge Pickering, who unfortunately was bottled up in Democratic partisanship." Lott's spokesman added, "Clearly, [blocking judicial nominees] did not help the Democrats' chances of either retaining control or gaining control of the Senate. . . . It backfired completely."[16] One analyst noted,

> The GOP strategy of raising the judicial issue succeeded. . . . Senate Republican polling indicates that the 2002 fight over Pickering brought judicial nominations into the top three factors in the Democrats' negatives, helping drive those negatives to historical highs. The judicial debate has remained among the top three negatives every month since, except for the month of the Iraq War. . . . The same polling indicates that in close-fought Senate contests in November 2002 in Georgia (Saxby Chambliss), Missouri (Jim Talent), and Minnesota (Norm Coleman), the "Pickering factor" helped motivate Republican base voters as well as swing moderates into the GOP column, thereby returning the Senate majority to Republicans. . . . Coleman . . . knew what he was doing when he focused voters' attention [on Pickering] during his one televised debate opposite Walter Mondale. . . . Coleman readily asserts that judicial confirmations in general, and the treatment of Pickering in particular, helped him win his seat. . . .[17]

The *New York Times* confirmed that White House and Senate aides expected President Bush to re-nominate both Priscilla Owen and me.[18] Meanwhile, the *Washington Post* suggested the election mandate empowered Bush to obtain confirmation of his judicial nominees: "Officials in both parties agreed that the elections brought Bush an unparalleled opportunity to win confirmation of the men and women he wants on the Federal bench."[19]

The *National Law Journal* reported, "Two whose nominations were considered dead in the water—Charles W. Pickering, Sr., and Priscilla R. Owen, both nominated to the 5th U. S. Circuit Court of Appeals—will likely get the floor vote they were denied by the Senate Judiciary Committee earlier this year."

Haunting all this good news was a subterranean threat creeping up in the *New York Times* story:

Sen. Edward M. Kennedy of Massachusetts, said Democrats would continue to oppose any candidates they regarded as extreme conservatives—even, he added, to the point of filibustering. . . . But a filibuster is considered an extreme tactic. Democrats did not use it even during one of the most contentious Senate battles in modern history, involving the first President Bush's nomination of Clarence Thomas in 1991.[20]

Republicans did not take the warning of a filibuster seriously. The Democrats didn't filibuster Robert Bork, and they didn't filibuster Clarence Thomas. In fact, neither party had ever employed the filibuster to deny confirmation to a nominee enjoying majority support. Blocking nominees in committee was bad enough, but blocking judicial nominees by filibuster would be unprecedented. The Democrats had just taken a licking at the ballot box in part due to their obstruction of judicial nominees. Election losses historically are effective teaching techniques utilized by voters. Those of us who doubted the Democrats would follow through on the threatened filibuster did not comprehend the control that the Far Left—out of the mainstream—special-interest groups held over the Democrats in the Senate.

After the election of 2002, fellow judges and friends were congratulating me and assuring me that I would now be confirmed. When I reminded them there would still have to be a vote in the Senate, well-wishers would tell me, "The voting took place last Tuesday [election day]." I was not so sure; I had been there. I was hesitant about being re-nominated, but a week to ten days after the election, my reluctance evaporated and I again was excited over the prospect of being re-nominated and confirmed. I thought the Senate would finally be given the opportunity to provide "Advice and Consent." However, before re-nomination, there were turbulent times ahead for Senator Trent Lott that would affect all of Mississippi, the Senate Republican leadership, and my confirmation.

CHAPTER TEN

Re-nominated

IN DECEMBER 2002, a little over a month after the election, Washington D.C. celebrated Senator Strom Thurmond's one hundredth birthday. He had served in the United States Senate for forty-seven years and five months, longer than any person before him. He was the Dixiecrat segregationist candidate for president of the United States in 1948, but had lived, served, and changed beyond the days of Jim Crow. He was chairman of the Senate Judiciary Committee when the 1982 Voting Rights Extension Act he supported was voted out of his committee to the full Senate. He voted to designate Martin Luther King Jr.'s birthday as a national holiday. In recent years, he was best known for his frugality, his support of a balanced budget amendment, and his commitment to a strong military.

At his century birthday party he was in failing health, frail and confined to a wheelchair; he found it difficult even to talk. Sometimes he could comprehend conversations, sometimes he could not, but things needed to be simple. He understood praise, he understood gestures of friendship, and that night Washington D.C. gathered to extend both and honor him on his birthday.

All were praising Senator Thurmond's long years of service. It came time for Trent Lott—soon to be majority leader of the Senate again thanks to the Republican gains in the recent election—to make comments. Lott's prepared remarks were covered by other speakers—all the old jokes had been used. So he spoke extemporaneously. In the excitement and exuberance of the moment, he reminded Thurmond that when he ran for president in 1948, he carried Mississippi (it helped that his vice-presidential running mate was Mississippi governor Fielding Wright). Lott then told Thurmond, in a gesture of praise, the country would have been better off if he had been elected president in 1948.

It took a few days, but a furor developed over these remarks. Trent's political opponents sought to brand him a modern-day segregationist. Some Democrats wanted to make Trent the Republican poster boy for racial insensitivity. Some Republican senators wanted more power in the new Republican majority and thought pushing Trent overboard could help them move up the ladder. In addition, it was December—the holiday season—and there was nothing in the news to displace the story. The story brewed like a hurricane with no atmospheric pressure to push it away: it was just dead in the water, not moving anywhere, just swirling around Trent's future.

Trent called a press conference. He said several times that segregation and racism were wrong—"immoral." He said, "I apologize for reopening old wounds and hurting so many Americans. . . ." He called his remarks "a mistake of the head and not of the heart."[1]

Trent took a pounding. He had been under fire for nine days with no indication of the pressure letting up. I must confess, I found this time personally difficult as it brought back memories of the accusations leveled against me. Those memories were not easy for Margaret Ann, either.

I neither wanted to experience those attacks again, nor did I wish my pending nomination to contribute to Trent's turmoil. On Saturday morning, December 14, I prepared a statement withdrawing my nomination. I was ready to put the confirmation fight behind me and remove any impediment it might have on Trent. Chip counseled me to hold my fire and wait. He feared a withdrawal might actually hurt both Trent's situation as well as undermine other judicial nominees. Chip spoke to Trent and the White House and all agreed I should hold tight.

Less than a week later—on the Friday before Christmas and just over two weeks after his Thurmond remarks—Senator Lott announced he would not stand for election for Senate Republican leader. This was a big loss for Mississippi, but Trent rededicated himself to his work in the

Senate and to reestablish his effectiveness for Mississippi. In 2006, Mississippi voters reelected him to a third term.

Even in families deeply involved in public service, you cannot stop living because politics is in turmoil. In Pascagoula, the Lotts could finally relax just before Christmas as the news encampment on their front yard packed up to chase the next story. For the Pickerings, Chip and I took his boys deer hunting in the flood plains of the Big Black River and in the Mississippi Delta along the mighty Mississippi. These two areas boast some of the finest white-tail deer hunting in the country. Chip's oldest son Will killed his first buck: a nice six point. I killed two nice bucks, both worthy of mounting, with one being the longest shot of my life at almost three hundred yards. It was a good hunt and good to get away from the pressures of politics, if only for a short time.

In early January 2003, I had the pleasure of swearing in Bob Helfrich as circuit judge in Forrest County, Mississippi. Helfrich was the state prosecutor responsible for the successful 1998 prosecution of Sam Bowers for the 1966 fire-bombing death of Vernon Dahmer. He requested I swear him because of my fight against the Klan and Sam Bowers in the 1960s. I was honored to administer over Helfrich's investiture and thankful for the reminder that regardless of what my opponents had said in Washington D.C., my community in Mississippi knew the truth.

At the beginning of 2003, my nomination had expired without being considered by the full Senate. I remained a federal district court judge with a lifetime appointment. The seat to which I had been nominated on the Fifth Circuit Court of Appeals remained empty. President Bush prepared his first batch of nominees for federal judicial vacancies in the new congress.

President Bush and Republican Senate candidates had campaigned against Democratic judicial obstructionism. The issue resonated with voters and was one of the most effective lines in stump speeches across the country. Republicans retook the Senate and nominees would no longer be bottled up in committee.

The news media, sure President Bush would re-nominate me after the election, now speculated he would not due to the flap over Senator

Lott. But on January 6, I received a call from the White House advising me that the president wanted to re-nominate me if I was willing to go forward. He had campaigned about the abuse his judicial nominees were receiving at the hands of Democrats; it worked, and the president was determined to stick by his choices.

It had been two years since that duck hunt with Chip when Trent had called advising that he and Thad were recommending me for the Fifth Circuit. Had I known in 2001 what lay ahead, I probably would have declined the honor. (Sadly, if the judicial confirmation process is not improved, more and more prospective nominees will say "thanks, but no thanks.") Now the Republicans controlled the Senate, so we all expected the committee and confirmation process to run smoother for President Bush's nominees.

After consultation with Margaret Ann and Chip, I advised the White House I was honored and ready to go forward again. Previous obstruction abused the confirmation process. Democrats misused race against me for political advantage to divide Americans. Backing down could give credibility to the charges against me. Mississippi was being judged and condemned on its past and not on its present; I wanted to help change that image. I thought I could serve honorably as an appeals court judge and that accepting the re-nomination was the right thing to do.

On January 7, President Bush re-nominated me along with twenty-nine other "candidates for federal judgeships who had been blocked or defeated when Democrats controlled the Senate." A senior administration official said the administration was "eager to allow well-qualified judges to get a fair hearing . . . we don't believe many of them got a fair hearing the first time around under the Democratic control." The White House spokesman specifically complained of the "gross distortions" of my record.[2]

Immediately, liberal Democrats let out a howl over my nomination. All the "nice" things they said about me before the committee vote the previous March—about how I was good man who had been wrongfully accused of racism—flew out the window. Now—according to Kennedy, Schumer, Durbin, and others—I was racially insensitive, a threat to civil rights, and an insult to the American people following the Lott fiasco. Senator Ted Kennedy said Democrats "will use every tool in our arsenal to insure his nomination is rejected again this year." Senator Chuck Schumer said, "I'm going to do everything I can to stop the Pickering nomination from going forward." He predicted a "strong filibuster effort in the full Senate."[3]

A conservative writer wrote,

> there are serious doubts about whether a Democratic filibuster would be successful. Schumer's news conference was attended by just one other senator, Dick Durbin, of Illinois. Beyond that, only Massachusetts's Edward Kennedy has publicly supported a filibuster. . . . a successful filibuster would guarantee serious and possibly long-term reprisals from the GOP.[4]

I did not believe, and I think hardly anyone believed—certainly not the White House, certainly not the Republicans in the Senate—that the Democrats in the Senate could be talked into filibustering judicial nominees after the beating they had taken at the polls. However, we underestimated the persuasive ability of the intense and constant pressure of the special-interest groups with Senators Kennedy, Schumer, and Durbin leading the charge.

I must confess that the Democrat's reaction to my re-nomination was more harsh and the news coverage much more extensive than I had expected. My re-nomination was described as a "fire storm."[5] As the barrage continued night after night, repeated on national television and in the national newspapers, I could not help but wonder if I made the right decision. I wondered if I could accomplish what I wanted to achieve or whether the result would somehow backfire. Each time I reanalyzed the question, I always came back to my original conclusion: the job was not worth it, but the principles involved were worth the fight.

Some wondered why President Bush had re-nominated me. Marty Wiseman, a political scientist and director of the Stennis Center at Mississippi State University said the nomination was a vindication for Pickering. A Southerner hates to be accused of racism when he considers that he bent over backwards to live a life that had demonstrated otherwise. . . . If Bush had failed to re-nominate him after promising he was going to do so, that would have been a tacit admission that what the critics had said about Judge Pickering was right all along.[6]

Stuart Taylor Jr., writing in the *National Journal*, said, "maybe Bush's reason—or part of it—was that taking on the distorters and smear artists and race-baiters, rather than throwing a decent man to the wolves, was the right thing to do."[7] Byron York wrote in *National Review*, "It would also have sent a message to Democrats that their tactics worked—thus encouraging more."[8]

Paul Weyrich, a longtime conservative activist, wrote,

I think federal judges are the most important legacy an Administration can leave. They can out last the presidency by a generation. Everything else a president does can be rescinded or repealed by his successor. . . . To be honest about it, President Bush's nominees for the federal bench have been better than either those nominated by Reagan or his father. They are extraordinary. If Bush can fill all the vacancies in the federal court system, even if he should be denied a second term, then he will have made the greatest contribution a president can make.[9]

A number of writers recognized Senator Schumer's attack as race-baiting demagoguery. An editorial in the *Wall Street Journal* reported,

Sen. Chuck Schumer . . . has started the New Year with a harangue, playing the race card and vowing to filibuster the nomination of Charles Pickering. . . . Mr. Schumer's threat came just two days after Ralph Neas of People for the American Way released a memo urging Democrats to filibuster President Bush's judicial nominees. . . . The Schumer Democrats are smearing Judge Pickering as racist in order to smear Republicans as anti-black. . . . This race-baiting is all the more offensive because it is demonstrably false about Judge

Pickering's career. . . . Judge Pickering's whole life story, not just his experience on the bench, suggests that he has repeatedly gone out of his way to help African Americans. . . . Mr. Schumer knows all of this, but none of it matters because his agenda is to stir up the black vote against Republicans going into 2004.

A bold byline in the editorial proclaimed, "Judge Pickering has done more to advance racial harmony than Senator Schumer."[10]

Republicans also responded to Schumer's attack:

The Republican leadership contends Mr. Schumer is engaging in demagoguery in order to court minority voters and attract attention to himself. "What Schumer is doing with this nomination is just politics at its worst," said Dan Allen, spokesman for the National Republican Senatorial Committee. "It reminds me of that joke in Washington about the most dangerous place being between Chuck Schumer and a camera."[11]

Senator Bill Frist of Tennessee, the new Republican leader and Senate majority leader, said, "I think this unfortunately is trying to use race and racial issues to play politics."[12]

African American columnist Donald V. Adderton, then editor of Mississippi's civil rights paper of record, the *Delta Democrat Times*, wrote,

As much as we try, some people with deep-rooted personal political agendas are hell-bent on rubbing Magnolia's [Mississippi's] face in its racist past. . . . this has been one federal judge who has shown more courage than his gutless critics. . . . his judicial record speaks in a louder cadence than the racial drivel being spewed by his misguided detractors.[13]

Senator Schumer had his own problems. In March 2003, the FEC ordered Schumer's 1998 senatorial campaign to pay a civil penalty of $130,000.00. The campaign was also ordered to return $120,455.00 in illegal contributions, bringing the total of fines and restitution to slightly more than a quarter-million dollars. The campaign paid the sum in April. . . . No senatorial candidate has ever been so severely penalized.[14]

This did not make Schumer any less partisan, less strident, or less self-righteous.

The process was harder on Margaret Ann than on me. I think it is always harder to hear criticism of one's spouse than criticism of one's self. Even though I felt the fight needed to be made, I realized there was just so much that I could expect of Margaret Ann. I was also aware that Chip's political future lies ahead of him, and my public life is mostly behind me. So when the attack came so hard in early January, I told Margaret Ann and Chip that if at any time either wanted me to withdraw, I would do so. Margaret Ann never reached that point, and Chip, the eternal optimist, thought we could win and use the process to bring Mississippians together. He wanted to demonstrate that Mississippi has made progress and that Mississippi's whites and blacks can work together.

Besides making ourselves more available to the press, Chip decided to start contacting Democratic senators and trying to break the possible filibuster. He also was reaching out to African Americans, trying to build bridges.

> Rep. Chip Pickering (R-Miss.) has launched a one-man lobbying effort in advance of the coming battle over the nomination of Judge Charles Pickering. . . . Rep. Pickering has been setting up meetings with key Congressional Democrats and making the case for his father's elevation to the 5th U.S. Circuit Court of Appeals. . . . But Pickering is hoping that he can use the nomination fights to not only restore his father's image, but also that of the state of Mississippi. . . . "To overcome Mississippi's past image, I would hope that we can use my father's confirmation to bring the community in my state together," he said in a Friday interview. "We can use this to redefine our state."[15]

Other reporters quickly noticed the efforts of my most staunch supporter and defender. Mississippi's Charlie Mitchell wrote,

Liberal, conservatives and middle-of-the-road folk should all respect
U.S. Rep. Chip Pickering for the way he has declared, "If you're going
to say that about my daddy, you're going to say it to my face."
Pickering . . . is a Republican's Republican. . . . But . . . Pickering is
not uptight or stiff or distant. He shakes your hand and looks you in
the eye. If you don't believe what he believes, he accepts you. He may
try to convert you, but he won't mock or revile you. . . . That's defined
as class. . . . Last summer's debates between Rep. Pickering and fellow
incumbent Rep. Ronnie Shows were, for the most part, yawners . . .
but during those debates when Chip got on the case of other
Democrats who had railroaded his daddy, there was passion in his
voice. And it wasn't just that no one likes to be called a racist. Chip
knew it to be a lie—a lie on his family—and his outrage was real. . . .
Those who want to say something bad about Chip's dad between now
and the Senate vote may still say it. But their phones are going to ring.
It's going to be the nominee's son. And the name-callers are at least
going to be offered a chance to hear the truth.[16]

When Chip was questioned as to the strain of the confirmation
process, he also discussed the importance of the fight at hand:

U.S. Rep. Chip Pickering says his father, Judge Charles W. Pickering,
is feeling the strain of his controversial judicial nomination, but that
the principle of winning the battle out-weighs personal considerations.
"In many ways, it's larger than him," Pickering said on Thursday. "It is
about standing up to those groups who would make false charges, false
allegations, that would misuse race to divide us."[17]

As a part of his effort to win support and overcome opposition,
Chip decided to make another effort at talking with Congressman
Bennie Thompson behind the scenes. But Chip's visit with
Congressman Thompson was leaked to the press. Whether this was
Thompson's way of keeping control of the situation, or whether it was
someone in the African American community who did not want to see
blacks and whites come together, I do not know. Chip responded to the
press, saying, "I'm trying to reach out to people back home and talk, not
only about my father's confirmation, but how to work together for

what's best for Mississippi." Thompson's office said he urged Chip "to meet with some of the black leaders who oppose his father's nomination, especially those who live in the lawmaker's district." Thompson's spokesman "mentioned Eugene Bryant, the head of Mississippi's Chapter of the National Association for the Advancement of Colored People; and Phillip West, a state representative, who heads the state legislative black caucus." The article continued, "Chip seems to have taken Thompson's advice. Phillip West acknowledged that Chip had contacted him about meeting . . . and that he said that he was willing to meet. Eugene Bryant, head of the Mississippi NAACP Chapter, also said 'I'm willing to listen to anyone.'" But the same article reported that Congressman Thompson had not changed his position.[18]

Nevertheless, on February 10, Chip and I met with the Mississippi Legislative Black Caucus at the State Capitol. I told them my experiences in providing equal protection and civil rights under the law and responded to their questions about my record. Afterward, the press wanted to know why we had met. I told them "For twenty-five years I have strongly advocated that African Americans and whites should sit down and talk in a positive and constructive manner to try to promote better understanding. This I've done." Since my nomination was pending, I declined to comment any further.

The response from the black legislators that evening was positive. Representative West, a longtime civil rights activist from southwest Mississippi and chairman of the caucus, said, "I'm glad that we had the opportunity to exchange thoughts and get a better understanding of each other and I know that it's going to be something positive, hopefully, for all of us." Chip responded,

> I believe my father has a good record, a courageous record on race and civil rights, and he has a record of bringing people together, of reconciliation . . . . Only in Washington has he become divisive. I think here in Mississippi, we have a chance to show the rest of the country that we can come together, find common ground and use this to show a new Mississippi and to define who we are.[19]

Vicksburg representative George Flaggs said, "I'm absolutely emphatically convinced that he's not the man he's being portrayed as, because I think we had a heart to heart fruitful conversation."[20] Mississippi's largest daily newspaper opined, "[Pickering] didn't have to meet with the . . . Black Caucus . . . , but it speaks well to his character that he chose to do so."[21]

Whatever the outcome, we made progress at that meeting, not just for my confirmation but for all of us to find common ground and common understanding. Representative West later advised Chip that twenty-six of the forty-five black legislators were going to withdraw their opposition and support my nomination.[22]

It was a great surprise to the Washington press when Phillip West, chairman of the Legislative Black Caucus, announced he was withdrawing his opposition to my nomination and now supporting my confirmation. The *New York Times*, the *Clarion Ledger*, and other newspapers carried headlines announcing the switch in which the *Clarion Ledger* said, "Black Caucus leader praises Bush nominee. Pickering support a surprise."[23]

Phillip West, or "Bucket," his nickname from childhood by which friends and legislators alike addressed him, released a statement:

> It would . . . be "politically correct" for me to remain silent; however, I cannot support a position that may be "politically correct" but I feel is "morally wrong." . . . After having listened to Judge Charles Pickering during his meeting with the Mississippi Legislative Black Caucus, reviewed materials concerning Judge Pickering's record as a Jones County attorney, and spoken with some of the members of the Institute of Racial Reconciliation, I have decided to reverse my position regarding Judge Pickering's nomination to the Fifth Circuit Court of Appeals.[24]

When Phillip West announced his support, those close to Congressman Thompson began an effort to remove West from his position as chairman. This is an unhappy but frequent occurrence when African American leaders do not echo the liberal position and hue the party line. It was reminiscent of Bennie Thompson's "Judas" comment. I felt badly about what was happening to Phillip West, that he was encountering these political difficulties for supporting me. However, Phillip had been a civil rights activist at a time when it was hazardous to your health. He told me he had faced down much worse opposition in his life for doing the right thing. He survived and remained caucus leader. Shortly afterward, he was elected the first black mayor of Natchez—his hometown.

I suspect Congressman Thompson put a stop to our meeting with other African American groups, even though he had suggested these meetings in the first place. I don't think he liked the progress we made. State NAACP president Eugene Bryant, who had said he was willing to meet with anyone, suddenly was no longer willing to meet with me. (An African American friend of mine approached Eugene Bryant about meeting with me, and afterward he told me that conversation convinced him the NAACP's opposition to me was purely political and had nothing to do with my record.) The same was true of Melvin Cooper, president of the Magnolia Bar Association (a black lawyer organization), who likewise would not sit down for a conversation. Some who know Congressman Thompson tell me that if he cannot control something, he will destroy it, that he has an inordinate appetite for control. He uses race to divide Mississippians, and when he could not control my meetings with other black leaders, he decided to prevent them.

We did have success in picking up support in other areas. Jorge Rangel, a Hispanic nominee of President Bill Clinton from Corpus Christi, Texas, who was blocked from confirmation by Republicans during the Clinton years, announced his support for me and challenged the caricatures that had been alleged against me. Jorge had conducted the background investigation on me for the ABA Committee that had investigated my record in 1990. He knew me, he knew the abuses of the confirmation process, and he wanted to do his part to support me and reform the process. His is an outstanding example of someone putting politics aside to do the right thing for the judiciary.

Throughout my confirmation fight, I took a beating with most of the national press, primarily because they simply regurgitated the talking points fed to them by the Democrats and special-interest groups on the

Left. However, in most instances, when the press took a close look at my record in Mississippi, the stories were positive and refreshing.

In February and March 2003, two extensive reports on my nomination were published. Stephen Henderson with the Knight Ridder papers visited Jones County and researched primary sources to put together a story debunking many of the accusations by the left-wing special-interest groups. Afterward, Henderson told me that I would likely be surprised to know how liberal he considered himself. Like Jorge Rangel who put aside his personal politics to do right by the judiciary, Henderson put aside his personal beliefs to do right by the press and is a tribute to good journalism. He wrote,

> Rarely does a selective short hand of someone's biography do them justice. And Washington's affinity for caricature almost never produces accurate portraits. . . . This Mississippi Judge . . . is not the person his opponents have depicted. His political views are more mainstream and his judicial record is more balanced. . . . a man whose thirty year public record reflects deep compassion and a penchant for inclusion. . . . Those closest to Pickering say the church and his faith are the only filters through which you can truly decipher what motivates him.[25]

A team of writers—Janita Poe, Tom Baxter, and Bill Rankin—at the *Atlanta Journal Constitution* wrote exhaustive articles and analyses. The *Atlanta Journal Constitution (AJC)* is one of the great civil rights newspapers of the South, and I was pleased at the headlines: "Evidence Doesn't Support Charges of Racism Against Charles Pickering" and "Fairness, Not Bias, at the Root of Ruling" and "Jurist's Record Belies Racism Charge." They wrote, "In Mississippi, however, many describe a different man than the one feared and vilified by critics inside the Beltway. Rather, their up-close description of Pickering is that he is a relative progressive on race."[26]

Jonathan Groner, a "Legal Times" writer, published an analysis of the cases the left-wing special-interest groups used to oppose my nomination. He wrote, "A Legal Times analysis of Pickering's important rulings, as well as interviews with community leaders in his home state, offers an alternative view to the liberal's conclusions that Pickering is racially insensitive and indifferent to Constitutional rights." Groner reported interviewing a Hattiesburg Democrat who recounted my testimony against Sam Bowers in the 1960s and who said, "that required a great deal of personal courage for someone with four young children." This Democrat continued, "it's unfortunate that some members of my Party are making a political football out of this nomination."[27]

With these reports, along with two excellent articles detailing the circumstances, law, and facts of the cross-burning case by Byron York in *National Review*, publicity shifted my way for a change. Some members of the press began telling me they were hearing that Senators Daschle and Leahy were going to let my confirmation go forward without filibuster.

Maybe that is why the left-wing groups swarmed to the offensive. We began hearing all sorts of false negative rumors the left-wing groups were spreading among the press. We also heard they were looking for a reporter to come to Mississippi and do a negative article on me to counter the recent positive press.

The first rumor involved Daniel Swan whom I had sentenced to jail in the cross-burning case. The left-wing special-interest groups were spreading the rumor that Daniel Swan was a relative of Jimmy Swan, a local Democratic politician of note who once ran for governor of Mississippi and had helped my son Chip in his first race for Congress; therefore, I went easy on Daniel Swan. There are many problems with that rumor, starting with the fact that I was not easy on Daniel Swan by sentencing him to twenty-seven months in the federal penitentiary. Beyond that, Daniel Swan was not related to Jimmy Swan at all. Jimmy's son, Randy, is the television anchor for WDAM, the local NBC television station for Laurel-Hattiesburg. When I told Randy about this rumor, he told me his father died two years before Chip first ran for Congress. Furthermore, Randy said his father's family was from north Alabama and he did not even know Daniel Swan or his family.

Two weeks later, Randy called and told me that while he was at a station pumping gas into his car, a young man walked up and said, "I'm Daniel Swan. I have been wanting to meet you." Daniel Swan told Randy that reporters from the *New York Times* and the *Washington Post* had recently contacted him. They wanted to know if Daniel Swan was related to Randy; they also wanted to know if he had any family connection with any important person that might have played a role in the sentence I imposed. Reporters were following up on these left-wing rumors. To their credit, they did not report the false allegations. Unfortunately, they also did not report that the left-wing groups were spreading these rumors and sending them on wild goose chases, important pieces of information for the public to know because it strikes at the credibility of those making such charges.

The left-wing groups were looking in vain for a local story they could use to undermine the public's disconnect between their accusations in Washington D.C. and the truth in my home community in Mississippi. One day a lawyer friend called and said there was an attempt to get a busload of folks from Mississippi to go to Washington in opposition of my nomination. The opposition had found a plaintiff who had a case for oilfield contamination that I had dismissed. This group would charge me with being anti-environmental because I dismissed the action. I dismissed the lawsuit because the same lawsuit had already been dismissed on its merits in state court. Plaintiff's counsel had tried to circumvent the adverse ruling in state court by filing in federal court. Any first-year law student knows you can't do that under the Doctrine of *Res Judicata*. The issue had already been litigated and the plaintiff lost. You don't get two bites at the apple; dismissal was the proper recourse and to suggest otherwise was not only ludicrous, it was obviously frivolous. That bus never left the station; it was as empty as the charges against me.

I have told lawyers in open court that I strongly discourage trying lawsuits in the press. One reporter, following up on a left-wing rumor, called the local television station asking if I had ordered the station not to carry a certain story. The news director told the reporter that nothing like that had happened. But reporters kept following these left-wing dead-end tips.

I own a small interest in an oil production company. I have nothing to do with the operation of the company and never have. I received four or five telephone calls advising me that an environmental investigative reporter was working on a story to determine if this company had ever been cited for environmental violations, to brand me guilty by association as anti-environmental. If there were any violations, I was unaware of them, and if the story was ever written, I missed it.

I received a call telling me that Senator Ted Kennedy's staff was talking with a man who had been before me in a case regarding a pipe bomb. He was not a lawyer, but he was later back before me advising a plaintiff who brought action for excessive police force. I'm unsure what allegations Kennedy and company thought this man could make against me, but I knew there was nothing there. As usual, the facts and law of both those cases comported to my actions on the bench. Still, it shows that no rumor, no incident, regardless of how ill founded or insignificant, was too small for these groups or Senator Kennedy's staff to research in their effort to throw mud and spread rumors.

In the attempt by the special-interest groups to find a reporter to do a "hatchet job" on me, a New York reporter came to Mississippi. The special-interest groups surely thought this reporter would do a negative piece on me. Instead, he wrote an article that, though not totally favorable, was balanced. I was satisfied; the special-interest groups were disappointed. They did not get their negative from the *New York Times*, so next came a call from a *Washington Post* reporter that I discussed in detail in my previous book *Supreme Chaos*. This reporter came to Mississippi with his mind made up. He had already talked to those opposing my nomination and was not interested in talking to those who supported my nomination. Apparently, their side of the story was not consistent with the story he wanted to write, so he did not mention them at all.

The *Washington Post* reporter carried me on another wild goose chase supplied to him by my opposition. He wanted to know about a case that came before me in which a white sheriff was accused of using excessive force on an African American. We spent considerable time providing material to him: transcripts, public documents, and the facts and law of the case. In the end, he concluded that I had handled the case appropriately, but did not see fit to mention this in his article. Had he thought I mishandled the case, it certainly would have been covered. But the fact that an accusation had been made against me about this case, and that he had determined the facts exonerated me, would have been positive, and that wasn't the story he was interested in writing. When his hit piece came out in the *Washington Post*, the special-interest groups had their negative story to counteract my recent positive press.

After being the object of left-wing target practice for so long, it was nice to get out in the woods as turkey season arrived again, the second season since my original nomination. Chip and I were able to get off that year on one hunt together. We had an old gobbler with double beards gobbling at us ferociously and worked him for about an hour and a half. Unfortunately, I changed positions and scared the bird off. But we had fun and were able to spend quality time together without focusing on my confirmation struggle in Washington.

As they have for several years, my friends Wesley Breland and Louis Griffin helped me host Supreme Court Justice Antonin Scalia for an annual Mississippi turkey hunt. Justice Scalia did not kill a turkey the first time he came to Mississippi, but he has killed turkeys every season since, sometimes killing the limit and sometimes bringing home only one. This season Scalia had good hunts and brought in three gobblers—the limit in Mississippi. So on his last day, he went out without a gun just to enjoy the experience and be in the outdoors. That same morning, I finished out my season as well. I heard gobbling at a distance and trudged through a thick brushy swamp area, crossed over a creek, and climbed up on a bluff where I was able to call the gobbler with a nine-inch beard into an open spot. He was my third bird of the season.

Hunting has always provided me a special time with family and friends, or even alone, to recharge, relax, and reexamine my life. It may seem out of place in a book on judicial confirmation, but it isn't out of place in a book on my life.

Meanwhile, the gobbling and strutting in Washington D.C. continued. Miguel Estrada had a hearing before the Democrat-controlled Judiciary Committee in September 2002, but he did not have a Judiciary Committee vote until late January, twenty months after he was nominated and only after the Republicans regained control of the Senate.

Miguel Estrada was extraordinarily qualified for the D.C. Circuit Court of Appeals. He graduated Magna Cum Laude from Harvard, was editor of the *Harvard Law Journal*, and served as a law clerk to an appointee of President Clinton on the Second Circuit as well as a law clerk to Supreme Court Justice Anthony Kennedy. He served as an assistant United States attorney and an assistant solicitor general. He argued fifteen cases before the U.S. Supreme Court and won ten. The American Bar Association gave him its highest rating, "well qualified." Nevertheless, the Democrats, according to leaked strategy memorandums, did not want a conservative Hispanic on the appellate bench, nor did they want the Republican Bush to get credit for appointing the first Hispanic to the Supreme Court. And they were convinced President Bush intended to nominate Estrada to one of the anticipated Supreme Court vacancies.

I was the first casualty before the Judiciary Committee in the war over the confirmation of the Bush Appellate Court nominees in March 2002. However, Miguel Estrada was the first of the Bush Appellate nominees to face escalation of the battle by filibuster—an unprecedented action for a nominee with majority support, a practice never before employed in the entire 214-year history of the United States Senate.

According to Democratic pollster Sergio Bendixen, the Democrats had nothing to worry about by filibustering Estrada:

> "The Hispanic electorate doesn't care. They don't know about it, they are not well informed and they don't consider it to be an important issue." . . . He said . . . many of those who supported Mr. Estrada were also confusing him with actor Erik Estrada, who was on the 1977–1983 television police drama "CHiPS" and is now a popular Spanish-language soap-opera star. "Many of them think President Bush nominated Erik Estrada—I'd say a good third think that way."[28]

Democrats were also concerned about Republicans drawing Hispanic voters into their base:

Hispanic leaders are telling Democratic officials that Hispanics are no longer part of the party's political base because President Bush and the Republicans have made inroads into the nation's largest minority voting bloc. In closed-door Democratic strategy meetings to plan for the elections next year, Hispanic leaders and pollsters have painted a picture of declining Hispanic support for the Democrats, warning party officials that if they do not reach out more aggressively to this pivotal group, Republicans likely will make further gains in the 2004 elections.[29]

Thus, the Democrats saw a political advantage and a political necessity. One, they could fight Estrada without a backlash, and two, they could prevent the Republicans from successfully naming the first Hispanic to the D.C. Court of Appeals and ultimately to the Supreme Court, and deny the GOP this endearing achievement among Hispanic voters.

Besides election politics, the left-wing ideologues could not tolerate someone of Estrada's value system on the court. As an assistant solicitor general, in 1994, Miguel Estrada successfully argued a case before the Supreme Court prohibiting pro-life groups from blocking abortion clinics. Later, he told Patricia Ireland, president for the National Organization for Women, that he considered abortion to be the killing of a human being.[30] Estrada was not pro-choice. He was pro-life. But Estrada did believe in the rule of law, and his constitutional fidelity committed him to following and arguing on behalf of the law even though he might have personally disagreed with it. To rule consistent with one's personal beliefs is easy, but to rule contrary to one's personal beliefs is the mark of an impartial judge, one committed to the rule of law. These left-wing groups were not interested in that kind of judge; they want judges committed to their agenda, and Democratic senators were ever willing to do the bidding of the groups.

Estrada was royally abused by Democrats. During his committee hearing, he was grilled for some eight hours and required to answer 125 questions. Still, Democrats objected to the fact the he did not answer questions as to how he would rule in the future, even though this was consistent with the response of Ruth Bader Ginsberg, a liberal nominated to the Supreme Court by Democratic President Bill Clinton.

She stated she would not prejudice herself by answering hypotheticals about the future. This response has become known as the "Ginsberg Rule." Now that it was Estrada answering in this manner, Democrats attempted to use it as a justification for not supporting his nomination.

Democrats also complained that the White House refused to provide them the memos Estrada wrote as an assistant solicitor general. However, "every living former U.S. Solicitor General, both Democrats and Republicans, opposed the release of the information."[31] This, too, was a charge by Democrats full of sound and fury, but signifying nothing.

Now, in control of the committee, Republicans gave Priscilla Owen her second hearing in March. The committee approved her nomination on a straight party-line vote. Like Miguel Estrada, the American Bar Association gave Priscilla Owen their highest rating, "well qualified." She had an excellent resume and would two years later find herself on President Bush's short list for the Supreme Court. When her nomination reached the Senate floor, the Democrats filibustered her, too. By the first of May, Democrats had filibustered Miguel Estrada four times and Priscilla Owen once.

Republicans were frustrated. Some Republican lawmakers contemplated filing a lawsuit to declare the filibuster unconstitutional. Others suggested various rule changes to prevent the filibuster, but those too could be blocked by the minority. Senator Lott raised the prospect of imposing confirmation by majority vote by ruling on a point of order, a parliamentary procedure pioneered by Democratic senator Robert Byrd in previous decades. Lott's plan became known as the "Constitutional option," the "Byrd option," and unfortunately the "nuclear option" because of the expected response by Democrats. There was no immediate resolution.

One writer wrote, "The one real power Republicans have over the Democrats in this fight is the recess-appointment power. It's the only threat that could force Senate Dems to budge."[32] At the time, I did not realize that I would be called upon to consider such an appointment just nine months later.

To add suspense to the confirmation drama playing out in the U.S. Senate, news stories again surfaced in late May and June that both Supreme Court Justice Sandra Day O'Connor and Chief Justice William Rehnquist were considering retiring, which would provide President Bush with two appointments to the Supreme Court. However, these vacancies would not materialize for another two years.

In July, Chip's office called and said I needed to come to Washington for a meeting with Senator Jim Jeffords of Vermont. Jeffords, the former Republican who became the only independent in the Senate in 2002 and gave control of the Senate to the Democrats, truly did have an independent streak. He did not just accept the left-wing special-interest groups' talking points; he wanted to weigh the facts and make his own decision. His staff listed several areas of concern, and my supporters put together a documented briefing book that answered each concern.

My visit with Senator Jeffords was pleasant and thorough, and we discussed my life and record in some detail. He was particularly interested in my friendship with another of Vermont's public servants: Fred Parker.

Fred Parker and I met in 1990 while both attending a new judge training session in Denver, Colorado. Fred was a great big old bear of a man, a large presence at some six feet seven and with a heavy black beard; but he had a kind and gentle spirit. Mississippi and Vermont are far apart, but we hit it off immediately. When we would attend conferences together, he and his wife Barb, and Margaret Ann and I, would often attend dinner or rent a car and travel together.

Like me, Fred Parker was appointed to the district bench by the first President Bush. He was later elevated to the Second Circuit Court of Appeals by President Bill Clinton on Senator Patrick Leahy's recommendation. He was close to both Jeffords and Leahy and had worked with both of them in Vermont. Fred told me he thought our friendship and his affirmation of my record would be helpful with Jeffords. He was right.

After our meeting concluded, Senator Jeffords called Fred, who encouraged Jeffords to support me. Jeffords told Fred that while it would probably not sit well with Senator Leahy, he had to face himself in the mirror every morning, and he was going to do what he thought was right and vote for me. Fred also spoke with Senator Leahy and told him I was worthy of his support, but the power of the special-interest groups on Leahy was stronger than Fred's influence. A few weeks after these conversations, Fred passed away—an untimely death, a great loss to the judiciary. Margaret Ann and I still stay in touch with Barb Parker.

As Jeffords's support for my nomination leaked out, the left-wing groups turned up the pressure on him; nevertheless, he made his support public and issued a statement supporting me. In that statement he mentioned he had talked to the late and respected Judge Parker about my confirmation and he had vouched for me.

Chip felt like the endorsement of Senator Jeffords, since he was the only Independent in the Senate, would encourage some of the other Democrats to reconsider my nomination and vote against the filibuster. While it was some momentum in the struggle, it did not bring any additional votes on board. But I was and am grateful to Senator Jeffords.

While in Washington on the trip, I also visited with Senator Mark Pryor, a young Democrat from Arkansas. Pryor had previously been attorney general for Arkansas, and his father had been governor and senator. He came from a similar place, he and Chip had worked together in the past, and one of Chip's close friends was a strong supporter of Pryor. We thought he could be persuaded to support me in the face of a filibuster, and with his support might come the support of Arkansas' other Democratic senator, Blanche Lincoln. Senator Pryor listened courteously and told us he recognized that I had a good record, but said he wanted to run the traps—translated: he wanted to check out the politics. Well, the Democratic politics in Washington were clear, and they pressured his base in Arkansas, and the People for the American Way was a contributor to his campaign. In the end, he voted against me and for the filibuster.

As the Republican leadership and the White House began to make plans for what would be my third hearing, I wanted to testify and I started preparing. No one else in the process thought I should testify. They said Democratic senators would just cross-examine me, try to create inconsistencies in my testimony to exploit, and simply build a case to justify their previously made decision to vote against me and then support a filibuster. Facing near unanimous advice against testifying, I relented, despite my desire to attempt to clear my name. Later, when I watched the hearing—or more like it, interrogation—for William Pryor, I realized my advisors were absolutely right.

Next, we discussed who would testify on my behalf. We discussed various Mississippi Democrats and African American leaders, but eventually decided that I had already had two hearings, my record had been fully discussed, and there was no need for either me to testify or to have witnesses. These discussions took until July to resolve, and because the Senate would be in recess all during August, my hearing was put off until September.

The Senate left Washington for the August recess. What had happened to Miguel Estrada and Priscilla Owen did not bode well for me. My nomination was scheduled to come before the committee in September. I undoubtedly would be reported out of committee, although I was now convinced it would not be that simple. The new challenge of facing a potential filibuster on the Senate floor began to dominate strategy.

Filibustered

IT WAS NEARING the end of Congress's 2003 summer recess. My nomination would soon be back before the Judiciary Committee. Before that
happened, however, Miguel Estrada withdrew as a nominee to the
District Court of Appeals, "the first high profile Bush judicial nominee
to ask that his name be removed from Senate deliberation."[1] When
Estrada finally withdrew, his nomination had been blocked for twenty-
eight months and he had been filibustered seven times.

Byron York wrote about the pressures Estrada faced because of the
confirmation process, unnecessary pressures unrelated to his qualifications:

> Estrada was concerned about both his family and his career. . . . the
> nomination limbo had affected his law practice. He . . . expressed
> concerns about his family . . . he couldn't make any plans . . . . He had
> to change his phone number because he was getting crank calls . . . .
> His wife was upset. . . . Some of the accusations thrown at Estrada
> during the filibuster were distressingly personal. . . . [O]pponents
> went so far as to charge that Estrada . . . was insufficient Hispanic to
> merit the support of Hispanic groups. . . . He thought he was going to
> be a federal judge, and he ended up being a political football.[2]

The Washington press establishment was a willing accomplice. They
framed the debate by giving equal validity and credibility to the
Democrats' bogus charges against Miguel Estrada as they gave to his
sterling credentials. If the press had done its job and reported that the
charges against Estrada were as meritless as in fact they were, Miguel

Estrada would have been confirmed. What these groups and the Democratic senators did to Miguel Estrada was shameful. He deserved better. He was treated more unfairly than I or any of the other Bush nominees. His confirmation would have been an inspiration and a challenge to immigrants and minorities across our land, and he would have served with distinction in the federal judiciary. Any sensitive and thinking American should be offended by what Far Left special-interest groups did to Miguel Estrada. The price of public service should not be so high.

At the time Estrada withdrew, there were two other nominees being filibustered—Texas Supreme Court justice Priscilla Owen and Alabama attorney general William Pryor. The time when my name could be added to that list was fast approaching, but the White House feared any additional withdrawals would empower the Democrats and give the filibusters unstoppable momentum. The White House approached Chip about the possibility of giving me a recess appointment. Senator Orrin Hatch as chairman of the Judiciary Committee had reservations about recess appointments, as did Senator Trent Lott, who generally preferred the executive branch to use those powers rarely. Chip and I both agreed we should continue to work toward confirmation; and if we did not succeed, then I would give further consideration to a recess appointment.

At that time, my nomination was still in committee and would be until at least the end of the month. So I focused my time on the district court in Hattiesburg and returned to more relaxing work on the farm on weekends.

Throughout my adult life, I spent most Saturdays working around the farm: building bridges and maintaining roads through the timber, clearing brush, developing food plots for wild game, and whatever needed to be done. I enjoy the physical work, and I have an affinity for land and its wise stewardship and utilization. I planted many trees, mostly pine for commercial purposes, but also dogwood, redbud, poplar, ash, sycamore, and oaks of various kinds for aesthetics, conervation, and food for game. More than twenty-five years ago, I personally planted a row of some thirty-five live oaks alongside the lane leading to our farm home. (During Hurricane Katrina we lost three trees in that row, as well as some beautiful old oaks and other trees around the house and many across the farm.) During the almost three years my nomination had been pending, somewhat drained of energy, I had oftentimes let my farm work go. I intended to reclaim this portion of my life, and in September, I started trying to get back out on the farm to get both it and me in better shape. The work provided therapy and reminded me of— and tempted me to return to—normal life.

Momentum also seemed to improve regarding my confirmation. Several times throughout September and into October, I spoke with Chip, Senator Lott, or others connected with the confirmation process and heard encouraging information leading me to believe I just might dodge the filibuster and be confirmed. But for every call received indicating that I would be confirmed, I received a like number of calls indicating I would be filibustered.

Nevertheless, Chip had been meticulously and systematically counting votes to secure my nomination and avoid filibuster. He felt I had fifty-five solid votes—all fifty-one Republicans, plus the Senate's independent Jim Jeffords, and three Democrats: John Breaux of Louisiana, Zell Miller of Georgia, and Ben Nelson of Nebraska. He thought three more votes were in sight. Democratic senator Mary Landrieu of Louisiana told Chip she would support my nomination, but she did not make this public. (The White House staff was elated at that news; they had been unable to get her support when the Democrats successfully filibustered Estrada, Owen, and Pryor.) Chip thought I still had a chance at the vote of Senator Pryor, and if I got his vote, the vote of Arkansas' other Democratic senator, Blanche Lincoln, would likely follow. That would put us two Democratic votes shy of breaking the filibuster, and Chip was looking to personal relationships with Senator Bill Nelson of Florida and Senator Fritz Hollings of South Carolina to close the gap.

Chip and Leisha were friends with Senator Bill Nelson and his wife; they worked together with the fellowship that sponsors the National Prayer Breakfast. Senator Nelson's wife had often called Leisha to ask her help with various faith-based projects. Senator Nelson had voted against the filibuster of Miguel Estrada (Florida has a large Hispanic vote), and Chip was hoping he would also oppose my filibuster. Chip's repeated calls to Senator Nelson went unreturned, as did Leisha's calls to Mrs. Nelson.

Senator Hollings of South Carolina and Chip had a close relationship going back to when Chip was a staffer on the Senate Commerce Committee and Senator Hollings was the committee's ranking Democrat. They worked closely together on the Telecommunications Act of 1996. When Chip was first elected to Congress, Senator Hollings attended Chip's ceremonial swearing in at the Supreme Court Building where Justice Antonin Scalia presided and I administered the oath. In February 2002, Senator Hollings reviewed the charges against me and said, "I'll still vote for him . . . I think he is a fine Judge."[3]

However, Senator Hollings was facing reelection or retirement in 2004. From the right, he resented that the Republicans were going to field a major candidate against him if he ran. From the left, he had been roundly criticized for aiding the confirmation of Judge Dennis Shedd, who had been recommended to the Fourth Circuit by Senator Strom Thurmond. Between the attacks on Judge Shedd by civil rights groups in his own state and the furor over Senator Lott's comments, Hollings was concerned about his legacy. Still, Chip remained hopeful Senator Hollings would stand by his original commitment and vote for me. Again, Chip saw Hollings as the key to persuading other Democratic senators to follow his lead. If Hollings came on board, Chip thought Hollings could perhaps bring along Senators Inouye and Akaka of Hawaii. Except through Hollings, we had little access to the senators from Hawaii, although neither seemed strident in their opposition. Chip also thought that perhaps Biden was no longer considering a presidential race and might reconsider. Additionally, we thought, Evan Bayh of Indiana—despite his presidential ambitions—and Senator Byron Dorgan of North Dakota could be in play. If all of these came through, that would be sixty-five votes, more than enough to defeat a filibuster. Chip was optimistic. He thought my confirmation was in reach. Nevertheless, we knew everything had to break our way in order to be able to defeat a filibuster.

During this period, a lawyer friend was on a conference call with Senator Patrick Leahy's chief of staff and a number of attorneys. During the course of the conference call, Senator Leahy's chief of staff said the Democrats were going to let me go through without a filibuster. About the same time, a reporter told me that Senator Leahy had been asked if Democrats were going to filibuster me, and he had evaded the question. This was encouraging. It was also consistent with word that the staffs of the Democratic senators felt badly about what they were doing to me and that Democratic senators wanted to find a way out of the obstruction. But their expressions of empathy and sense of regret failed to produce action, especially when the special-interest groups engaged.

The Feminist Majority Foundation issued a press release titled "Opposition to Anti-Women Nominee Pickering Wavering." The piece cited a recent article in *Roll Call* that reflected "small signs of wavering opposition."[4] The left-wing organizations rallied and renewed the pressure on the Democrats.

On September 25, my nomination was scheduled to be voted on in the Senate Judiciary Committee. But Senator Leahy forced my nomination over for one week, saying I had not updated my Senate questionnaire. There had been no request to do so, but I reviewed the forms to see if there were any changes since January of that year. By now I was used to delays and used to Democratic requests for more information. Since I had not been reversed during my confirmation process (beginning in 2001), there were no significant changes to be made. As Yogi Berra said, it was déjà vu all over again.

On September 29, Paul Kane wrote an article in *Roll Call* describing my plight. He reported that voting me out of committee was a foregone conclusion, and that I would likely come up for a vote before the full Senate around mid-October. He said that my confirmation

> rested in the hands of a half dozen undecided Democrats. . . . Despite the mountain of media attention given to the nomination, at least six Senate Democrats said last week that they were undecided on Pickering or hadn't heard enough about the judge to take a position. With 55 Senators publicly in his corner—the 51 Republicans, plus

Miller, Jeffords, Breaux and Ben Nelson—Pickering will need to win over five of the six undecided votes, five of whom hail from the South.

Kane listed Democratic senators who were uncommitted: Bill Nelson of Florida, Mary Landrieu of Louisiana, Blanche Lincoln of Arkansas, Mark Pryor of Arkansas, Fritz Hollings of South Carolina, and Byron Dorgan of North Dakota. These, of course, had been our targets, but now that they were in print, the special-interest groups would certainly turn up the heat.

Just before the committee voted on my nomination, the Committee for Justice—an organization supporting the Bush nominees—ran a full-page advertisement in *Roll Call* featuring a letter supportive of my nomination. The letter was on Mississippi Democratic governor Ronnie Musgrove's official stationery, addressed to Senators Bill Frist and Tom Daschle, and signed by Musgrove, Secretary of State Eric Clark, Attorney General Mike Moore, Commissioner of Agriculture and Commerce Lester Spell, and Commissioner of Insurance George Dale. It read in part,

> The nomination of Federal District Judge Charles Pickering to the U.S. Fifth Circuit Court of Appeals is once again coming before the U.S. Senate in Washington for consideration. We are the Democratic statewide officials of Mississippi. We know Charles Pickering personally and have known him for many years. We believe Judge Pickering should be confirmed for this appointment and serve on the court. Judge Pickering chose to take stands during his career that were difficult and often courageous. He has worked for racial reconciliation and helped unify our communities. . . . We are all active Democrats. Charles Pickering was, before rising to the Federal Bench, an active Republican. It is our hope that Party labels can be transcended in this fight over his nomination. We should cast a blind eye to partisanship when working to build a fair and impartial judiciary. The U.S. Senate has a chance to demonstrate a commitment to fairness. Judge Pickering's record demonstrates his commitment to equal protection, equal rights and fairness for all. . . . In the 1960s, Charles Pickering stood up for the voting rights of African Americans, and for the equal protection of all. In the 1970s and 1980s he led his community,

children's schools, political party and church in integration and inclusion. Today, he is a voice for racial reconciliation across our state. As a judge, he is consistent in his fairness to everyone, and deemed well qualified by those who independently review his rulings, temperament and work. Mississippi has made tremendous progress in race relations since the 1960s and Charles Pickering has been part of that progress. We ask the United States Senate to stand up to those that malign the character of Charles Pickering, and give him an up or down vote on the Senate Floor.

On October 2, 2003, my nomination once again came before the Judiciary Committee. Supporting my nomination in Washington, among the usual players, were my friend Wesley Breland; Representative Phillip West, chairman of the Mississippi Legislative Black Caucus; and Reverend Ed King, a Mississippi civil rights era activist who, though white, had been a member of the Mississippi Freedom Democratic Party and had personally faced violence from segregationist forces.

One newspaper reporter described the hearing as "more than two hours of impassioned debate."[5] Senator Hatch delivered a lengthy introductory statement defending my nomination, saying,

> Unfortunately, there has been an unjustified campaign against Judge Pickering, driven largely by Washington special-interest groups. . . . Make no mistake about it: These groups' political agenda is to paint President Bush's fair and qualified nominees as extremists in order to keep them off the federal bench. . . . It's time to give him the dignity of an up or down vote. . . . I expect we will hear today a recycling of the tired arguments and well-worn parade of horribles—which are horrible in large part because of their gross distortion of Judge Pickering's upstanding reputation and record.[6]

Senator Ted Kennedy's statement against me that day was the harshest of all, although I am told he read it without emotion. Kennedy said that my nomination "signals the Administration's lack of respect for civil rights concerns"[7] and proclaimed that I was not a "decent Judge."[8] In my previous hearing, Kennedy had said I was "certainly a decent and generally kind individual."[9] Over the duration of the battle, Senator

Kennedy became more political and his rhetoric more strident. For whatever reason, Senator Kennedy has emerged as the leading spokesman for extreme feminism in the U.S. Senate.

Senator John Cornyn, the freshman Republican senator from Texas and former state supreme court judge, said, "some Republicans call Pickering a victim of anti-Baptist and anti-Southern bias. . . . We should stop using religious views or stereotypes, about Southerners or any other people, against a nominee."[10] The *New York Times* reported that Cornyn, "[e]ngaged in an argument shorn of the usual formal courtesies . . . as a freshman, . . . was dismayed to discover that the confirmation process was broken and that there was discrimination against nominees from the South."[11]

Senator Leahy was so strong in his mocking response to and dressing down of Senator Cornyn that Senator Jon Kyl and Senator Hatch rebuked him and suggested that Leahy apologize to Cornyn. Leahy refused to do so, rejecting even the idea he might be fallible.

Senator Russ Feingold described me as "an extraordinarily fine man" while at the same time claiming he was concerned about my ethics involving letters of support for my nomination from lawyers in Mississippi, some of whom from time to time practiced before me. Feingold read off some of the names: Raymond Brown, Leonard Melvin Jr., Frank Montague, and others. Feingold seemed pleased with himself, as if this charge would surely stick and justify his opposition.

But Senator Hatch grabbed a file and read through my relationship with each person Feingold mentioned at such dismissive speed that the press largely ignored the exchange. Hatch noted that Raymond Brown and I were fraternity brothers and law school classmates and that our children played together. I met Leonard Melvin when I was in high school; he and his wife hosted a pre-wedding dinner for Margaret Ann and me; today I teach him in Sunday school. Frank Montague and I shared clients and have had a close working relationship for decades. I had similar relationships with the other lawyers specifically mentioned by Senator Feingold.

Hatch basically told Feingold that if the worst thing he could do was to complain that one of Judge Pickering's Sunday school friends had sent a letter of support, he hardly had a reason to block me from the Fifth Circuit. He said that this was just another attack like every previous attack, a smoke screen, an attempt to derail my nomination with false charges, and like all the rest it was easily answered. I am told Feingold looked a little stunned.

In all candor, I do wish the letters of support had been handled differently. Letters of support from lawyers and judges often are solicited for controversial nominees in both Republican and Democratic administrations. Because both the White House and I were caught off guard when opposition to my nomination surfaced just two days before my first hearing, no letters of support had been written. Then, when faced with opposition at the first hearing, we had the compounded problem that a letter with anthrax had been delivered to Senator Tom Daschle's office, causing a several-week delay for screening purposes of all mail to the Senate.

To overcome this delay, Sheila Joy—a Justice Department career employee who had worked with both Bush and Clinton nominees—advised for the sake of convenience that I have letters of support faxed to my office and then faxed to her office in the Department of Justice. She would in turn fax the letters to the Judiciary Committee for filing.

It is difficult for those from larger states to appreciate that a judge in a rural state like Mississippi is going to know and have close contact with many of the lawyers who appear before him. A judge who cannot put aside these relationships simply cannot sit as a judge. However, judges are to avoid even the appearance of impropriety or impartiality, and if I had it to do over again, I would distance myself from the letters for my own reasons—even though I did nothing wrong and nothing unethical.

The American Bar Association considers judicial ethics in making its evaluations. The ABA reevaluated my record as part of my re-nomination, and once again, even after the issue over the letters of support was raised, gave me its highest approval rating, "well qualified"—the "gold standard" by which to judge nominees. The ABA would not have given this evaluation if it had found an ethics problem.

All this made no difference to Feingold and his Democratic colleagues. Their main concern was politics—abortion politics, culture war politics—not ethics.

Under the subheading "Decorum fades in a debate over a renewed nomination," Neil Lewis described the hearing for the *New York Times*:

> The usual fragile shell of courtesy that surrounds such events had . . . shattered. . . . Before the straight party-line vote of 10 to 9 in favor of the nomination, there were several heated arguments. . . . The atmosphere was made more tense by the presence in the room of Representative Charles W. Pickering, Jr., the nominee's son, who could hardly contain himself. At the conclusion of the hearing, he went near some Democratic staff aides and said in a low, intense voice: "You have participated in the smear of a good man and you know that. You know what you have done."[12]

Byron York, writing for the *National Review Online*, described the scene vividly, from a different perspective:

> Even though the rhetoric was pointed and the stakes high, there was a sense of listlessness in the room. . . . Both sides have recited their lines so many times that even the Senators making the arguments seem to get bored. . . . As Kennedy spoke, repeating the allegations of Pickering's alleged insensitivity, Hatch got up and walked around the table. Other Senators milled about. Some reporters read newspapers. . . . The Committee was on autopilot—until the speaking order got down to one of the panel's newest members, South Carolina Republican Lindsey Graham. . . . Up until now, Graham has kept a relatively low profile on the Committee, but as he spoke, his voice rose and his sense of outrage began to radiate throughout the room. His speech, quoted here at some length, gave a tired committee a newcomer's sense of what the judicial deadlock has done to the Senate.
> "If I thought that Judge Pickering somehow condoned cross burning, it would be the easiest decision in the world to vote no," Graham began. . . . "And if you really believe that, then you're absolutely right, you should vote no.

"The truth is, the man's been under siege for a couple of years now, and I can only imagine what he and his family went through and . . . It's been total hell . . . . there's nothing worse you can say about a southern white person than that they're a racist. We have to live with that all the time, and it's our own fault to a certain extent. . . .

"In my state, 31-percent African American, we're a long way away from South Carolina being where it should be. The incomes in my state of African Americans are dramatically lower than the population as a whole. So I don't want anyone to leave this room today thinking that we've fixed our racial problems in the South. We have not. . . .

"But I tell you, you need to look at your own states and see if you've fixed them in your state. There's a long way to go, and beating on this good man is not going to make us a better nation. . . .

"The reason we're here is that you all have chosen a handful of nominees—and there are not many, but one is too many—and you've used the tactic of stopping them from having a vote up or down on the floor. And we will respond in the future, and the country will be the great loser. . . .

"What's happening is going to doom the future of the U. S. Senate, because if you think the people on my side of the aisle, when there's a Democratic president, are going to sit back and not do the same thing—that's just naïve. . . .

"This is history being made in the United States Senate. This is horrible history. It's happening on our watch. God, I wish I could fix it. But I don't see it being fixed. . . .

"Senator Schumer said let the fight begin. The fight has begun, and the fight needs to be taken to its logical conclusion. We need to break these filibusters, we need to bring reason back to the table, and we need to stop taking good men and women who are well qualified by the bar association and saying that they are racists. . . .

"Do you know what it must have been like in 1967 to get on the stand and testify against the Ku Klux Klan in Mississippi? Do you have any idea what courage that took? Shame on you."

By the end, Graham was nearly in tears and the room was silent. It was an almost stunning conclusion to a meeting that had just a few minutes before seemed entirely recycled and pre-scripted. Of course, no minds were changed; when Graham finished, Hatch ordered that the roll be called, and Pickering was approved, with all ten

Republicans voting for him and all nine Democrats voting against him. But Graham's speech hinted at the depth of Republican anger over the filibusters that have so far stopped three appeals-court nominations and threatened others (including Pickering's).[13]

When Senator Graham had finished his speech, the three Democrats who remained in the hearing room came over and shook hands with him. My friend, Wesley Breland, heard Senator Schumer say, "It's not too late. Maybe we can still work something out." That was not the first time that Schumer had talked about working something out. But he never followed through.

The *New York Times* reported, "Democrats have not yet decided if they will try to block the Pickering nomination with a filibuster."[14] As soon as the committee reported my nomination to the Senate floor, Chip, Senator Hatch, and Senator Lott held a press conference in an effort to build support for my confirmation and avoid a filibuster. They released a video reflecting the widespread support for my nomination by Mississippians. The video through photographs, news articles, and interviews—of Republicans and Democrats; blacks and whites—visually told my story to the Washington press corps in a way words alone can never convey. Unfortunately, by this point, their template had been written and it was coming down to the decisions by a few Democrats as to what my future would be. One Democrat, Senator Joe Biden, approached Senator Lott and told him he could not vote to confirm me, but he would vote to stop the filibuster against me. This was a huge step forward.

Wesley called and kept me posted of what was going on throughout the proceeding; I had remained in Mississippi. That afternoon after the vote was taken and I was voted onto the Senate floor, I went to where I was having some timber thinned and burned brush until eight-thirty that evening.

Following my vote out of committee, Nat Hentoff wrote,

As a reporter, I've covered stories where people's reputations have been badly distorted by their opponents and then the media. One such victim, after being unequivocally cleared, plaintively asked, "Where can I go to get my reputation back?" . . .

I have been teaching my New York University journalism students about one such classic case—the savaging of a judge who did justice—Federal Judge Charles Pickering of Mississippi. . . .

But, once again, Democrats have trumpeted the same charges against Pickering, echoed by journalists who fail to do their own reporting and recycle the allegations in news stories and editorials. . . .[15]

Hentoff wrote in another article,

What the Democrats on the Senate Judiciary Committee—led relentlessly by Charles Schumer—have done to distort Pickering's record on and off the bench has been the antithesis of due process and plain decency. . . . I focus on Pickering . . . because, since he became a national figure, he has had to hear himself tarred as a racist.

Hentoff then excoriated the *New York Times* editorial writers for ignoring what their reporters wrote about me. He described Senator Schumer as "an unabashed, ideological partisan." He continued, "There is now no charge too low and too inaccurate that is beyond the bounds of trying to terminate a judicial nomination. It has become disgusting."[16] Hentoff queried,

Are there any Democratic members in the Senate with the decency and honesty to show Pickering that he can get his good name back as a judge who has already proved with his record—as extensively laid out in the Atlantic-Journal Constitution [sic]—that he does justice for all who come in front of him?[17]

Two weeks after the committee sent my nomination to the full Senate, Chip told me I needed to come back to Washington to meet with Democratic senators thought to be wavering or leaning in my direction. Senators Mary Landrieu of Louisiana and Evan Bayh of Indiana had indicated a willingness to meet with me, and Chip was still working on Senator Bill Nelson of Florida. Meetings with Landrieu and

Nelson never materialized. My meeting with Bayh was courteous and friendly and he said he would give me careful consideration. Apparently, when the other Democrats learned Bayh was not committed to my filibuster, they turned up the pressure on him. A January 3, 2004, *Washington Post* story describing the leaked Democratic strategy memos reported, "Another memo indicated that Senator Evan Bayh (D-Ind.) was dragging his feet over the filibuster. The Kennedy aide urged his boss to cajole Bayh."[18] Those opposing my nomination even enlisted Senator Bayh's father, former Senator Birch Bayh, to make sure he stayed hitched.

In late October, Senator Joe Biden backed away again. He told the newspaper *Roll Call* that he had considered voting for cloture—to end the filibuster—and then to oppose me on final passage; but he was upset that the White House re-nominated me after I had been blocked in committee. This was disingenuous; he would have never had the opportunity to vote against my filibuster unless I had been re-nominated. Furthermore, he knew these circumstances when he spoke with Lott just a few weeks prior. People who supported my nomination spent more time with Biden than any other senator. He acknowledged to my supporters that the charges against me were not valid. He was always telling them that either he was going to support my nomination or he was trying to find a way to support my nomination, but his support never materialized. This was another case of the pressure being too great and a Democratic senator looking for cover.

Senator Lott talked to every Democratic senator with whom he had any kind of rapport and whom he thought might be persuaded to vote against the filibuster of my nomination. He went again to Senator Tom Daschle and told him he would personally appreciate his help in preventing a filibuster. Daschle was warm and cordial but told Trent the groups were putting lots of pressure on him; still, he would see what he could do. He was not encouraging.

Chip met with many Democratic senators privately, including members of their leadership. On one occasion, he met with Senator Harry Reid, then Senate minority leader. He was courteous and professional and frank with Chip. Chip began arguing my qualifications, but Reid told him, "It has nothing to do with substance or merit."

Reid said he knew my reputation and my record and the Democratic leadership regretted what had happened to me. But the matter had gone too far. If the Democrats let me through, their power of the filibuster would weaken or perhaps break. "Our constituency wants us to filibuster your dad. We have forty-five Democratic senators committed to do that. We are going to filibuster him."

When he did not respond to Chip's argument on the basis it was the right thing to do, that I deserved confirmation, Chip then addressed the political. Chip said my filibuster would cost the Democrats in Mississippi and the South. That argument also fell on deaf ears. Reid replied it would cost them more politically across the country if they did not filibuster me. The Democrats had expended so much effort demonizing me that if they let me through, it would dishearten their base approaching the 2004 election season. They would not pull the rug from under the feet of their special-interest groups. They told Chip they were sorry, it was politics and not personal, but they had the votes to block me and Chip should quit trying to change the outcome. Whether they were bluffing and fearful Chip might succeed or whether they truly meant what they said, we don't know. But in the end, they had the votes, and in the end, they did block me; but Chip did not give up.

The Republican Senate leadership decided to file for cloture on Friday night, October 24, with debate on my nomination set for the following Tuesday.

On Thursday before the cloture was to be filed, *Congressional Quarterly* reported, "Some opponents said they were concerned that Pickering's supporters had persuaded wavering Democrats to back him. . . . But Democrats have been under intense pressure from their leadership—as well as scores of civil and women's rights groups that oppose Pickering—to present a united front against the nominees." The article noted that Senator Lott had talked to half the Democratic caucus on a personal basis, and they wanted to be helpful because they wanted to respond to Trent and they knew I had been treated unfairly.[19]

On Thursday night before cloture was to be filed, Senator Harry Reid, the Democratic minority whip, approached Senator Lott and requested that he not file for cloture until after the weekend. He told Trent that the Democrats would not work against me over the weekend and gave Trent names of Democrats who might be persuaded to oppose the filibuster. Trent called me and told me it could be the Democrats were trying to firm up opposition to my confirmation, or that it could be a genuine gesture of conciliation in response to Trent's conversation with Senator Daschle and Chip's private meeting with Democratic leadership. Trent felt that in respect of Senate comity we should acquiesce and put my vote off once again. I concurred. I thought we had more to gain than lose.

The left-wing groups and their leaders opposing me now saw this fight not only as a means to send a message to the White House, to keep me off the circuit bench, but also as a referendum on their power. They could not allow the Democrats to buck them on this issue; they could not afford the loss in the press and public opinion. Today I have come to believe Senator Reid and Senator Daschle probably wanted to allow me to go through without a filibuster, but other factions in their party would not allow it. Representative Bennie Thompson and the Congressional Black Caucus met with many of the Democratic senators to reinforce those who might be wavering. The secularist groups and abortion rights organizations also turned up the heat and issued warnings. Reid and Daschle may have been inclined to let me through, but they didn't have the strength or resolve to stand against the special-interest groups that were in charge.

On Tuesday night, October 28, a cloture motion was filed on my nomination. That meant that I would either be confirmed or filibustered on the following Thursday. On Wednesday, I learned that Mark Pryor had called our mutual friend in Arkansas and told him that he realized I was qualified but that he didn't have political cover so he would not be able to vote to stop the filibuster. He made a similar call to the White House, but he couldn't bring himself to tell Chip when he saw him. As to this vote, Mark Pryor was not a profile in courage.

Without Pryor, Biden, Bayh, or Hollings, it didn't seem possible that I could be confirmed.

As the time approached for the showdown vote on my nomination, analysts were weighing the impact of what was about to happen.

While Republicans are not giving up the fight, the Committee for Justice is attempting to make Democrats pay politically for blocking an up-or-down vote on the nomination. . . . Republicans and their conservative allies have accused liberals of painting Pickering as a caricature of segregationist Mississippi in the civil rights era. . . .

Republicans believe their message will resonate with their conservative base, particularly in rural regions of the South. And they point to several victories in Southern Senate races last year as examples of where that theme fit their strategy.

But nowhere will the impact of a Pickering filibuster have an immediate impact as in Mississippi, where Barbour and Musgrove are still in a heated battle, with less than two weeks to go. "It looks tight," Lott said of the race. . . . "This could be the difference." . . . "This is a big deal in the Mississippi gubernatorial race," one conservative strategist said. "There will be an angry reaction in Mississippi even among Democrats," said Senator Trent Lott (R-Miss).

But Democrats don't appear to have been swayed at all by a fear of backlash by southern voters, either in Mississippi or other states.[20]

The White House continued to discuss a recess appointment but no decision had been made. I conveyed to the White House that I wanted to get the process behind me.

On the day that my nomination came before the Senate, the *LA Times* noted, "Two years, five months and five days after President Bush tapped him for a promotion, U.S. District Judge Charles W. Pickering, Sr., of Mississippi today expects to get his first vote from the full Senate."[21] Senator Orrin Hatch in a guest editorial in the *Washington Times* noted, "After more than 880 days since President Bush nominated him, Judge Charles Pickering's nomination to the U. S. Court of Appeals is finally, and properly, before the Senate." Senator Hatch noted that twenty-four currently serving Democrats were members of the Senate when I was unanimously confirmed in 1990 and that "the case for the same result now is compelling. . . . His most deeply-held beliefs including the religious ones some find so troubling, commit him to fairness, justice and respect. He worked for racial equality long before it was popular."[22]

Hatch argued that the real issue was abortion and since I had never ruled on an abortion case, "At the end of the day, Judge Pickering's opponents believe that personal opposition to abortion disqualifies him from federal judicial service. I believe that is an unacceptable standard for confirming judges."[23]

The news media and Democratic senators noted that the debate on my nomination was only five days before the hotly contested election between incumbent Democratic governor Ronnie Musgrove and former Republican national chairman Haley Barbour. The *Los Angeles Times* reported, "To help drive the wedge, Senate Republican leaders scheduled the Pickering vote to occur five days before the closely fought Mississippi gubernatorial elections. That will give Republicans a well-timed opportunity to portray Democrats in Washington as out of step with a region where many Democratic incumbents are struggling to hold onto office."[24] The *LA Times* did not mention that Senator Leahy delayed my committee vote by one week in late September and Senator Reid requested the vote on my nomination be delayed several days. The article did mention the letter of support for my nomination from Governor Musgrove and the other statewide Democrats. Unfortunately for Musgrove, while he could claim he had done what he could to support me, the Barbour campaign could point to my defeat as an example that national Democrats do not care about Mississippi Democrats and it would be a mistake to elect an ineffective Democratic governor.

Debate on my nomination was scheduled for nine o'clock Thursday morning, October 30, for an hour and fifteen minutes. The Senate was approaching the end of the session and other important matters had to be addressed as well. But after nearly three years since my first conversation with Senator Lott about the Fifth Circuit, and after debates in public and committee over my record stretching back nearly forty-five years of my life, I thought seventy-five minutes of debate was anticlimactic.

Family and friends joined Margaret Ann and me at our farm home to watch the Senate debate on C-SPAN. I had prepared two statements earlier in the week—one if I was confirmed, the other if I was filibustered. I had submitted copies to the Department of Justice and the White House.

About the time the debate commenced, I started receiving phone calls. Dabney Friedrich, my contact in the White House Counsel's Office, called asking me not to issue a statement withdrawing. Senator Hatch, likewise, called and requested that I not withdraw and expressed the same thoughts from Senator Frist. Apparently they had interpreted my comments that I wanted certainty and finality as an indicator I would withdraw my name. Senator Hatch said he and Senator Lott were—in light of the bitter and unprecedented Democratic attack—shedding their reluctance about a recess appointment. I told Senator Hatch I would "keep my powder dry" and not withdraw. I told Judge Alberto Gonzales the same when he called from the White House a few minutes later.

On the Senate floor, one of the strongest speeches made on my behalf was by Senator Lamar Alexander of Tennessee. He argued,

> The Fifth Circuit played a crucial role in desegregating the South. Judges Tuttle, Rives, Brown, and Wisdom were real heroes at that time. Crosses were burned in front of their homes. . . . Judge Pickering is a worthy successor to the court of Judges Wisdom, Tuttle, Rives, and Brown.
>
> While those judges were ordering the desegregation of Deep South schools, while crosses were being burned in front of their homes, Judge Pickering was enrolling his children in those same newly desegregated schools, and Judge Pickering in his hometown was testifying in court against Sam Bowers, the man the *Baton Rouge Advocate* called the "most violent living racist," at a time when people were killing people based on race.
>
> Many of my generation have changed their minds about race in the South over the last 40 years. That is why the opposition to Judge

Pickering to me seems so blatantly unfair. He hasn't changed his mind. There is nothing to forgive him for. There is nothing to condemn. There is nothing to excuse. He was not a product of his times. He led his times. He spoke out for racial justice. He testified against the most dangerous of the cross burners. He did it in his own hometown, with his own neighbors, at a time in our Nation's history when it was hardest to do. He stuck his neck out for civil rights.[25]

The Democrats made their usual arguments. I had fifty-four votes to stop the filibuster, a majority, enough to be confirmed, but not enough to break the filibuster, not enough to obtain an up or down vote on the Senate floor. Every Republican voted to end the filibuster and give me an up or down vote. They were joined by Independent Jim Jeffords and Democrats John Breaux and Zell Miller. Democrat Ben Nelson of Nebraska publicly gave me support before and afterward, but he was unable to be present for the vote; still I have no doubt he would have done as he said.

The reaction to my filibuster was immediate. Assistant Senate Majority Leader Mitch McConnell of Kentucky told Chip on the Senate floor, "This is one of the lowest points in the history of the United States Senate. We ought to be apologizing for what's happening here."[26]

Chip stated,

"This is not just about one individual, my father. This is a broader example that goes to the very heart of . . . the Senate, the confirmation process and the independence of the Judiciary." . . . He said his father's supporters should be assured "his legacy is not determined by this. It is just one more chapter of his courage, his character. And I cannot be more proud of who he is or what he has done in his lifetime."[27]

When the vote was concluded, I issued a statement:

Although I am disappointed that a minority of the Senate kept the majority of the Senate from confirming my nomination, and while this has been a painful process for me and for my family, what has happened to me personally is of no great importance. But what is happening to the confirmation process is tremendously important. That should be a matter of great concern for all Americans. . . . Most of all, I am grateful, and humbled by the widespread support of the people of Mississippi, people that I have worked with over the years, the people who know me best, both Republican and Democrat, both black and white. I am also grateful for the strong editorial support from all of the major newspapers in Mississippi. So many people offered words of encouragement and said a prayer on behalf of Margaret Ann and me. For this outpouring of support, I will be forever grateful.

I was disappointed at the filibuster; however, I was humbly grateful for the affirmation following. Hattiesburg's NBC affiliate WDAM editorialized,

> A tragic, disgraceful and despicable disservice was perpetrated upon the people of our Nation and a very outstanding and honorable man today by forty-three Democrats in the United States Senate. . . . Judge Pickering's critics continue to unfairly label him as racist and a segregationist. Nothing could be further from the truth. . . . He has been shamelessly mistreated and mischaracterized beyond all bounds of decency. But his legacy and character have not been diminished as all who are privileged to know him will attest.[28]

My friend from the conference call with Senator Leahy's chief of staff who had said the Democrats would let my nomination go through called for an explanation. The staffer explained, "We were prepared to let the judge go through. He probably would not have served more than two, three or four more years. But the groups put so much pressure we were not able to do so."

After the vote, I was drained. But, on Friday afternoon, Chip called Margaret Ann and asked her to go with him and Leisha to a campaign event on the coast where President Bush was campaigning for Haley Barbour. As a federal district court judge, I couldn't join them, so I had a more pleasurable experience: football and grandchildren.

Saturday morning, I worked on the farm and during midday watched the Ole Miss/South Carolina football game on television. Near the end of the third quarter, Ole Miss had a 43-14 lead and they almost blew it. South Carolina raced back with a powerful offense including a 99-yard touchdown pass and bungled plays by the Rebels. But Ole Miss was able to run the clock out, barely winning the game. Afterward, I took Chip and Leisha's boys to Hebron Baptist Church where I added my truck and trailer loaded with hay to two others for a community trick-or-treating hayride. We finished up at the Hebron Community Center for the annual Halloween festival and auction: a feast of hotdogs and hamburgers. That night, I found another tight football game on television—Arkansas and Kentucky. The game went into five or six overtimes before Arkansas finally won. A filibuster can block a judicial confirmation, and truly that is harmful to our judiciary and nation; but fortunately, it cannot block the other joys of life.

The following week I conducted a jury trial on Monday and Tuesday in the district court where I continued to serve. Tuesday was Election Day. My nephew Stacy Pickering was running for the state Senate seat I held in the 1970s. Margaret Ann and family went to the election party, which turned out to be a victory celebration. Stacey won handily. Again, as a federal judge I could not attend so I watched state returns on television as Chip joined a Jackson television station as a commentator. Republican Haley Barbour defeated Democratic incumbent Ronnie Musgrove 53 percent to 46 percent.

The immediate issue for me was whether President Bush would offer and whether I should accept a recess appointment. If I refused a recess appointment, I could remain a federal district judge with a lifetime appointment. If I accepted a recess appointment, I would give up my district judgeship and lifetime appointment. Without confirmation, I would serve on the Fifth Circuit of Appeals only until the end of the congressional session, at which time I would have to retire—no lifetime guarantee. However, my nomination would remain before the Senate, and if I were confirmed, I would still have a lifetime appointment, but to the Fifth Circuit. I pondered my choices.

Recess Appointment

NEVER HAD I wanted to get away and rest anymore than right after the filibuster vote. But I had commitments. There was the passing of the gavel from Chief Judge Tom Lee to Judge Henry Wingate, a ceremony I had been instrumental in arranging, and there was the dedication of the new Dan Russell Courthouse in Gulfport. I didn't want to miss these events and give the impression that I was hiding. Margaret Ann and I did take a long weekend with our children and grandchildren in Alabama and Georgia.

In Washington D.C., the battle over judicial confirmations did not miss a beat. Votes on Priscilla Owen, Carolyn Kuhl, and Janice Rogers Brown had been scheduled. Republicans, anticipating filibusters, decided to draw attention to the debate by scheduling forty straight hours of discussion on the issue.

During the forty-hour debate, there was some discussion over my nomination. Senator Lott mentioned that my confirmation had been personal to him; Senator Lindsey Graham said he thought the most egregious mistreatment of all the judicial nominees was that of "Judge Pickering;" and Senator Mike DeWine made a spirited defense of my record.

Democratic senator Mary Landrieu of Louisiana, who had told Chip she would support me but did not, talked considerably about the nomination of Attorney General William Pryor and said she did not know whether she wanted to talk about me or not. She did mention that I had "an extremely fine son," that I had "cute grandchildren," and that I was "probably a good man," but that I represented the old South. I found her remarks both patronizing and an indication she had not been listening to the testimony, looking at the facts, or responding to folks like Dr. Ed King who spoke in defense of my record at the press conference that followed my hearing. Neither had she listened to Lamar Alexander's speech against the filibuster. Either she did not pay attention to the debate over my nomination, she conveniently ignored the discussion, or she politically disregarded the facts. Landrieu criticized conservatives for trying to divide people over religion because some conservative groups were saying Catholics need not apply, because of the abortion issue, and because of opposition to William Pryor and J. Leon Holmes, both of whom were Catholic. She almost became hysterical. Yet she did nothing when Democrats misused race against my nomination to divide.

Senator Ted Kennedy called the nominees "Neanderthals," and Hillary Clinton called the nominees "lemons." I had become somewhat numb to the process and to the criticism. Name-calling by these extremists no longer outraged me personally; it just made me sad for the Senate.

I often heard the question "Doesn't it bother you to hear these false accusations?" Knowing who I am helped sustain Margaret Ann and me. We know what I have done, what I have not done, what I have thought, and what I have not thought. It would have bothered me much more if the accusations had been true.

There were a few on each side of the aisle who said the issue should be resolved and called for a solution. But when the votes came for cloture on Owen, Kuhl, and Brown, the filibusters continued.

As the month of November passed by and I moved further from the actuality of the confirmation fight, I had three strong impressions. First, I wanted to get the process behind me one way or the other so I could make plans for the rest of my life. Secondly, I realized this battle was far bigger than I and the other current nominees. This struggle involved the whole of the federal judiciary—the entirety of the third branch of government, its future, its independence, quality, diversity, fairness, the confirmation process itself, the power of the president to nominate and appoint members of the judiciary, the role of the Senate as to Advice and

Consent, how the Constitution is to be interpreted, the appropriateness of filibustering judicial nominees—all of these issues and more were at stake. Third, I wanted to play some part, no matter how small, in helping find a solution to this grave threat, which could undermine and seriously weaken the judicial branch of government over a relatively short period of time.

The White House raised the possibility of a recess appointment with Chip in September and again with me when the motion to invoke cloture failed on October 30; but during the month of November I heard nothing further about a recess appointment.

Around Thanksgiving, I called Jorge Rangel in Corpus Christi, Texas, who did my background investigation for the American Bar Association in 1990. When I was confirmed to the district court, Jorge came to my investiture. When President Bill Clinton nominated Jorge to the Fifth Circuit Court of Appeals, I tried to help him move through committee, but discovered the holds were from the Texas senators and there was nothing I could do to help. Eventually, after experiencing committee limbo, Jorge withdrew his name. He knew what it was like to be denied the opportunity for an up or down vote on the Senate floor, and when I encountered my opposition, Jorge wrote a strong letter of endorsement for my confirmation in which he also urged an end to the escalation of the confirmation fight.

Jorge and I discussed enlisting another Democratic nominee who had failed to gain confirmation (perhaps Ronnie White, a blocked Clinton African American nominee) and another Republican nominee who had been blocked (perhaps Miguel Estrada, the Hispanic Bush nominee) to join the two of us in issuing a statement calling on the Senate to stop the confirmation war. His reaction was favorable. We were not going to contact either of these other blocked nominees until we had a draft statement and a better idea of the details of our prospective effort. No specific timetable was established; we just agreed to get back together.

I felt some reluctance jumping back into this fight, but I knew I wanted to improve the judiciary and I thought this would be a way I could help. Then, later that month, the Democratic Senatorial

Committee sent out a fundraising e-mail from New Jersey senator Jon Corzine using my nomination to raise money. An article appeared in the *Weekly Standard*:

> Why must the Democrats continue their fight against Charles Pickering? Miguel Estrada, Janice Rogers Brown, Patricia Owen, and Carolyn Kuhl had their turn in the spotlight . . . but a recent Democratic fund raising memo reveals that Charles Pickering—the first Bush nominee [to be blocked in Committee] for his "racist and reactionary" tendencies—maintains a firm hold on the imagination of the Democratic senators. And donors.[1]

It became obvious to me that it wasn't a matter of getting back into this fight; they wouldn't let me leave if I wanted to. They had created a boogey man to scare their grassroots into voting and their donors into giving—and that man had my name. I wanted to take my name back and help protect the reputations of future nominees.

I still had not decided whether I should accept a recess appointment, but one had not been formally offered. I was generally inclined toward accepting, but that is the kind of thing you cannot be sure about until truly faced with the choice. It was my assumption at the time that a recess appointment would have to be made during the interval between the time Congress adjourned in late 2003 and reconvened in January 2004. If I were to go onto the Fifth Circuit in January, I needed some time to wrap up matters on the district court. So as we moved into December, I conveyed to the White House Counsel's Office and to Senator Trent Lott that I was willing to consider a recess appointment, but I would like to know by December 15 for the sake of my work on the district court. I also made it clear to Senator Lott and the White House that they should not feel any obligation to offer me a recess appointment. I told them I felt what was going on in the confirmation war was wrong, and I wanted the president to offer a recess appointment only if he felt this was the most effective way of fighting back. On December 10, Dabney Friedrich with the White House Counsel's Office called and told me they had made no decision.

RECESS APPOINTMENT | 171

During the month of December, I talked a number of times with Dabney Friedrich and Judge Alberto Gonzales. They told me they were operating under an opinion written by the Office of Legal Policy in the Department of Justice a number of years prior that a recess appointment could be made during any senatorial recess of more than ten days. Dabney told me she understood that if the president made a recess appointment after Congress reconvened, the appointee could serve almost two years. I had not thought that possible until I reread the constitutional provision for recess appointments. Article II, Section 2[3] of the Constitution provides, "The President shall have Power to fill up all Vacancies that may happen during the Recess of the Senate, by granting Commissions which shall expire at the End of their next Session." A congress lasts two years, divided into two annual sessions. Consequently, if the president makes a recess appointment before a session begins, the appointee can only serve until that upcoming session of Congress adjourns, which would be a little under a year. But if a nominee is appointed after a session begins, that appointee can serve through the remainder of that session and until the "end" of the "next session," for an aggregate period of almost two years if the appointment is made early in the session.

To me a recess appointment of one year was perhaps more attractive than a two-year recess appointment. I thought at the time if I were not going to be confirmed, I would rather have conclusion to this episode in my life earlier rather than later. Plus, my seat on the Fifth Circuit needed to be filled permanently. I told Dabney and Judge Gonzales that whatever decision they made, waiting for the Senate to recess for ten days in order to take a two-year rather than a one-year appointment was not an added incentive for me.

The White House and Senate Republicans engaged in a delicate strategy over how to proceed with the fight for judicial confirmations. In politics, you always want to be playing on the field you pick and by the rules you choose—reacting to the unexpected can put you on defense and stall, stop, or reverse your political momentum. I think the White House could sense my weariness and feared I might decide to throw in the towel and withdraw. Certainly had I reached that point I would have given them notice.

Shortly after my conversation with Dabney and Gonzales, I received a call from Senator Orrin Hatch encouraging me to hang in there a few more days and reassuring me the White House was working on recess appointments but wanted to do a combo—they were looking for a second nominee to give an appointment so that I wouldn't be the only one. I wished Senator Hatch a merry Christmas, thanked him again for his support, and told him I would hold tight. Later Judge Gonzales confirmed with me that they were indeed looking for another nominee to give a recess appointment, and I assumed they were speaking with Priscilla Owen and Janice Rogers Brown. I did not know until it was given that they had discussed a recess appointment with Alabama attorney general William Pryor.

In early December, Chip and President Bush were speaking when he asked Chip if I wanted a recess appointment. Chip told him I was inclined to accept if he felt it was the best way to help solve the judicial confirmation problem.

On Tuesday before Christmas, I called Judge Gonzales. He said the president had not decided on the recess appointment and he expected the decision after the first of the year. I told Judge Gonzales that although I realized he might not want to know the details, I had spoken with Jorge Rangel and we were contemplating a bipartisan appeal to stop the bitter confirmation fight. He acknowledged he did not want to know the details—in other words, he wanted to keep his distance. I'm sure he did not want the perception the White House had any part in any statement I was going to make. That was understandable, and for our statement to be effective, it needed distance from the White House. Before we finished, he assured me the White House was very serious about the recess appointment.

The day after Christmas, Trent Lott called. He wanted to know what the White House was telling me about a recess appointment, so I updated him. Trent told me President Bush told him he wanted to make the recess appointment but wanted to do it in February. The prospects of a recess appointment looked good, but I became more and more focused on the bipartisan statement.

On Monday after the New Year, I faxed Jorge Rangel a draft of an open letter to the Senate leadership. The next morning he told me he had revised the letter but his wife, Lupe, had asked him if he really wanted to get back into the fray. Margaret Ann and I understood what she meant. Jorge and I both felt it was the right thing to do, and after he and his wife had lunch, he called me back ready to go forward. I told a national news reporter of our intentions, and he assured me such an effort would require the attention of and coverage by the press—especially in that atmosphere of confirmation conflict.

In the draft I submitted to Jorge, I addressed the filibuster and giving every nominee who had a hearing an up or down vote before the full Senate. Jorge also wanted to eliminate the senatorial holds that had prevented his nomination from moving forward. We agreed we would call for an end of senatorial holds, an end to the filibuster, and—after a reasonable time to investigate charges—that every nominee would receive a respectful and civil hearing and an up or down vote before the full Senate with confirmation by majority vote. We were going to recommend the bipartisan solution be agreed to that year, but not implemented until 2005 after the presidential election, so neither side would know who would benefit from the agreement. We felt this would make it easier to gain support for the reform.

We wanted to time the announcement near the reconvening of Congress on January 20. After Jorge and I had agreed on our plan of action, I felt a rush of adrenaline. For so long I felt I had no control over my life, and I felt I was beginning to gain some control. I had a sense of relief that a decision on at least one issue had finally been made, though the plan of action we had adopted produced some uncertainties. I did not know what impact if any our bipartisan statement would have on my possible recess appointment. I wanted to do both. I wanted to make the bipartisan statement, and I wanted to accept the recess appointment if it were offered.

I contacted Ed Haddon, who was judicial counsel to Senator Jeff Sessions, and asked him to make sure the administration was fully aware of what I was contemplating. They did not need to be linked to my statement; but they also did not need to be surprised. Ed and I worked closely on my confirmation, and I was confident Ed would deliver the message.

Less than two weeks later, Ed called to tell me Judge Gonzales would be calling me to discourage me from making the statement. I told Ed I had pretty well made up my mind and if the White House decided not to give me a recess appointment after I made the statement, then so be it. Ed was affirming and told me that's why he was supportive of me and had enjoyed working with me. He said he told the administration how he expected I would feel about the matter; he was accurate.

On January 15, Jorge and I were up to a deadline on making a decision on when to make the statement. The two of us only had two free days in common around our target time: January 26 or January 28. One of the dates was the day before the New Hampshire primary; the other was the day after. We decided on the day before and had a room reserved at the National Press Club. I booked a flight to Washington and began drafting letters to newspaper editors to release after the statement.

But the next morning around 7:15, I received a call from the White House. Judge Gonzales was direct and to the point: "President Bush is offering you a recess appointment today. If you accept the recess appointment you cannot issue the bipartisan statement." The White House seemed to have a fear that if I made the bipartisan statement and they gave me a recess appointment, it would appear that there was a quid pro quo and they were orchestrating the statement. I told Judge Gonzales I was reluctant to give up the bipartisan statement, but that it was difficult to turn down the president.

Judge Gonzales and I discussed the plans that Jorge and I had made. He wanted to know when we were planning to make the statement. I told him "January 26," just ten days away. I told him I wasn't sure that I would take the recess appointment if I could not make the bipartisan statement. Judge Gonzales suggested that if I decided to go ahead with my plans with Jorge, then a good time to withdraw my nomination would be when making the bipartisan statement. It was good political advice in that the media would give more coverage to the statement, and the withdrawal might have given the statement greater credibility. The advice also reiterated the White House would not give me a recess appointment if I intended to go forward with the statement. I told him I would call back in an hour.

I wanted to challenge the degradation of the confirmation process and I wanted to do my best to try to improve the judiciary. Whether I took the recess appointment or made the bipartisan statement, both were battling back, not only for me but also for the other Bush nominees and for future nominees. I had to decide which approach would be the most effective.

Chip, Margaret Ann, and I quickly conferred. Chip's initial reaction was I should follow my heart. Margaret Ann started calling our daughters and other friends who had given us such tremendous prayer support. I tried to reach Senators Lott and Cochran and then called Judge Gonzales and told him there was no way that I could give him an answer within an hour, that it would be noon before I could give him a response. Judge Gonzales told me he understood I might not accept the recess appointment, but the White House would go forward with the paperwork just in case.

We have two hard lines for phones in our home, and Margaret Ann and I each have cell phones. It was a frantic, hectic morning; sometimes we had two or three calls on the lines at the same time. When I reached Trent shortly after eight o'clock, I briefed him on the statement Jorge and I planned to make, as well as the White House offer of a recess appointment, conditioned on my not making the joint statement. I asked Trent if he wanted time to think about my situation before sharing his advice. He said he did.

Chip called back, and even though he left the decision entirely to Margaret Ann and me, I knew he hated to give up on the struggle, he hated not to win, and he wanted me to take the recess appointment. He expressed serious reservations as to whether a bipartisan statement at that time would be effective. He thought the Democrats and groups were not finished fighting, and it would take another election before there could be any serious effort at trying to find a bipartisan solution. In retrospect, there was tremendous rancor at that particular time.

I began methodically to call all who had been closest to me and supportive of my confirmation efforts. I called my brother Gene; Margaret Ann called my sister Ellen; I called my friends Wesley Breland and James Huff. I spoke at length to Paul Walters, my career law clerk who had worked closely with me in responding to questions from the Democratic members of the Judiciary Committee and been with me since I came on the bench and even before had practiced law with me.

I called Jorge Rangel, and while he was cordial, I perceived he wanted to go forward with the joint statement. He said he hated to see me appointed to the Fifth Circuit with the blemish or asterisk that I was never confirmed. I would have preferred no asterisk as well. His advice and thoughts were important to me before I made my final decision.

Trent called back and said his two most trusted political advisors— his wife and his daughter—both felt strongly I should take the recess appointment. I will always be appreciative that Trent finished the conversation by saying, "You and Margaret Ann make the decision, and I'll be supportive whatever you decide."

When Judge Gonzales told Karl Rove about our conversation, apparently Rove thought I was planning on turning down the appointment. While I was on the phone with family and friends, Karl called both Trent and Chip and asked them to encourage me to accept the appointment. Rove spoke to Chip for half an hour and asked him to convey that the administration hoped I would accept the recess appointment to the Fifth Circuit.

One of the last people I called put the decision more clearly in perspective. I shared with Ed Haddon my conversation with Judge Gonzales. Once he understood that if I made the bipartisan statement, I would have to withdraw my nomination, he became adamant in his advice, "If you withdraw, Schumer and the Far Left secularist groups will react just as they did when Miguel Estrada withdrew. They will point to your withdrawal as proof that you were not worthy of confirmation." He said, "Schumer will dance on your grave." That thought was more than I could take.

Every person I spoke to, with the exception of Jorge Rangel, thought I should take the recess appointment, although all said it was my and Margaret Ann's decision to make. I've never felt you should let others make decisions for you, but I've always felt when there is a strong consensus among your friends and advisors, you should seriously take that into account.

Around noon, I called the White House and told Judge Gonzales I was accepting the recess appointment. My next call was to Jorge to let him know my decision. He might have been disappointed, but I hope he understood. (Later that year I visited Jorge and Lupe in Corpus Christi when he invited me to make the Annual Law Day speech for the Corpus Christi Bar.)

The afternoon was even more hectic than the morning's flurry of calls and advice. When President Bush made the recess appointment, he said,

> For the past two and a half years, Judge Pickering has been waiting for an up-or-down vote in the Senate. A bipartisan majority of Senators supports his confirmation, and if he were given a vote, he would be confirmed. But a minority of Democratic Senators has been using unprecedented obstructionist tactics to prevent him and other qualified individuals from receiving up-or-down votes. Their tactics are inconsistent with the Senate's constitutional responsibility and are hurting our judicial system. . . . I call on the Senate to stop playing politics with the American judicial system and to give my nominees the up-or-down votes they deserve.[2]

There were two Fifth Circuit judges from Mississippi. Grady Jolly was the senior judge and had sworn me in as a district judge in 1990. He was in Houston with his wife for a cancer checkup. I contacted Judge Rhesa Barksdale, and he agreed to swear me in. I called Chief District Judge Henry Wingate, who was on the bench, and asked his secretary to take him a note asking if he would introduce me. He promptly sent word back that he would be happy to do so. Margaret Ann called Chip and told him that I would be sworn in at six o'clock that evening at the federal courthouse in Jackson. I had promised two local television stations I would make a brief statement at four o'clock that afternoon at my home, which I did:

Today President Bush made a recess appointment elevating me to the Fifth Circuit Court of Appeals, which I accepted. I am grateful to the President for his continued confidence and support. I look forward to serving on the Fifth Circuit. I would be remiss if I did not express my gratitude to Senators Lott and Cochran for their friendship and for their strong and continuous support, and to my son, Chip, who did so much to defend my record. Most of all, I am grateful for the outpouring of support and prayers from so many in Mississippi and around the country. I will serve in a manner to justify this confidence and support.

By the time I finished, we had to leave immediately for Jackson. As I traveled to Jackson, a couple of my friends, Roy Ward and Dudley Bozeman, who had heard the news of my recess appointment, called to congratulate me, and we invited them and their wives to join us for the swearing in ceremony, which they did as well as our friend Bill Lampton and his wife. My two law clerks drove up from Hattiesburg and brought my robe.

Nehemiah Flowers, the U.S. marshal for the Southern District of Mississippi, met me at the parking lot. He offered to escort me into the back door, but avoiding the press can create the appearance you have something to hide. I told him we would go through the front door. Two local television stations were there and wanted live interviews at six. They asked me about the criticism leveled against President Bush for nominating me on the weekend of Martin Luther King Jr.'s birthday and asked me about Bennie Thompson's negative comments. I told them that I had a good record that spoke for itself; I would leave it to the senators and others who were supporting my nomination to defend.

I followed Judge Barksdale and Judge Wingate into the courtroom. Judge Wingate, who is currently the only African American federal district court judge in Mississippi, gave me a great introduction. He said that he had visited in our home, shared meals, and enjoyed conversations. He continued,

Over the years, once this nomination was proposed, I have heard things about my friend that surprised me. . . . I have heard that he is a racist; that's not the Charles Pickering I know. I have heard that he is antagonistic toward African Americans, and that's not the Charles Pickering I've grown to know.[3]

He spoke about the courage and "intestinal fortitude" that I had to speak out against the Klan during the civil rights movement. He related that before my nomination to the Fifth Circuit, he and I had discussed the need for racial reconciliation and spoke of plans that we had to speak jointly at civic clubs promoting racial reconciliation and improvement in race relations. We had to put those plans on hold when the confirmation battle started.

I made a brief statement,

It's been a long journey. At times it's been painful. It has also been rewarding. One of the most humbling things that Margaret Ann and I have ever experienced in our lives was the outpouring of support from the people of Mississippi with whom we have worked over the years—both black and white, both Democrat and Republican.

As Margaret Ann held the Bible, with Judge Wingate standing by my side and Judge Rhesa Barksdale administering the oath, I became a member of the Fifth Circuit Court of Appeals.

It was a brief ceremony, probably lasting no more than ten minutes. Judge Barksdale's staff, the clerk's staff, staff from the U.S. attorney's and U.S. marshal's offices, Chip's staff, and the few friends we had been able to notify of the swearing in filled the courtroom. It was one of those occasions where everyone had warm, positive, and fuzzy things to say. It was an affirming experience.

That was in Mississippi; those in Washington D.C.—and Bennie Thompson—had other words. Congressman Thompson said it was "quite unfortunate that the President would choose to seat Judge Pickering as the Nation prepares to celebrate the life and legacy of Dr. Martin Luther King, Jr."[4] Senator Kennedy said my appointment "serves only to emphasize again this Administration's shameful opposition to civil rights."[5] Wesley Clark, candidate for the Democratic presidential nomination, called the president's move "reckless, irresponsible and wrong" and said that I had an "unforgivably dismal record on important civil rights issues." Howard Dean called the president's action "an ultimate hypocrisy" and called me a "racist."[6] Senator Leahy said, "This is a cynical, divisive appointment."[7] "Ralph Neas, president of People for the American Way, called the appointment 'absolutely outrageous.'"[8]

An editorial by Dennis Smith, news director of Jackson television station WLBT, noted that Gen. Wesley Clark had called me an "anti-American Judge." He said, "Gen. Wesley Clark was sacked as NATO commander a few years ago for shooting his mouth off and making dumb statements. From my point of view, he won't be elected president for the same reason."[9] The *Atlanta Journal Constitution* recorded, "Those who know Pickering well including black and white Mississippi residents and political leaders, describe him as a relative progressive on racial issues."[10]

Reaction of the pro-family groups was just the opposite to that of the Democrats: "Tony Perkins of the Washington, D.C.- based family research council says it was a 'bold and necessary move,'" adding, "Charles Pickering is exactly the type of judge this country needs on our Federal bench. . . . President Bush has taken the first step to ensure that our Federal courts are filled by jurists who understand their role is to follow the Constitution—not reinvent it." Chuck Colson with Prison Fellowship called the appointment "a win for the President, a win for Pickering, and most importantly, a win for justice." Colson pointed out that the opposition to my nomination had been "tantamount to religious discrimination and blatant injustice." He said the recess appointment was "the right move not for just Judge Pickering, but also for our judicial process." Don Wildman, chair of the Mississippi-based American Family Association, said, "[Pickering] is a good man, a deserving man, a good Judge. An injustice has been done to this man; it has been rectified now. . . . At least Bush has shown some backbone—and that's good news." Gary Bauer said, "It is unfortunate that the President was forced to take such action," but it shows a renewed commitment by the White House to "spotlight the Senate's liberal obstructionists who are abusing Senate procedures and running roughshod over the Constitution."[11]

Deborah Gambrell-Chambers, civil rights attorney from Hattiesburg, said the appointment was "excellent. I think it's long overdue. . . . I know him as a person to be compassionate and fair." The chairman of the Forrest County Democratic Executive Committee, Bill Jones, said, "The notion that Charles Pickering is a racist is kind of ridiculous. . . . I think his troubles are indicative of what happens to good people who get involved in politics."[12]

The *Laurel Leader Call* headline proclaimed, "Mississippi Reaction Favorable to Bush Appointment of Pickering." The front page of the *Jackson Clarion Ledger* announced "Pickering Prevails." Outside Mississippi, the headlines were equally descriptive: the *Maui News*, "Bush Bypasses Congress to Install New Appeals Judge"; the *Washington Post*, "Bush Bypasses Senate on Judge—President Fills Judgeship During Recess . . . Bush Names Judge Despite Filibuster"; the *Salt Lake Tribune*, "Bush Snubs Senate, Puts Pickering on the Bench"; CBS News, "Bush Taps Pickering in End Run"; CNN.COM, "Pickering Appointment Angers Democrats"; the *Tacoma Washington News Tribune*, "Bush Raises Stake over Judges"; and back home, the headline for an editorial in the *Biloxi Sun Herald* on January 17 said, "President Uses a Rare Process to Give a Judge a Little Justice."

An article by Steve Henderson put the recess appointment in perspective:

> Recess appointments are not unusual. President Bill Clinton used one in 2000 to name Roger Gregory, the first African American on the U. S. Court of Appeals for the Fourth Circuit in Richmond, VA., after Republicans refused to hold a Senate hearing on his nomination. . . . Harry S. Truman in 1949 used a recess appointment to put the first African American on a Federal Appeals Court: William Henry Hastie to the Philadelphia based Third Circuit. John F. Kennedy used the same maneuver to put women and minorities on the bench when segregationist Southern senators threatened to block their nominations. . . . The Senate rarely unseats a judge after a recess appointment expires; more than 85% eventually win permanent commissions.[13]

After the recess appointment hit the news, I received calls of congratulations from all around the country. Wherever Margaret Ann and I went, people greeted us warmly and congratulated us. The same was true of Chip. In my church where political figures are seldom recognized, the pastor acknowledged the journey that we had traveled and the congregation responded with great warmth. When Chip went to church the following Sunday, the same thing happened with him.

I received a call from Nancy Albritton, who covered me when I was in the state legislature while she was working for the Memphis *Commercial Appeal*. She was now working for the *Atlanta Journal Constitution* and wanted to come do an in-depth interview. I did not want to get into the partisan issues, but I did agree to discuss the human side of the equation. I believed I could utilize the recess appointment within judicial guidelines to ease the bruising confirmation battle and bring a sense of decency to the process by doing interviews showing the human side of the equation. Judges are permitted and encouraged to make efforts at improving the judiciary as long as we do not stray into politics, so I was careful to stay away from discussing the partisan aspects of the confirmation battle. Nancy Albritton wrote,

> Stung and bruised by more than two years of political wrangling over his nomination to a federal appeals court, Charles W. Pickering says if he'd known then what he knows now, he might not have taken President Bush's offer in the first place. Pickering relaxed in jeans Saturday afternoon after a frenzied Friday in which he accepted Bush's offer of an unusual "recess appointment" to the appellate court—an end-around-run that bypassed the Senate, which had first defeated, then stalled the Mississippi jurist's confirmation. In the den of their spacious country home, as three of their 20 grandchildren played, Pickering and his wife Margaret Ann gave a glimpse of the anguishing 2 1/2 years they endured before he finally took the oath Friday night. Pickering said he thought long and prayed hard with family and friends on Friday before he decided to accept the recess appointment, which meant giving up his federal district judgeship for an appeals courts post that could be temporary. Margaret Ann Pickering said her

home, which overlooks a tranquil 10-acre lake at a former dairy farm, was bedlam the day before as she and her husband scrambled to reach a decision. "It was a madhouse yesterday," she said. "It was just wild." She said phones rang two and three at a time throughout the day. Events moved so rapidly that only one of their four grown children, U.S. Rep. Chip Pickering (R-Miss.) was able to get to the swearing in.[14]

I granted one other interview for a personal interest story to Julie Goodman with the *Clarion Ledger*. In the Saturday, January 31 edition of the *Clarion Ledger*, she wrote,

Hebron—Charles Pickering, settling on a couch, surveys the interior of his cypress farm house, from the carefully mounted deer heads and stuffed mallards to the dozen of family photographs hung squarely on the walls. The dark corridor behind him leads to a spotless cast iron tub, unused pear-shaped soap and a neatly folded hand towel. There is welcome order here, unlike the chaos that has come to characterize this Judge's recent political life. . . . "I don't regret not having backed down. Do I wish it had worked out differently? Of course. I wish there had never been a controversy and I wish I had been confirmed, but I can't change history. So we live with it and we will follow it," he says as his wife, Margaret Ann, looks on. "He slept," she says. "I was the one who didn't sleep." . . . "It was a fight I felt had to be made. I feel that if I had withdrawn, it would have given some credence to the charges and it would have been wrong to back down."[15]

Veteran political columnist Sid Salter wrote,

Racist. Extremist. Civil rights opponent. That's what his Democratic opponents called . . . Charles W. Pickering. . . . President Bush decided those same Democratic critics could call him something else—a Federal Appeals Court Judge. . . . Senate Democrats who in truth disagree more with Pickering's Baptist faith and the impact that faith might have on his personal views on abortion and other questions attacked the Judge as a racist. . . . But the smear to which Pickering's reputation was subjected on the question of race was

simply unconscionable given the fact Pickering stood up against Ku
Klux Klan intimidation in the '60s—an act of political and social
suicide in many circles of the state in that day. Pickering's progressive
stance on race in Mississippi . . . is one that should have been praised,
not castigated. . . . Pickering was qualified to serve and is a mighty
good man caught in a political quagmire not of his own making . . . .
But clearly this is a president who recognized that advice and consent
does not give the Senate unlimited power to usurp presidential
appointments.[16]

It was obvious my confirmation fight would become a campaign
issue in the elections of 2004. *Washington Post* writers Mike Allen and
Helen DeWar noted, "both parties are now likely to make Pickering an
issue in November's election as an engine for motivating their core
supporters."[17] Another writer noted, "Bush invariably gets a big round
of applause during campaign stump speeches when he mentions the
fight for his judicial nominees."[18]

According to news reports, the Democrats had picked up rumors
that I might be given a recess appointment and there were questions as
to whether there would be other recess appointments. A *Mobile Press*
article reported, "It is unclear whether Bush is considering a similar
appointment for Alabama Attorney General Bill Pryor, whose nomination to the 11th U.S. Circuit Court of Appeals in Atlanta is also being
filibustered. At the White House, a spokesman would only say that the
President seeks to fill all judicial vacancies as quickly as possible."

The groups and Democrats apparently thought I was the only
nominee willing to accept a recess appointment. People for the
American Way spokesman and legal director Elliot Mincberg said that
he had heard nothing indicating Pryor would receive a recess appointment. He "noted that Pickering is already on the Federal bench and
close to retirement. 'Pryor, on the other hand, is much younger, with
more to lose by taking an appointment that would last only a year,' he
said. 'If I were William Pryor, I'm not sure I would accept a recess
appointment,' Mincberg said."[19] Mincberg did not know Bill Pryor. The
confirmation battles would continue and President Bush had not yet
finished.

Meanwhile, I had a new job and it was time to get to work. On my way to Jackson to be sworn in, Carolyn King, chief justice of the Fifth Circuit, called and left a voice message as well as a fax that the Fifth Circuit would have a meeting on administrative matters on the following Wednesday, January 21, and an *en banc* (the full court) hearing on the following Thursday. By overnight mail she sent me my homework— the briefs in two cases that I needed to be prepared to discuss on the following Thursday when I would sit for the first time to hear a case with the Fifth Circuit. I was anxious to begin my work on the Fifth Circuit, but just after I was sworn in, there was one more request to tell my story, a surprise request that brought both excitement and fear, and one I could not resist.

60 Minutes

WILLIAM FAULKNER WROTE, "The past is not dead. In fact, it's not even past." The president utilized his constitutional powers to place me on the Fifth Circuit Court of Appeals; but the fight over and interest in my confirmation continued.

On Tuesday afternoon following my swearing in, just before my drive to New Orleans for my first meeting as a judge on the Fifth Circuit, I returned a phone call to the CBS news program *60 Minutes*. The person who had called me was away, but the receptionist asked me to hold and said, "Mr. Wallace wants to talk with you." That familiar, smooth voice—decidedly American in speech but absent regional accent—spoke on the phone. The dean of broadcast journalism said, "Judge, I read a story about you in the *Chicago Tribune*. I saw you on ABC. I want you to come on *60 Minutes* and let me tell your story." Mike Wallace read aloud the article from the *Tribune*—one of those reports that told my story, my history, but that the Washington D.C. establishment reveled in ignoring. However, the story had seized the attention of Mike Wallace and could now reach a greater audience.

Leftist secular groups and Democratic senators had assailed my reputation for more than two years, disseminating charges through the national media and providing the slander fodder for many large city editorial writers. Mike Wallace's offer to tell my story sounded too good to be true. I told him, "That sounds fine to me, but I'll need to talk to some people." He gave me his home and cell phone numbers and we agreed to talk within a few days.

Within thirty minutes, Mike Wallace faxed me the following letter:

Dear Judge Pickering,

I hasten to add this note, in light of our telephone conversation half an hour ago. You told me you very much wanted to sit down for a *60 Minutes* interview, but that you had to run it by "some people." Candidly, I fear those people may be telling you: "You're out of your mind if you sit down with Wallace. He's sold you a phony bill of goods. He will crucify you."

Judge Pickering, I am a man of my word. When I read that piece from the *Chicago Tribune* from February 13, 2002, it pointed out that among your backers, ". . . are prominent African Americans including James Charles Evers, brother of slain civil rights leader Medgar Evers, and Henry Wingate, the first black federal judge in Mississippi." It goes on to say that, "In 1967, Pickering testified against Ku Klux Klan imperial wizard Samuel Bowers in a case involving the murder of civil rights worker Vernon Dahmer." Your old friend Chet Dillard said, "He does happen to be white and he does happen to be Baptist, but you couldn't find any person that I think is more morally conscientious about following the laws as set forth by the United States Supreme Court."

That's the Charles Pickering who deserves a hearing on *60 Minutes*, the man I want to talk to.

Sincerely,
Mike Wallace

I spoke with Mike Wallace at least half a dozen times at his home, his office, or on his cell phone over the next couple of weeks. He was the most accessible high-profile individual with whom I've ever had contact. I told him if I agreed to come on *60 Minutes*, I would not address partisan aspects of the confirmation fight, only my own record; I would not get "off the reservation." He took pause and responded that this was television and he had to make it interesting. I suggested a surrogate: "Well, if you want to interview Chip as well, he may be willing to get into politics and cover the areas you want to cover."

Chip spoke with Bob Anderson, Mike's producer, and provided requested background material. We proceeded with a certain amount of trepidation—a fear I could be walking into an ambush. When in doubt, his fax reassured me. I could not imagine Mike Wallace, at eighty-five years of age, putting in writing the story he would tell and then breaking his word. More so, I feared other members of the *60 Minutes* team not partnered with Mike or Bob would try to alter the story; that our left-wing opponents would intervene.

We grew comfortable with Mike and Bob the more we spoke with them, so without discussing it outside the family, Chip, Margaret Ann, and I decided to go for it. I hoped my appearance on *60 Minutes* would provide an opportunity to show America a different Charles Pickering than John Kerry's "cross burner," Wesley Clark's "un-American Judge," and Howard Dean's "racist Judge."

Mike Wallace selected the week of February 15 to visit Mississippi and conduct an interview with me at our farm home, and to interview several African Americans in Hattiesburg.

As CBS arranged for the visit, a friend in the local news media called to tell me he heard rumors that Mike Wallace was coming to do an interview. After I confirmed this, he warned me, "You can't trust the national press; they love to ambush people." His warning provided a shadow of doubt, but I still felt we made the right decision. Generally, I have fared better when I am open with the press. I told my friend I hoped he would not run the story until Mike Wallace had concluded the interviews so as not to put additional pressure on the interviewees. He agreed to hold the story unless his competition was about to break the news. I assured him if the news leaked out, I would immediately call him. True to his word, he did not break the story until after the interviews were finished.

A few days before Mike Wallace arrived, Charles Evers spoke at a Valentine's Day banquet celebrating Black History Month at the Elk's Lodge in Palmer's Crossing, an African American community just south of Hattiesburg. Margaret Ann and I attended. When Charles Evers stood to speak, he interrupted his remarks to recognize Margaret Ann and me and took several minutes to tell the audience why he supported me and why they should support me as well.

The banquet honored the memory of the late Dr. C. E. Smith, the African American physician who integrated local hospitals. During the '50s and '60s, Dr. Smith could not admit his patients to either of the hospitals in Hattiesburg: the Forrest General or the Methodist. All his patients in the area had to be admitted to the charity hospital in my hometown of Laurel, some thirty miles from Hattiesburg. After years of consistent and diligent work, Dr. Smith received privileges at Forrest General and Methodist, providing black patients with greater healthcare options. Dr. Smith participated in other phases of the civil rights movement as well—dangerous work during that time in our area of Mississippi.

Following Charles Evers's speech and a video tribute to Dr. Smith, his widow spoke and accepted the honor on his behalf. Mrs. Smith said she appreciated Dr. Martin Luther King and his nonviolent movement, but she appreciated even more Mr. Evers because he organized the Deacons of Defense. The Deacons of Defense were black men who armed themselves in the '60s and accompanied and protected African Americans engaged in civil rights activity who might be the object of Klan aggression. The bodyguards escorted Dr. Smith when he integrated the hospitals and even made rounds with him to see his patients. One of the Deacons of Defense attended that night, a Mr. Kaley Duckworth. Although now an elderly gentleman—very tall, very thin and angular, with a completely gray head of hair and a rather craggy face—he carried himself with quiet dignity and maintained the strength that surely made him an effective Deacon of Defense. Mrs. Smith turned to Margaret Ann and me and said she concurred with what Mr. Evers said; her family came from Jones County and she had known my family before she was married. She said my family had always treated everyone with respect, which I accepted as a gracious tribute to my parents.

As we were leaving, Margaret Ann and I walked over to the limousine that brought Charles and his daughter to the Elk's Lodge to speak to them before they left. As I approached, I shook hands with a man who identified himself as Clarence McGee. Mr. McGee said, "You might have heard of me; I am the president of the local NAACP. The things I have said about you have not been favorable, but I understand that you are a decent person." I almost challenged him for being contradictory but decided this was neither the time nor place. A few minutes later, Charles Evers told me that he and Mr. McGee were both going to be interviewed by Mike Wallace for *60 Minutes*. Charles said Clarence McGee was off base in his opposition to my nomination and that he was going to kick his butt at the interview—although Charles was a little more graphic in his speech.

Margaret Ann and I usually attend church Sunday evenings and rarely watched *60 Minutes* because of that schedule. So Margaret Ann suggested we should read up on Mike Wallace and know something about him before our meeting. We checked out *Close Encounters: Mike Wallace's Own Story* from our local public library and learned about his life, family, background, and his "no-holds-barred" interviewing technique.

Mike Wallace, his producer Bob, and his camera crew arrived at the Best Western Motel in Collins—a small Mississippi town eleven miles west of our farm home—on Monday afternoon February 16. Margaret Ann and I joined Mike and Bob for dinner at the Covington House, a restaurant just outside Collins (the same restaurant where I met Bennie Thompson some two years earlier). Mike is a schmoozer: when we met, he said "Oh no, you're not the older Pickering."

Dinner was served with engaging yet relaxing conversation. We surprised him with our research on his life and background. Mike Wallace pours color and energy into the room: simultaneously salty and respectful, boisterous and demur, rowdy and relaxed, cosmopolitan and earthy, questioning and knowing—the twinkle in his eyes says there is a wonderful joke in the world all around us, and he is about to deliver the punch line. We had a delightful two hours.

The following morning at seven o'clock, his technical crew arrived at our home right on schedule. Margaret Ann and I live in a lodge on the "back forty" of the small farm where I grew up. In the 1970s, when my parents grew older, it became too much for us to bring our four children and spend weekends in their home, so we built a lodge with one great room and three small bedrooms downstairs. This allowed us to visit the farm, not burden them, and I could still do my farm work on

Saturdays. Our home and my law office in Laurel were only three minutes apart either by walk or by car. But when I went on the bench in 1990, it would be necessary for me to commute forty minutes whether from Laurel or from the farm. So we sold our house in Laurel, added on to the lodge, and lived at the farm with room for twenty-one grandchildren.

Margaret Ann prepared sausage, biscuits, coffee, and juice for the crew and Mike and Bob. The crew enjoyed the Southern hospitality as they moved every piece of furniture in our great room and transformed it into a television production studio in less than two hours. They waited until later in the morning to try Margaret Ann's pound cake and sandwiches. Shortly after nine o'clock, Chip arrived and right behind him drove up Mike Wallace and Bob Anderson.

Mike and I sat down facing each other, a camera over each shoulder, the room lights low but the shooting lights aimed inward, forming almost an enclosed circle around just him and me. The rest of the room seemed distant, and I could understand how someone with something to hide would be intimidated in this situation. I imagined Mike Wallace going up against corporate executives or world leaders much like a tough cop and a nervous hood in an old black-and-white film or movie: a musty police station with a light in his face and pressure all around. I must admit that while I was very comfortable with the interview, when you sit across from Mike Wallace, you get a tinge of doubt and trepidation.

With the cameras recording, he looked down and closed his eyes for a moment, then looked at me and began, asking something like, "Federal judges do not typically give interviews. Why are you talking to me today?" The question threw me off guard, and I stumbled in response. My first thought was "That's a good question. Why *am* I doing this?" My second thought was to say, "Because you wrote me a letter and said you would tell my story." I thought neither of those responses appropriate, so I explained I wanted to tell the truth of the confirmation battle and my record.

For the next hour, with a wood fire burning in the hearth behind us, Mike Wallace interviewed me and despite the slow start, I grew more confident and bold with my responses. He gave me an opportunity to answer the questions raised by my critics. For a man eighty-five years of age, his mind was sharp as a tack, and I could see why no one does this better than he does.

After an hour, the producer said that Mike and I needed to walk around outside so the camera crew could get some actions shots. Between the moisture of the river and the lake, the February coldness bit when the wind blew, but while chilly, it was not cold when the wind was at rest. Bob started giving Mike his overcoat, and Mike said he wasn't going out with an overcoat if I didn't have one on, so I grabbed mine and we walked outside. Mike and I walked around the front yard next to the lake and out onto the pier. Margaret Ann joined Mike and the camera crew took shots of them as well.

Next Chip and Mike walked around and visited before sitting down for a thirty-minute interview. In the final cut, none of Chip's conversation was used. The producers thought the material was fine, but it really added little drama that a son supported his father, even if the son was a congressman. They had plenty of material for the piece without Chip's interview.

Later that day I left for Hattiesburg for a scheduled appointment, and Mike's camera crew divided. Two crewmembers went to Laurel to take shots of the courthouse, City Hall, First Baptist Church where we attended, the house where we lived, and the private school nearby where we didn't send our kids during integration. The other two crewmembers went with Mike and Bob to the Forrest County Courthouse to conduct interviews with Charles Evers and two civil rights attorneys who appeared before me frequently: Deborah Gambrell and Charles Lawrence.

After their interviews, Mike Wallace sat down with Clarence McGee, the head of the local NAACP who was opposing my nomination, and whom I had met for the first time just three days before. Charles Evers said, "I want to stay and make sure that he tells the truth." Mike Wallace turned to Clarence McGee and asked if that was okay and McGee said, "Sure." During the course of the interview, Charles Evers took over the interview and started questioning Clarence McGee. Mike

Wallace sat back and allowed it, and while it was a little unorthodox, it certainly could make for good television, and it did.

After the *60 Minutes* team returned to New York, I followed up with a call to Bob Anderson about some photos he had requested to let him know they were in the mail. I told him I still struggled with that first question and I was still asking myself why I let myself be interviewed by Mike Wallace. Bob assured me I would be glad I did the interview, and when it was all over "the world will know that you were not soft on cross burners."

Meanwhile, my friends and neighbors expressed excitement about the visit. The local newspapers and television news carried extensive stories about Mike Wallace's visit to Collins and Hattiesburg and his interview at the farm and the courthouse in Forrest County.

Mike had wanted the piece to air on March 14, but management and colleagues at CBS News pushed back the piece. Bob contacted Chip and faxed over a list of concerns and questions, and Chip responded with documented answers. Bob told him that he and Mike knew the truth about me and that was the story they were sticking with, but the materials Chip gave them made it easier to go to bat against the naysayers at CBS.

I called Mike and he told me the piece had been pushed until March 21. The next week, he called me and said that the segment would not air on March 21 but on March 28. He said I would be pleased with the segment, that "Margaret Ann looked beautiful," and for me to give her his regards. Throughout this entire process, Mike Wallace impressed me with his kindness and friendly manner, which was not entirely consistent with his reputation for aggressive reporting.

The CBS web page began promoting the piece on the Thursday prior to the showing and I started getting calls from the local press. The Associated Press called and asked that same question that had haunted me: "Why did you do the interview?" I responded, "*60 Minutes* is a reputable national program and, consequently, that gave me the opportunity to reach people who otherwise would not have access to my side of the story." A representative for *60 Minutes* said it was "extremely rare for a Federal judge to grant an interview, and Judge Pickering's story is illustrative of the partisan scrutiny nominees must go through in the judicial confirmation process."[1] The CBS spokesman told another reporter, "Mike and his producers had a pleasant experience in Laurel when they visited Judge Pickering at his home on February 17. . . . He has become a controversial national figure in the process and therefore a compelling story for *60 Minutes*."[2]

Before the news broke, Chip called Trent Lott to let him know about the interview. Late Friday afternoon, Trent called and said, "I sure wish you had talked with me before you went on Mike Wallace's program." He was afraid *60 Minutes* would portray me in a bad light, and Trent's doubts made me a bit nervous. I had full confidence in Mike and Bob, but I wasn't sure of the rest of the staff at *60 Minutes*. However, Trent's brother-in-law Dickey Scruggs (they married sisters) had a good relationship with Mike Wallace from his lawsuits against the tobacco industry (made into a movie called *The Insider*) and called about my segment. Mike told Dickey not to worry; we would all be pleased with the piece.

All of our children with the exception of our youngest daughter, Christi, were able to come to the farm with their children—my grandchildren—to watch the *60 Minutes* segment with Margaret Ann and me. In Washington D.C., all of Chip's staff gathered to watch the segment; and folks around the country who had been supportive of my nomination tuned in.

In the segment, Mike Wallace let me explain what I had done over the years in regard to race relations and providing equal protection, including my testimony and fight against the Klan. We discussed the cross-burning case, and viewers saw the facts of the matter and that justice was done: that I was not sympathetic to cross-burners. We also talked about the days of integration when Margaret Ann and I kept our children in public schools and urged others to do the same to build a stronger, more unified community. Senator Chuck Schumer made an appearance, but his attack came across as tired and stale.

The end of the piece was the best. They pulled a clip of President Bush, who said, "Pickering has got a very strong record on civil rights. Just ask the people he lives with." With shots of Laurel, Mississippi, with blacks and whites mingling on the street, a voiceover said, "*60 Minutes* did, and found that in Mississippi, Pickering enjoys strong support from the many blacks who know him." One writer described this portion of the piece:

> The high point of the segment came near the end, when black citizens from . . . Mississippi spoke out on Pickering's behalf. One black attorney, a man named Charles Lawrence, said of Pickering, "I trust him because I have been in front of him. I have had cases in front of him. And that's not to say I've always won. I haven't always won. But . . . he has an understanding of the law and he applies it fairly across the board." Another black attorney, Deborah Gambrell, said, "This man makes for a level playing field. . . . And that's the thing that I admire about him."[3]

The obvious star of the *60 Minutes* presentation was Charles Evers. The *60 Minutes* announcer said, "When Clarence McGee, who heads the NAACP in Hattiesburg, sat down for *60 Minutes* with a Pickering supporter, Charles Evers, brother of murdered civil rights leader, Medgar Evers, the NAACP president got an earful."[4] The *American Spectator* described it as a "priceless exchange."[5]

> EVERS: You know that Charles Pickering is the man who helped us to break the Ku Klux Klan. Did you know that?
> MCGEE: I have heard that.
> EVERS: Well, I know that. Do you know that?
> MCGEE: I don't know that.
> EVERS: Do you know about the young black man that was accused of robbing the young white woman?
> MCGEE: No.
> EVERS: So Charles Pickering took the case. Came to trial and won the case and the young man became free.
> MCGEE: I don't know about that.
> EVERS: Do you know that Charles Pickering is the man who helped integrate his churches?
> MCGEE: I don't know about that.
> EVERS: Well, you don't know a thing about Charles Pickering.

That was a fitting conclusion for the *60 Minutes* interview: Charles Evers defending my record as the NAACP spokesman was unable to articulate a valid reason for their opposition.

I was told that at one point, Evers asked Clarence McGee why he was opposing me, and McGee said because the national NAACP called down and said to oppose me. This quote didn't make the broadcast, but it is illustrative of what has happened to the NAACP: it is out of touch with grassroots blacks. The NAACP is now an organization more committed to Democratic politics than advancing the interest of the average African American. In addition to embracing irrelevance by tying itself too tightly to Democratic politics, the NAACP is following the lead of secularist groups in supporting abortion and redefinition of marriage—issues that do not enjoy wide support in the African American community, at least not in Mississippi. How many other worthwhile organizations have gone the same way as the NAACP—accomplished great good and then wandered off into other areas and squandered their effectiveness? When Medgar Evers (and later Charles Evers) was Mississippi field secretary of the NAACP, the organization responded to the needs of Mississippi African Americans. Now, it seems, time has reversed the roles.

That Sunday night after we watched the *60 Minutes* program and were getting ready for bed, the phone rang. It was the White House switchboard calling; former President Bush—George H. W. or "Bush 41"—was on the line. He and Barbara watched the CBS broadcast with friends in California. They were excited about the segment, congratulated me, and said they thought the program was great. President Bush commended me for a fine record and was glad to hear it finally worked out for me to be appointed to the Fifth Circuit. Barbara got on the phone and talked with both Margaret Ann and me. It was an unexpected but special call from the man who had originally put me on the federal district court.

The ratings showed the number of viewers watching the *60 Minutes* broadcast on March 28 was 16.74 million, the sixth most watched primetime program for the week and the highest rating for *60 Minutes* during the first three months of 2004.[6]

In January 2006, while in New York to promote my previous book *Supreme Chaos*, I visited Mike Wallace and Bob Anderson at their *60 Minutes* studio. Mike and Bob told me that the segment on my confirmation won an award from the Columbia Journalism School's "Let's Do It Better" Workshop on Race and Ethnicity. It won in the category of "Finding the Untold Story"—the only piece portraying the role of a white person advocating racial justice that received an award.

Almost a month after the *60 Minutes* segment ran, a television critic confirmed what we had suspected behind the scenes. There was considerable opposition at CBS to the story that Mike and Bob Anderson produced. In a story about the retirement of Mike Wallace's boss, Don Hewitt, we read,

> Mike Wallace and boss, Don Hewitt, have waged legendary battles . . . . But this March morning, the mood is surprisingly collegial in the Ninth-floor offices of the CBS News Magazine. The two men confer happily about Wallace's feature on Charles Pickering, a judicial appointee of President Bush. It was an atypical meeting in that Hewitt and Wallace were on the same side against virtually everybody else in the screening room.[7]

On Monday after it aired, I called Mike and told him that I thought the program went well and expressed my appreciation for his work. Bob Anderson called back a couple of hours later and said that Karl Rove had called Mike and thanked him for the piece, and that Nat Hentoff with the *Village Voice* had called and said, "you gave the man his reputation back." He said Mike had also spoken with the president of Warner Books, who said, "This man is different than what I thought he was." Mike told me early on in our process that his favorite stories are the ones that take conventional wisdom that is false and correct it. He said you don't have to make a good story if you can find one where everyone else is telling fiction and you tell the truth. The truth can be shocking enough, and that makes good television. I think he succeeded again.

Of course, I wish Senator Schumer had not had as much airtime as he did. But I know with many of those at *60 Minutes* pushing back against Mike and Bob, they were fair to me and I could not have expected a better piece. I also learned that Wade Henderson of the NAACP had sent a letter to the executive producer of CBS News *60 Minutes* expressing outrage: the piece certainly shook things up.

My personal concern that other members of the Fifth Circuit might consider the interview inappropriate dissipated Monday morning when they began calling to express their congratulations and saying that under the circumstances, with the attacks that had been made on me, I was totally justified in making the appearance. In addition, a Clinton-appointed federal district judge from California called and told me he was "extremely appreciative of my appearance on *60 Minutes*."

Friends all around the country had seen it and called to share their thoughts. Deborah Gambrell and Charles Lawrence told me they received calls from family members in New York, Chicago, and North Carolina expressing appreciation for the piece and their involvement.

Another friend watched *Imus in the Morning* on MSNBC and said his guest was talking about Senator Schumer in regards to Condoleezza Rice. The I-man's guest commented that after Sunday night, "Schumer ought not be opening his mouth." I understand Don Imus responded, "Yes, I think that Pickering boy has gotten a bad deal."

Mississippi newspapers editorialized positively about the piece. The *Greenwood Commonwealth* opined,

Charles Pickering made the right decision when he gave an interview to *60 Minutes.* Pickering's opponents can holler all they like . . . the facts do not support the allegations against the Judge . . . any objective viewer of the *60 Minutes* segment would have to say the Judge has gotten a raw deal, and an unfair label, from the Senate.[8]

The *Meridian Star* wrote,

Given the tough, penetrating reporting that marks the program and the traditional reluctance of Federal judges to expose themselves to questions, we were surprised when Federal Judge, Charles Pickering agreed to an on-camera interview with Mike Wallace with the CBS news magazine *"60 Minutes."* . . . we are so happy he did. . . . He answered all his liberal critics' baseless accusations. . . . The Judge presented his defense in a non-partisan, non-threatening, orderly fashion that we believe went a long way toward clearing his name.[9]

I received copies of several letters from New Yorkers sent to Senator Schumer. One told him he was "quite unfair—and this smacks of partisan politics . . . I urge you to look closer at this decent man." Another letter to Schumer said, "Judge Pickering handled himself wonderfully on *60 Minutes* and the facts that were brought out by Judge Pickering and the number of other people speaking . . . were pretty overwhelming. . . . I think you picked the wrong guy to beat up on."

A New York lawyer wrote to me saying, "Sen. Schumer . . . should have been supporting you. . . . I am privileged to have a number of clients who are among Sen. Schumer's supporters. . . . If I can be of assistance to you in your confirmation . . . don't hesitate to call. . . . It would be an honor to be of service to you."

A letter from a self-described "solid liberal" related,

I've lived in the South most of my life and understand who is an honorable person with regard to race relations. . . . So when I first heard the smear campaign against you by my fellow Democrats, I was inclined to believe it. However, when I heard you speak on t.v. and understood the strength of your convictions, and saw photos of your children in mostly black schools, I understood immediately what you stand for and the leadership style you have lived and not just "talked" with regards to race relations. . . . I wish you a long and meaningful career on the Circuit Court.

Another letter came from the West Coast:

As a lifelong Democrat, and a California attorney for over thirty-two years . . . I want to express my appreciation for your visit with Mike Wallace on *"60 Minutes"* recently. At our Monday "debriefing" (i.e., lunch) at the office, those of us who saw the segment agreed you made your case eloquently and forcefully. I couldn't help but think that courage was involved as well—we've all seen clips over the years of Mr. Wallace skewering the rich and famous. It appeared to be the same kind of courage you demonstrated in promoting racial harmony and equality throughout your career, at times with considerable risk to you and your loved ones. . . . Keep up the good fight!

The outpouring of letters and calls and support was extensive and further confirmed to me that talking to Mike Wallace was the right thing to do.

A few days after the broadcast aired, Chip called and told me of the powerful impact the segment had on the members of the Congressional Black Caucus. One of the caucus leaders approached him and said he had a very liberal girlfriend who after viewing the segment said, "You have got to go back and correct a wrong—you all did that man an injustice." He told Chip he had spoken with other members of the caucus who had likewise been impressed. Another member of the caucus approached Chip on the floor and told him that if what she saw on *60 Minutes* was true, the caucus made two mistakes: the first was opposing me and the second was not trumpeting my nomination as exactly the kind of person who should be on the Southern courts. A picture can speak a thousand words, and I think the thing that impressed many people the most was the picture of our daughter Allison in public school with her black classmates. I think some of the Congressional Black Caucus members realized that in contrast, few if any of the Senate Democrats who condemned me in the Judiciary Committee had sent their children to integrated public schools.

Several members of the caucus asked Chip to get together material concerning my record, the video showing my support among African Americans, and a copy of the *60 Minutes* segment for them to share and review. They wanted to go back and try to get the caucus to withdraw its opposition. Despite their good intentions, I knew that was not going to happen. Bennie Thompson had invested too much in fighting me, and he loves to control even when it requires dividing people by race. Plus, the special-interest groups aligned with the NAACP would never allow it. After a couple of weeks of good vibes from caucus members, we heard nothing. In many minds, my story was over and many did not realize my recess appointment was temporary or that my nomination was still pending in the Senate. Legislative matters took priority and I faded from the daily Washington fights and headlines.

Several days after the piece aired, White House Counsel Alberto Gonzales called and said he had not seen the *60 Minutes* segment, but understood it went quite well. He mentioned the White House heard other television programs might contact me for an interview. He politely suggested I not do any more interviews.

Chip and I had already discussed the matter and decided it was better to quit while I was ahead. We realized there are always those who want to make a name for themselves, who want to portray the negative, regardless of the facts. We felt we had hit a homerun on the major league of news programs and there was no reason to bat in the minors. A 2004 Media Consumption and Believability Study by the Pew Research Center for the People & the Press noted that CBS's *60 Minutes* is tied with CNN at the top of broadcast and cable believability, with more than a third calling it *highly* credible. It is the third most credible program among Republicans; the second most credible program among Democrats; and the most credible program among Independents. There was little to gain and much to lose by going on additional programs at that time.

I told Judge Gonzales I generally agreed with him and my inclination was to refrain from additional interviews. But I told him it was my record under attack, my reputation slandered, and I was the one John Edwards cross-examined as if I were a criminal. I told Judge Gonzales I understood his concern, reminded him that I was a team player, but I reserved my right to do what was necessary to defend my name in the future, and he understood.

In August 2004, according to news accounts, Mike Wallace's driver was cited for double parking and Mike "spent part of Tuesday night in police custody." He had been "handcuffed and hauled away by peace officers with the Taxi and Limousine Commission. . . . [O]ne police officer reportedly said he thought that Wallace was going to lunge at the other inspector, so he handcuffed the 86 year old journalist and hauled him off to a police precinct where he was issued a summons for disorderly conduct." A witness said, "He is 86 years old. The poor guy cannot

. . . the inspector can say what he wants. It is a lie. It is a lie. Plain and simple. I saw the whole thing. If I have to, I will be a witness." Another witness said, "They threw him in cuffs. There were policemen and, I mean, it was unbelievable. It was appalling. He didn't do anything." The next day I called Mike and said, "As one who has been accused in the news, I just want to commiserate with you." We had a warm conversation and I thanked him once again.

The *60 Minutes* pieces provided a cathartic transition from the confirmation struggles in Washington D.C. to the actual judicial work of sitting on the Fifth Circuit Court of Appeals. Although I hoped for confirmation to a lifetime term on the bench, I realized I might be on the circuit for less than a year, and while I was there, I wanted to do my part. It was time to get to work.

Serving on the Fifth Circuit

THE UNITED STATES Fifth Circuit Court of Appeals convenes in the
John Minor Wisdom United States Court of Appeals Building—three
stories of marble and granite rising above Camp Street in New Orleans.
First constructed in 1915 of Mississippi pine, Louisiana gum, and
Tennessee marble, the building has housed a court that—like the levees
guarding the city from the Mississippi River and the Gulf of Mexico—
has guarded the constitutional rights of individuals in the South for
generations. This court ensured that equal rights became a reality. The
Fifth Circuit and our Constitution have held stronger than the levees of
New Orleans.

At each of the four corners of the building stands a sculpture of a
bronze woman. Daniel Chester French, also known for his sculpture of
the seated Lincoln in Washington D.C.'s Lincoln Memorial, created
these statues known as "The Four Ladies." They depict History,
Agriculture, Commerce, and Industry.[1]

Congress named the building for John Minor Wisdom in 1994.
Wisdom, with his fellow members of the "Fifth Circuit Four"—Elbert
Tuttle, John Robert Brown, and Richard Rives—decided and wrote the
important federal court decisions involving equal access, equal opportunity, equality in education, voting rights, and civil rights in the South
during the 1950s and 1960s. (At that time, the Fifth Circuit also
encompassed today's Eleventh Circuit: Alabama, Georgia, and Florida,
plus the Panama Canal Zone.) Wisdom wrote the opinion ordering the
desegregation of my alma mater, the University of Mississippi. Among

Wisdom's former law clerks are Tennessee senator Lamar Alexander and Judge William H. Pryor on the Eleventh Circuit.

Today the Fifth Circuit covers Mississippi, Louisiana, and Texas. I approached my new position on this distinguished institution with humility and honor and with a commitment to uphold the Constitution and judicial precedent.

Within two hours of my appointment to the Fifth Circuit, the court dispatched briefs to my home for an *en banc*[2] hearing in New Orleans on the following Thursday. All sixteen Fifth Circuit judges[3] would be present. I had previously met all my new colleagues at judicial conferences, but with the exception of one with whom I sat on a three-judge panel a few years earlier, I had worked with none of them.

Appellate court judges maintain chambers in their hometowns where they do most of their work researching the law and writing opinions, with a second office in the city where the circuit meets. Fifth Circuit judges travel to New Orleans to hear cases, do administrative work, and perform other judicial duties. They work out of their hometown chambers more than three-fourths of the time. Former colleagues in the Southern District of Mississippi were kind enough to allow the Fifth Circuit to take over the chambers that I had occupied in Hattiesburg for the past thirteen years, so I did not have to move and could do my circuit work in the same chambers where I worked as a district judge.

Before my recess appointment, the confirmation process occupied me for three years while my district court responsibilities continued. During the first year, because of the rigors of confirmation preparation, three major surgeries, and an increase in case filings in the Southern District of Mississippi, I fell slightly behind in my district work. After that year, the Southern District of Mississippi developed one of the heaviest dockets in the nation due to the increase of mass tort filings and class-action lawsuits. Defendants sought to move their cases to what they perceived as more protective federal courts, and plaintiffs filed for remand to what they saw as more friendly state courts. This greatly increased the workload of all district judges in Mississippi. Mississippi has since enacted major tort reform legislation. Combined with the excessive demands of Senate Democrats on my time, I fell further behind.

When I accepted the recess appointment, I vacated my district court seat. But a circuit judge can do district work if designated by the chief judge of the circuit. I requested the chief judge make the designation so I could finish some of my district court work, but gradually the demands of my circuit court duties required me to spend less and less time on district work. Fortunately, the federal district court judges from New Orleans have seen their workloads ease as offshore oil litigation has decreased. They previously helped the overcrowded and overworked district courts along the Texas-Mexico border with their backlogs, and under the leadership of Adrian Duplantier generously volunteered to do the same for my docket.

When I joined the Fifth Circuit, the three judge panels sat for four days—Monday through Thursday—usually hearing five cases per day. Each sitting requires a judge to read briefs in advance, prepare for oral arguments, and decide some twenty cases. Ordinarily Fifth Circuit judges seek to avoid back-to-back sittings: that is, sitting on panels during two consecutive months. I knew if the Senate did not confirm me, I would be retiring at the end of the year; I requested to be scheduled as much as possible.

I wanted to make the most of my opportunity for service and to grow as a judge while on the circuit court. My scheduling of matters was further complicated because I did not know when the Senate would adjourn. In an election year, the Senate tries to adjourn in October but instead often goes on recess and comes back after the election. It takes sixty to ninety days after hearing a case to write the opinion, circulate it among the judges, and approve and render it as the decision of the court. I had to schedule my sittings so I would have time to finish writing opinions and deciding cases assigned to me before the Senate adjourned. Unless confirmed, I could not sit past September, though I could and did continue to draft opinions and decide previously heard cases. I was scheduled for four back-to-back sittings, a strenuous schedule. I intended to attend a workshop on appellate work at New York

University School of Law, but the extent of my circuit duties simply would not allow it and I had to cancel.

One Sunday afternoon during this time, my grandsons—Jeremy and Thomas Dunkerton—and I were scouting for turkeys at a sandbar on our farm on the Leaf River. I saw a couple of men setting up a tent on the far end of the sandbar. I approached them and found they were canoeing down the Leaf River and on down the Pascagoula River to the Gulf of Mexico. They were recording their trip to write about the Pascagoula and its tributaries. One of the campers turned out to be Ernest Herndon (better known as Leather Britches), the outdoors editor for the *McComb Enterprise-Journal* and author of several books, including a guide to Mississippi's rivers called *Canoeing Mississippi*. We discussed their trip and they mentioned spotting on the lower end of the sandbar an area where hogs had rooted out extensively. Hogs make it difficult for deer and turkey because they consume the food supply and tear up food plots and roads. Consequently, I try to trap and remove wild hogs.

I told them I would investigate the hog rooting and left them to camp on the sandbar. I wished them a safe journey on to the Gulf. Herndon later wrote an article about our meeting on the Leaf River sandbar:

> Pickering put his love for the river into action thirty years ago by participating in the effort to preserve the Pascagoula River, into which Leaf River flows. That effort, which was both complicated and groundbreaking is detailed in the 1980 book *Preserving the Pascagoula* by Donald Schueler. . . . In a nutshell, the Nature Conservancy purchased some forty-two thousand acres of riverside land from the Pascagoula Hardwood Co. and sold it to the state, which set it aside in wildlife management areas. Many people were involved, and Pickering was one of the sponsors of the legislation. . . . [Pickering said,] "You've got a tremendously large tract of land that's preserved for this generation and for future generations so that they can have a wilderness experience and maintain the beauty of it. . . . I think it is very important that we have those kinds of areas that are available for the public."[4]

You never know whom you're going to meet on a riverbank in Mississippi. I had not expected to run into a reporter in a canoe; he had not anticipated talking to a federal appeals court judge and his two grandsons.

As we moved through August, I completed my sittings on the Fifth Circuit with the remainder of my service on the court to be in chambers, writing opinions. But I still had two remaining district court cases to come before me. While preparing for those sentencing hearings, I realized that unless the Senate took action on my nomination, this could be my final occasion to wear a judicial robe and sit on the bench.

Both defendants that day were African Americans. The first was a female who while on drugs robbed a postal employee; the guidelines mandated prison time. She needed drug treatment, and I extended as much leniency as the guidelines permitted and sentenced her to the penitentiary in such a way that she could get the maximum drug treatment.

The second defendant, a young man with two small children, was facing a drug charge. He had a good job and a side business doing body shop work. I was convinced this young man could be rehabilitated, care for his family, and make a positive contribution to society. The government moved for a downward departure, giving me complete discretion under federal guidelines to determine his sentence. I made a considerable downward departure with lengthy probation and home confinement, severe restrictions, and substantial community service. By avoiding the penitentiary, he could keep his job and support his wife and children. Later, I inquired on his status with the probation officer. He told me the defendant was doing great. The officer said, "He's making more money than me." His business has taken off. He quit his regular job and hired four employees.

This was one of those exceptional times when a guilty criminal defendant can come before a judge and still be helped. Too frequently, they have already committed themselves to a life of crime. That was not true of this young man. He had a good work ethic, a good job, family support, church support, and I felt he could make it. If I had sentenced him to the penitentiary, his two small children would have lost their father for a number of years, he would have lost his job, and his wife would have struggled. Then when he got out of prison, he would have had difficulty finding employment and may have returned to crime. Instead, the prosecution and I worked with this young man in sentencing and we salvaged a life.

As I wound up my final hearings on the bench, Peter Barrett, the Assistant United States Attorney (AUSA) representing the government, asked permission to speak. He related he had been the first AUSA to prosecute a criminal case before me (one in which—he could not help but mention—he had gotten me reversed), and considering this could be the last case I would handle, he thought the occasion should be noted in the official court records. He made gracious and moving remarks; he became emotional and I could not respond. I had not expected it to impact me, but it did, and the final time I wore the robe, I was speechless. I turned and walked off the bench.

Trent, Chip, and I continued to monitor the chances of my confirmation and discussed strategies to bring that to fruition. The Democrats were committed to the filibuster and there was no movement. Trent counted votes for the Constitutional Option—sometimes inappropriately called the "nuclear option"—which would end filibusters through a parliamentary ruling upheld by a simple majority. In June, Trent told me the Republicans were within two votes of being able to implement this procedure.

As the 2004 presidential election charged on, I continued to see news stories where John Kerry, John Edwards, Ted Kennedy, and other Democrats were criticizing me as a racial extremist. Kerry railed,

> George Bush has nominated some of the most radical, right-winged judges that our country has ever seen. For example, Bush appointed Charles Pickering through a recess appointment after Pickering testified in his confirmation hearing . . . that as a trial judge, he threw out cases alleging sex or race discrimination on the job, assuming that they all lacked merit.[5]

Kerry's extreme and inflammatory statement was false. I gave no such testimony. The record in the cases I dismissed clearly revealed there was no cause of action; the cases that did have merit were not dismissed. I was never reversed on any case regarding sex or race discrimination. But Kerry was running for president, and the truth could not interfere with his campaign.

Rather than adjourn before the election, Congress recessed. My recess appointment would continue at least into November or December.

There were a number of issues involved in the presidential and senatorial elections of 2004. The most visible and the one with the most impact of course was the war on terror and the fighting in Iraq. But with Democrats filibustering judicial nominees and obstructing the confirmation process, and with President Bush sticking with his nominees and daily campaigning on the issue, the confirmation of judges was also central. The Massachusetts Supreme Court redefined marriage, the Ninth Circuit found the Pledge of Allegiance unconstitutional, and both reminded voters of the importance of a judiciary committed to the rule of law. The Massachusetts ruling led to marriage amendment votes in eleven states, including Ohio, where the turnout on this issue contributed greatly—perhaps decisively—to Bush's win of the state and thus his reelection as president. Furthermore, when the dust settled, Democrats sustained a net loss of four seats in the Senate, including their minority leader.

None of this assured my confirmation. When the Senate came back after the election, Democrats and Republicans agreed on a list of judicial nominees to be confirmed. Senator Lott and other Republicans pushed to include me on the list, but the Democrats refused. Chip continued to talk to senators in late November and December about my confirmation. He thought perhaps in the waning hours of the session, the Democrats would relent and allow me to go through by unanimous consent. By this time, I think most everyone except Chip had given up on my confirmation.

On December 8, 2004, it became evident the Senate would adjourn just before midnight. I would either be confirmed or retired. I wanted confirmation; no one likes to carry on a fight for four years and lose. The White House assured me if I were not confirmed, the president would re-nominate me at the next session. But if the Senate did not confirm me, I would have to retire, for like Cinderella's carriage that disappeared at midnight, the ink on my commission would become invisible when the Senate went home. I would be off the bench. I would have to start the process all over again. My life would once more be in limbo, but this time I would not be a judge able to hear cases. No one could predict how long the process would drag on, or how it would ultimately be resolved.

I considered the White House's offer of another re-nomination, but even though the Republicans had increased their majority in the Senate, it was not a filibuster-proof majority, although I felt the Democrats could not continue to filibuster nominees. They could not afford to continue to lose elections over the issue, and if they triggered the Constitutional Option, they and their left-wing special-interest groups would lose the threat of filibuster against Supreme Court nominees even before a vacancy occurred.

On a personal level, Margaret Ann and I were ready to move on with our lives and, equally or more important, the White House should be allowed to nominate a younger candidate for the Fifth Circuit, for I was then sixty-seven. I advised the White House that I intended to do all I could to secure my confirmation before the Senate adjourned, but if the Senate adjourned without confirming me, I would announce my retirement and decline re-nomination.

As the Senate was winding down, I flew back from Washington by way of Memphis, where I would change planes en route to the Pine Belt Regional Airport near my home. Chip went to the Senate floor in a last-ditch effort to win my confirmation and to help with two telecommunication bills. He was successful with the telecom bills as the Senate came to an agreement, giving unanimous consent to the previously passed House legislation. Chip asked Majority Leader Bill Frist to make one last effort to bring my nomination to the floor. Senator Frist asked Minority Whip Harry Reid, who due to the defeat of Senator Daschle would soon become minority leader, if the Democrats would give consent for my confirmation. Senator Reid agreed to contact Senator Leahy to see if he objected.

A flight delay in Washington caused me to miss my flight home from Memphis. Another passenger bound for Hattiesburg also missed the same flight, and together we rented a car and began the drive. My cell phone had lost its charge, so on the way home, driving through a thunderstorm and on a borrowed cell phone, I learned that I had retired. Senator Leahy told Senator Reid he would not consent on my nomination. Chip fought to the end, but he could not overcome the influence the groups held over Democratic senators.

I arrived home after midnight. The next morning, surrounded by family and friends, I announced my retirement in front of the courthouse where I had served for fourteen years. My confirmation battle was over, my judicial services concluded. I retrieved my personal belongings from my chambers upstairs and once again became a private citizen.

I had the privilege of serving as a United States District Judge for a little more than thirteen years and of serving on the Fifth Circuit Court of Appeals for eleven months. My judicial career spanned fourteen years and two months. On the district court bench, I disposed of more than 5,000 cases. During my eleven months on the Fifth Circuit Court of Appeals, I helped render 355 panel decisions, writing 110 opinions. I entered 115 additional orders.[6] I consider each day that I served in the federal judiciary a privilege and an honor and appreciate the friendship and professionalism of the judges, clerks, and staff of the district and circuit courts. I have lived the great American experience from humble roots in Jones County to the Fifth Circuit Court of Appeals and am deeply grateful for the opportunity I had to serve as a member of the third branch of government.

While I have not reviewed in detail the biographies of all the filibustered Bush appellate nominees, I did review the records of Miguel Estrada, Janice Rogers Brown, Priscilla Owen, and William Pryor. They are and were all excellent jurists who were treated unfairly. The slander and attack and lies they faced are a price too high for public service; but they endured and they prevailed. As to whether I was treated fairly or unfairly, I will leave that to history and others; but you have read my odyssey. You be the judge. I hope by sharing my experience and insights

I can increase the awareness of the importance of this struggle and hopefully be a voice of reason for solutions fair to both sides.

Would it have been better for me to have made the bipartisan statement with Jorge Rangel rather than accept the recess appointment? Who knows for sure? I have the utmost respect for Jorge, and I believe he has the best interests of the judiciary at heart. He would have served with distinction on the Fifth Circuit had he not been blocked.

In the final analysis, Chip was probably correct with his advice that 2004 was not a good atmosphere for Jorge and me to make the bipartisan statement. There was great acrimony and turmoil over judicial nominations in 2004, and it is problematic as to whether a bipartisan statement by two judicial nominees who had been thwarted in their individual efforts to win a seat on the Fifth Circuit Court of Appeals could have fashioned a ceasefire. But one thing is for sure: the solution we would have proposed addressed only symptoms and not the underlying problem itself, the politicization of the Supreme Court.

The confirmation battle is fought because some judges interpret the Constitution as a changing document; a document to be fought over by opposing sides with the victor able to change its meaning and to change the rules while the game is being played. In fact, the Constitution is a contract between a government and its people that establishes once and for all the rules by which the game is played until the people themselves decide to change the rules, to change the Constitution; otherwise, it is nothing and meaningless. Interpreting the Constitution as a changing document has politicized the judiciary, which is ill equipped to make political decisions.

The attack on my nomination was about far more than me and whether I would sit on the Fifth Circuit Court of Appeals. It was and is about the future of the judiciary. Now that I am no longer on the bench, I can address the whole problem, not just part. If I had not taken the recess appointment, I would still have my lifetime appointment on the district court, but I would not be as free to discuss the problem and its solutions. I could not have written my previous book *Supreme Chaos*, nor this one. I have never enjoyed controversy, but one could argue that without the recess appointment, I would not have had the opportunity to speak around the country nor write these books to address the problems facing the judiciary. When considering the opportunity I had for public service and the ability it gave me to continue to address problems facing the judiciary, I have no regrets on the choice I made. I am glad I had the privilege of serving on the Fifth Circuit Court of Appeals.

Consequences

FOR EVERY ACTION, there is a reaction. For every reaction, there is yet another reaction, and on and on it goes. There were many consequences—affecting almost everyone involved—from filibustering the Bush judicial nominees.

There were consequences for the nominees. The left-wing special-interest groups targeted some twenty nominees, whom their Democratic allies attacked. Of these nominees, Miguel Estrada and Caroline Kuhl withdrew; and I, while not confirmed, served by recess appointment on the Fifth Circuit Court of Appeals. A fourth, Terrance Boyle, made it through committee only to have his nomination expire in December 2006 (he was not re-nominated). A fifth, Claude Allen, withdrew for an appointment as a White House Domestic Policy advisor. The United States Senate eventually confirmed most of these nominees savaged by the Left to lifetime appointments on the federal judiciary.[1]

There were consequences for the special-interest groups. Their attacks in the press were effective; they raised money and excited their base against the Bush nominees. But ultimately they overreached, and seven moderate Democrats joined with seven Republicans to form the Gang of Fourteen compromise in which these Democrats pledged not to filibuster except in extraordinary circumstances. This effectively removed the filibuster from play and weakened the ability of the special-interest groups to defeat nominees with their smear campaigns.

The loss of the filibuster and the weakened effectiveness of the special-interest groups provided the Bush administration with an open door to nominate solidly conservative and strict constructionists to the

United States Supreme Court. Following the retirement of Justice Sandra Day O'Connor and the passing of Chief Justice William Rehnquist, President Bush nominated John Roberts and Samuel Alito to the Court. The special-interest groups had cried wolf too many times, the Democrats had obstructed too much, and both had wasted their strength and capital in the minor leagues of appellate nominees. When it came time for the big game, the opposition had spent so much time and energy sending a message to the White House that they had absolutely no impact on the very subject about which they had been sending messages—confirming nominees to the U.S. Supreme Court. President Bush named two young outstanding conservative nominees of the precise judicial philosophy he promised, affecting the direction of the Court for the next thirty years.

Evan Schultz, a former Democratic counsel for the Senate Judiciary Committee, took note in *Legal Times* of how the Democratic obstruction of Bush's judicial nominees failed:

> . . . the Senate Democrats made opposing Bush's judicial nominees a signature issue, and they failed miserably. . . . So far, the Senate has confirmed the overwhelming majority of Bush's nominees—about ninety-eight percent. . . . [T]he Democrats hit them hard. . . . But after the dust settled, the Bush administration had the best of all possible comebacks—the sound of these nominees uttering their judicial oaths of office. Bush's two picks for the most important bench, Chief Justice John Roberts Jr. and Justice Samuel Alito Jr., also beat the Democrats' opposition.[2]

Perhaps the greatest consequence was in the political arena, at the ballot box. There should be a consequence for policy decisions, and the voters spoke loudly against the Democratic decision to obstruct the Bush judicial nominees.

In 2002, Republicans captured a net gain of two Senate seats in a year that historically should have provided the Democrats an opportunity to expand their majority, because it was a mid-term election for a new president and Republicans were defending more seats than the Democrats. After their brief stint in power, the Democrats lost control of the United States Senate to Republicans who prevailed at the ballot box.

Shortly after I was filibustered in 2003, Sean Rushton, executive director of the Committee for Justice, wrote a guest editorial for *National Review* titled "Judge Pickering's Revenge." He related:

> . . . with Tuesday night's Republican victory in the Mississippi guber-natorial race, as well as vulnerable Senate seats across the south and midwest in 2004, it may be Pickering who ultimately has the last laugh.
>
> . . . Democrats and their liberal allies from the New York-Hollywood axis opted for a strategy of hardball opposition, and settled on Pickering as their ideal target. Southern, white, middle-aged, conservative, and religious . . . Pickering seemed the ideal nominee for a good, old-fashioned borking. The only problem was, contrary to the stereotypes, Pickering had a long record in the new south as a racial reconciler and friend to African Americans. . . . he was supported by numerous Democratic officials and African American leaders in his state.
>
> . . . While Democrats had won the battle, Republicans were intent to win the war, especially in the south, where Pickering is well-known and highly regarded. In a region where "racist" is a deeply meaningful and serious charge, many were outraged by its casual use by Democrats and the elite media to smear a man of Charles Pickering's standing. Some saw the accusation as Yankee shorthand for Mississippian, religious, and conservative, and regarded the Left's tone and tactics as a sign of what the national Democratic party really thought of them.
>
> In Mississippi, Republican gubernatorial candidate Haley Barbour, no political novice, immediately seized the Pickering issue to bash his opponent, incumbent Ronnie Musgrove. Though Musgrove—like all state-wide elected Democrats—endorsed Pickering and called for his confirmation, Barbour was quick to jump on the issue and link his opponent to national Democrats: "They [Senate Democrats] have one thing against Charles Pickering, and this is the story of the Democratic Party today," Barbour said. . . . "We need a governor who has influence with his national party. . . . [Governor

Musgrove's] support for Judge Pickering didn't sway any of their votes."

. . . Democrats should be wondering why rural voters, especially in the south, are turning them out of power. With open or vulnerable seats next November in North Carolina, South Carolina, Georgia, Louisiana, Arkansas, Florida, North Dakota, Nevada, and South Dakota, Senate Democrats may end up regretting their treatment of Charles Pickering after all.[3]

In 2004, Republicans swept the Southern open seats in Florida, Georgia, Louisiana, North Carolina, and South Carolina, moving formerly held Democratic seats into GOP control. With the defeat of incumbent Senate Minority Leader Tom Daschle of South Dakota, Republicans netted four additional seats in the U.S. Senate.

I do not suggest that filibustering judges was the only reason Democrats lost a net of six Senate seats in two elections. But without question, obstructing Bush's judicial nominees was a major contributing factor. In fact, when retiring Democratic senator Bob Graham of Florida was asked why the Democrats lost every hotly contested Senate election in the South, he responded, "filibustering judges."

Besides the Senate contests in 2004, judicial confirmation politics played a role in the 2004 presidential election as well. John Edwards, seeking to build left-wing support for his primary campaign for president, ambushed my nomination in the Senate Judiciary Committee, but not without consequences.

Mississippi trial lawyer leader Richard Scruggs, the attorney responsible for the successful multibillion dollar lawsuits against the tobacco industry, said in a February 2003 *Roll Call* article that what Edwards did "wasn't the manly thing to do. . . . Not that he owes me a vote, but he owes me a phone call. . . . I sent a message through another trial lawyer: He can forget my support and that of anybody I have influence with." The article continued,

> To finance his national ambitions, Edwards opened a leadership political action committee, New American Optimists . . . $167,000 came from Mississippi attorneys, legal employees or their family members—

many of whom work at firms, such as Minor & Associates and Langston Law Firm, whose principals are also supporting Pickering.

On April 25, *Roll Call* followed up on these numbers:

In the last months of 2001 . . . Mississippi lawyers, their employees and their families accounted for $177,000 in contributions to [Edwards's] PAC, more than 20 percent of his total haul. During the past three months, Mississippi's legal community gave just $5,000 to Edwards—less than one-tenth of one percent of the hard and soft dollars the Senator raised during that time. The last check from Mississippi arrived Feb. 5, two days before Pickering's hearing, during which Edwards delivered a blistering cross-examination of the judge. . . . [Pascagoula trial lawyer leader Richard Scruggs] said he tried in vain to get Edwards to hear his arguments in support of the judge. But Edwards didn't return his calls, and Scruggs . . . vowed to rally opposition to the North Carolinian's presidential ambitions. "He's probably seen his last nickel out of here," Scruggs said Wednesday. While there have been no formal votes among Mississippi bar members, Scruggs said he has raised the issue and has found a generally positive response to his anti-Edwards crusade. . . . Scruggs, however, insisted there is more money to be had in Mississippi, funds that are now waiting for one of the other Democratic contenders. . . . "Had [Edwards] been more responsive, he could have gotten a lot more of it," he said of the campaign cash, vowing to find a way to exact more revenge in the future. "I'm just waiting for the opportunity to be relevant in his life again."

Whether this hurt the Edwards campaign, it certainly did not help to have some of the leaders of his biggest constituency—trial lawyers—standing opposed to him.

Once John Kerry sewed up the Democratic nomination and brought Edwards on as his running mate, Edwards's actions in the Senate Judiciary Committee continued to haunt the campaign in conservative Democratic circles.

State Insurance Commissioner George Dale—the dean of Mississippi Democrats who is serving his eighth statewide term, undefeated since 1975—went one step beyond endorsing my nomination. He said my treatment at the hands of Senator John Edwards was "a slap in the face of every American," and so he endorsed George W. Bush for president in 2004. I think he overstated things, but I appreciated his support. George Dale has always been conservative, but also a staunch Democrat. That says something about his feelings on John Edwards's behavior. Kerry-Edwards was never in a position to win Mississippi, but the Bush-Cheney campaign used Democratic endorsements like this in competitive states around the country, and it helped—if only a little—in a close presidential campaign.

When the Supreme Court of Massachusetts redefined marriage and the Ninth Circuit Court of Appeals held the Pledge of Allegiance unconstitutional, many voters who had been sitting on the sidelines suddenly connected the dots. They realized the importance of the judiciary and the results of activists on the bench. These voters took action, turned out, became involved in the election, and made a difference.

The Marriage Amendment—defining marriage as between one man and one woman—won overwhelmingly on the ballot in eleven states during the 2004 presidential election. In Ohio it passed by 62 percent of the vote. President Bush carried Ohio by less than 120,000 votes out of more than 5.6 million votes cast. Bush won Ohio with about 50.8 percent and in so doing won the White House. Had John Kerry's Massachusetts Supreme Court not redefined marriage, the marriage amendment would not have been on the Ohio ballot. If the marriage amendment had not been on the ballot in Ohio, Bush may well have lost the state. Had Bush lost Ohio, John Kerry would be in the White House today. The obstruction of strict constructionist judicial nominees and the action of liberal activist judges may have done what all the Republican strategists otherwise could not have done in 2004—reelect George W. Bush.

At home in Mississippi, the Democratic obstruction of my nomination played a role in two major campaigns. As already noted, in 2002, my son Chip ran for reelection against another incumbent due to the combination of House districts after census-imposed redistricting. His opponent, Democrat Ronnie Shows, was reluctant to alienate national

Democrats who opposed my nomination, as well as Mississippi congressman Bennie Thompson. At first, this made him reticent and slow to endorse me, and later it made him hesitant to embrace fully my nomination. Chip's campaign capitalized on those mistakes and made the argument that Ronnie Shows would be working with the same liberal national Democrats who had blocked my confirmation and attacked my reputation and impugned the progress of Mississippi. The campaign further argued that if Ronnie Shows did support my nomination, the fact that national liberal Democrats ignored him demonstrated his ineffectiveness as a Mississippi representative. My nomination certainly did not win the race for Chip, but it helped to run up the score.

In 2003, Haley Barbour challenged a conservative incumbent Democrat—Ronnie Musgrove—for governor of Mississippi. Again, Musgrove fully supported my nomination and I am grateful for his help. Unfortunately, both for him and for me, the national Democrats would not listen to him. The Barbour campaign used the same strategy as Chip's campaign to show that Musgrove would be an ineffective leader because his party would not pay attention to him. Again, my nomination did not win the election for Haley Barbour (which was decided by 20,000 votes statewide), but, when nothing would go Musgrove's way, this was another issue advantage for Barbour.

There were consequences for me personally. When the Senate did not act on my nomination following my recess appointment, I had no alternative but to retire from the judiciary. Had I been confirmed, I could have continued for life with a full workload, could have served for life, but could have taken senior status with a reduced workload and opened my seat up for another appointment, or I could have retired. The left wing made a pragmatic mistake to attack me when most of Bush's conservative nominees were much younger than I and will be spending many more years on the bench than I would have even if confirmed.

Once retired, my life changed. I suddenly realized I was without a secretary. Sonja Gatlin had served me faithfully and well for some thirty years, and she understood me and could anticipate what I needed. I told people I did not miss the robe, nor the power of the pen, as much as I missed not having a secretary. Although I said this jokingly, it was also a reality.

Margaret Ann and I were at peace with my retirement. When the judiciary door closed, new opportunities opened. I am now able to speak out and more fully discuss the fight over the judiciary. In doing so, I wrote my previous book, *Supreme Chaos: The Politics of Judicial Confirmation & the Culture War.* I wrote this book to follow up and complete the story of *Supreme Chaos.* And I have spoken to legal, civic, religious, and political groups across the country on the issue of judicial confirmation politics and reform. Meanwhile, my federal district court seat was taken by a qualified judge who is healthy and younger and can serve for more years than could I. Furthermore, President Bush has nominated a capable conservative nominee to fill my seat on the Fifth Circuit, and so the battle continues.

No longer on the bench, I became senior counsel at Baker Donelson Beerman Caldwell and Berkowitz and joined the board of directors of the Magnolia State Bank, the board of directors of Mission Mississippi (a faith-based group working for racial reconciliation), and the board of trustees of William Carey University. I started an education trust fund for my twenty-one grandchildren. I am also co-chairing with Judge Reuben Anderson (the first African American elected to the Mississippi Supreme Court) a gubernatorial commission to make recommendations to establish a national civil rights museum for Mississippi. There is life beyond the robe.

And looking back at the consequences of the judicial confirmation struggle, the left wing lost, and lost badly. The Senate confirmed almost all of the Bush nominees. The Gang of Fourteen neutralized their ability to block nominees to the Supreme Court and devastated the effectiveness of the filibuster against other nominees. Democrats facilitating the attack lost control of the Senate as well as a net loss of six seats. The people reelected President Bush. Voters defeated conservative Democrats in Mississippi. And I ultimately served on the Fifth Circuit Court of Appeals, though only briefly. The left wing made a bad political miscalculation. Their strategy backfired, and they have few results to show for their effort other than spending the contributions of their supporters.

There will be future consequences as well. So long as the Democrats allow these narrow, out of the mainstream special-interest groups to control them, they will continue to pay a price. Unless we correct the confirmation process, the judiciary will suffer as qualified nominees decline to participate in a procedure that could tarnish their lives or reputations. Nominees with less experience and little paper trail will tend to be the norm, costing the federal courts a great deal of judicial and life experience. Unless we correct the confirmation process, the Senate will continue to be a body of extreme partisan conflict unable to resolve with comity or collegiality nominations or legislation. Unless we correct the confirmation process, the judiciary will continue to be politicized as each side of the culture war attempts to control it like they do the legislative and executive branches.

Only time will tell whether I will make any effective contribution whatsoever toward improving the confirmation process or depoliticizing the judiciary. But the consequences of doing nothing are far too great to sit on the sidelines.

A Problem that
Cries Out for Solution

THE POLITICIZATION OF the judiciary threatens the federal judiciary with irreparable harm. Our Founders never intended the judiciary to become a political branch of government, and the majority of Americans oppose a political court. Americans want judges to interpret the law, not judges who make it up.

This politicization of the judiciary has created a bitter, mean-spirited, highly partisan process for the confirmation of federal judges. Special-interest groups often target nominees to the federal judiciary with smear campaigns, innuendoes, downright false accusations, and contentious hearings that are the antithesis of due process, fair dealing, and civility. Many nominations are blocked in the Senate for years.

At the time of the 2004 election, Democrats had filibustered ten Bush appellate nominees and threatened six more with the same treatment. Seven Democrats and seven Republicans joined together for the Gang of Fourteen compromise to grant a reprieve and finally deliver confirmation to many nominees, who had dwelled in nomination limbo for four years—not in control of their lives, unable to plan for the future, unsure of their careers, and silently at the mercy of extreme partisan politics. Democrats filibustered Miguel Estrada seven times before he said enough is enough. The nomination of Terrence Boyle to the Fourth Circuit languished for more than five years before finally expiring in December 2006.

A survey jointly sponsored by the Heritage Foundation and the Brookings Institute "found that fifty-one percent" of judicial nominees "believe that the process is embarrassing, and sixty-six percent found it to be an ordeal."[1]

This same Heritage/Brookings survey study "found that one out of every two candidates finds the process so unbearable as to decline nomination." Potential candidates are not willing to have unscrupulous people with ideological axes to grind probing into every nook and cranny of their lives, calling family, friends, and neighbors trying to find dirt at any expense, of any kind, to harass, intimidate, and cause nominees to withdraw or face defeat by filibuster. They are unwilling to submit themselves and their families to the kind of grilling experienced by Sam Alito, Clarence Thomas, Robert Bork, Miguel Estrada, William Pryor, Janice Rogers Brown, Priscilla Owen, and me. The pool of prospective nominees willing to subject themselves to such a firing squad grows smaller each day. Had I known what I would go through, I might have been with those hesitant candidates in declining the honor of nomination.

Senator John Cornyn, recognizing this "dangerous pattern in American politics," wrote,

> I am deeply troubled and concerned about how hostile and destructive the Senate's judicial confirmation process has become . . . . and the problem seems only to be getting worse. . . . senators are not merely delaying nominees; they are destroying them—destroying their names and their reputations and doing so by any means necessary. Nothing seems beyond the pale any more; every conceivable line has been crossed.[2]

Within a year of leaving their positions, clerks at the Supreme Court can make more than the justices. In America's large cities, partners in big law firms often make five times more money than justices on the Supreme Court. The disparity of salary grows greater between successful lawyers and lower court judges. The financial sacrifice for public service increases, while the emotional and public attacks discourage future judges. With a broken and chaotic confirmation process and judges making far less than lawyers in private practice, the brain drain from the judiciary will increase if we do not find a solution.

If the confirmation fight continues, we will see mediocre nominees with lackluster credentials, few writings, and little paper trails. This bodes ill for the judiciary and the American people. Unless a reasonable, practical solution to the confirmation conflict can be found, the lack of experienced and established nominees will severely weaken the federal judiciary in the not-distant future.

Justice Clarence Thomas, speaking in Alabama in spring 2006, said he is already hearing that the best and brightest of our law school graduates are directing their careers away from a judicial path. They are simply not willing to devote the necessary effort to a judicial career, nor subject their families to an uncertain and brutal confirmation process. Americans should have serious concern when one out of two nominees says "no thanks," and the brightest and best refuse the option before they ever enter the starting gate, greatly endangering the competence of our courts.

A crisis of confidence also confronts the judiciary. In September 2005, the American Bar Association *Journal & Report* revealed disturbing results of an extensive poll:

> A majority [fifty-six percent] of the survey respondents agreed with statements that "judicial activism" has reached the crisis stage, and that judges who ignore voters' values should be impeached. Nearly half agreed with a congressman who said judges are "arrogant, out-of-control and unaccountable."

The ABA report summarized poll results: "More than half of Americans are angry and disappointed with the nation's judiciary." For the first time ever, a majority of Americans disapprove of the Supreme Court.[3]

Any civilized nation seeking to provide an orderly society and protect the rights of its citizens must have qualified members of the judiciary and public respect for the courts. The venom of the judicial confirmation process and the politicization of the courts poison both these necessities.

This fight over nominees weakens another leg in our government's tripod besides the judiciary. During the confirmation battles over the Bush appellate nominees, civility, comity, and collegiality in the Senate spiraled to a new low, held hostage by the bitterness of the fight. Those opposing judicial nominees saw them not as flesh-and-blood human beings with family, friends, feelings, and pride in their records and reputations, but rather as mere pawns in a political game. Just before Democrats filibustered my nomination in October 2003, the *New York Times* reported the intensity of this partisan struggle. Under the descriptive headlines "Sharp tongues and hard feelings in the Senate Judiciary Committee" and "Where the Gloves Are Nearly Always Off," Neil A. Lewis wrote, "Such is the level of partisan rancor at Senate Judiciary Committee meetings that some staff aides recently suggested that the Department of Homeland Security screen senators for weapons and 'sharp objects before they enter the hearing room.'"[4]

A couple of months later, the *Washington Post* quoted one participant as saying, "The level of rancor and acrimony is at an all time high." The reporter noted things were being "said off the record that could not be printed in a family newspaper." The article said,

> Hatfield's and McCoy's, Montague's and Capulet's. The intractable feudists of lore have nothing on the Republicans and the Democrats of the Senate Judiciary Committee. . . . "Each party ratchets up the politicization of the process," said Peter Berkowitz, a fellow of the Hoover Institution. "There were Republican abuses that are now taken a step farther by the Democrats—and I expect when we see the next Democratic president, the Republicans will ratchet it up one more step."[5]

The tension from the confirmation fight made it difficult for the Senate to discharge its constitutional responsibilities. The confirmation battle drained the energy of senators, and they accomplished less. Longstanding relations became fragile; some fractured. The enmity created will be difficult to erase.

Any problem that threatens the ability of two of our three coequal branches of government to perform their constitutional responsibilities and weakens those institutions cries out for a solution. The politicization of the judiciary is just such a problem. The responsible solution must be fair to both parties, to the president regardless of party, to prospective nominees, and more importantly to the American people. Unless a commonsense solution can meet these needs, it will fail. We— Republicans and Democrats and Independents; conservatives and liberals and moderates; all Americans—cannot afford to neglect the problem; we cannot afford to fail.

Restoring Civility,
Respecting One Another

MY PERSONAL ODYSSEY through confirmation chaos did not reveal a reasoned and rational debate on the qualifications, integrity, or judicial temperament of nominees. Opponents mischaracterized statements, maligned reputations, portrayed court proceedings inaccurately, and used inappropriate racial attacks to obstruct and finally block my confirmation and those of other Bush nominees. Personal, social, procedural, and cultural failures create this breakdown of the confirmation process.

If we want to bring order to the chaos of the confirmation process, we have to address each area. We must individually and corporately return civility to our discourse. We must seek racial reconciliation and harmony and repudiate both the personal and institutional vestiges of racism, as well as the misuse and abuse of race through racial demagoguery. We must institute a clear procedure in the confirmation process. And we must remove the confirmation of federal judges from the culture war by passing a constitutional amendment to prevent judges from legislating from the bench and restricting them to interpreting constitutional provisions as they were understood at the time of their adoption.

Restoring civility is the first step in improving the judicial confirmation procedure. This is not a matter of partisanship; parties in the American system have effectively advanced their members' beliefs for centuries and can do so in a respectful manner even in opposition. This is not a matter of disagreement; the old saying "we can disagree without being disagreeable" applies when we all have the best interests of our country at heart. This is a matter of common decency, of polite engagement, of common human respect for persons.

On June 9, 1954, Senator Joseph McCarthy grilled Special Counsel for the Army Joseph Welch during hearings of the Senate Permanent Subcommittee on Investigations, seeking to determine whether or to what extent communists had infiltrated the State Department and other federal agencies, including in this instance the United States Army. After suffering interrogations and facing snide and sometimes sinister innuendos, and having seen the destruction of reputations of many Americans, Welch responded to McCarthy in those now famous words, "Have you no sense of decency, sir, at long last? Have you left no sense of decency?" McCarthy responded that he knew these questions hurt Welch, to which Welch interrupted and replied they did hurt him, but also, "Senator, I think it hurts you, too, sir."

The McCarthy-Welch encounter splashed cold water on the face of the American public, and within six months, the United States Senate had censored McCarthy. Welch was correct: when we abandon civility, we damage not just others but also ourselves.

On January 11, 2006, Samuel Alito faced the Senate Judiciary Committee for his second day of questioning on his nomination to replace Sandra Day O'Connor on the United States Supreme Court. The Democrats had attempted to paint Alito as a racist and a bigot, hoping they could make a case that he would be hostile to the rights of minorities and women on the Court and thus would not be qualified for that high office.

When Republican senator Lindsey Graham began his questioning, he asked Alito, "Are you really a closet bigot?" Alito replied, "I'm not any kind of a bigot." Senator Graham continued,

> No, sir, you're not. You know why I believe that? Not just because you said it, but that's a good enough reason, because you seem to be a decent, honorable man. I've got reams of quotes from people who have worked with you, African American judges . . . glowing quotes about who you, the way you've lived your life, law clerks, men and women, black and white. Your colleagues, who say that Sam Alito,

whether I agree with him or not, is a really good man. . . . Because the way you have lived your life and the way you and your wife are raising your children. Let me tell you this, guilt by association is going to drive good men and women away from wanting to sit where you're sitting. . . . Judge Alito, I am sorry that you've had to go through this. I am sorry that your family has had to sit here and listen to this.

Martha-Ann, Judge Alito's wife, left the room in tears. She sat behind her husband for hours and days as Democrats—especially Ted Kennedy—directed insulting questions and innuendo at him in an attempt to smear him and wreck his nomination. Those opposing him sought to destroy his chances for serving on the Supreme Court by any means necessary and regardless of casualties, including his life's reputation and the feelings of his family. She could no longer bear the lies directed at the man she loved.

Just like the McCarthy hearings, this moment of awakening shook the American public. Every television network carried the footage of Martha-Ann leaving in tears. Every major newspaper featured the photograph of her troubled face with tears in her eyes. Every radio news program discussed it, and people around the country were outraged. The Democrats overplayed their hand, and a nation with a civil conscience reacted.

The attacking Democrats did not view Alito as a real life-and-blood human being with feelings and pride in his record and reputation. This was nothing new; this was the modus operandi against many conservative judicial nominees. Priscilla Owen, Janice Rogers Brown, Bill Pryor, others, and I all experienced the treatment as mere political pawns, dehumanized, and fair game for attack to reach the left wing's political goal.

Jim Wright warned against such cannibalism when he resigned as Speaker of the House of Representatives in 1989 as a result of ethics charges. William Safire selected Wright's speech of resignation as Speaker of the House as one of the "Great Speeches in History." Wright posited that he resigned as "a propitiation for ill will." The Speaker intoned,

> . . . it is grievously hurtful to our society when vilification becomes an accepted form of political debate. . . . Have I contributed unwittingly to this manic idea of a frenzy of feeding on other people's reputation? Have I been too partisan? . . . When vengeance becomes more desirable than vindication, harsh personal attacks on one another's motives, one another's character, drown out the quiet logic of serious debate on important issues. . . . Surely, that's unworthy of our institution, unworthy of our American political process. . . . All of us in both political parties must resolve to bring this period of mindless cannibalism to an end. There's been enough of it.[1]

Whether it is 1954 and Republican Joe McCarthy, or 2006 and Democrat Ted Kennedy, we must say we will not tolerate incivility. Unfortunately, incivility permeates much of our culture. America is becoming a nation of shouters and pouters where the response to shrill discourse is personal attack and demagoguery rather than polite correction or respectful rebuke. A hopeful future requires a return to public manners and civility—that basic code for community cooperation and productive dialogue.[2]

A country of diverse beliefs built the world's finest democracy by civil discourse based on debating problems, not by attacking people. Foundational rules in the formation of George Washington's character include 110 rules of civility that he transcribed as an exercise in personal development.[3] Washington, at age sixteen, affirmed the first rule: "Every action done in company ought to be with some sign of respect to those that are present." We must return to such other-oriented values. The National Civility Center in Pontiac, Michigan, suggests that, in governments, churches, businesses, and schools, "Civility is a variation of the 'Golden Rule.' It is being kind, courteous, polite, and avoiding overt rudeness."[4]

Today's charged culture war challenges such basic community decency. In government, media, and commerce, a win-at-all-cost attitude strains our treatment of each other. Boorish behavior and coarse conversation, being uncivil and shrill in civic discourse, and being meanspirited and hostile toward each other do not make us a better nation.

In government, Massachusetts senator Ted Kennedy calls the Bush nominees including Janice Rogers Brown, Miguel Estrada, and Priscilla Owen "Neanderthals," and no Democrat publicly rebukes him.[5] California senator Barbara Boxer, in a televised congressional hearing, questions Rice's "respect for the truth," and Rice must politely defend herself.[6] Democratic Senate Leader Harry Reid unapologetically calls President George W. Bush "a loser" and "a liar," then-Federal Reserve chairman Alan Greenspan a "political hack," and Supreme Court Justice Clarence Thomas an "embarrassment."[7] NAACP chairman Julian Bond announces, "The Republican Party would have the American flag and the swastika flying side by side" after making previous statements that President Bush "has selected nominees from the Taliban wing of American politics, appeased the wretched appetites of the extreme right wing, and chosen Cabinet officials whose devotion to the Confederacy is nearly canine in its uncritical affection."[8]

In media, celebrities add to the onslaught of boorish behavior. Dixie Chick country singing star Natalie Maines announces in a London, England, concert, "Just so you know, we're ashamed the president of the United States is from Texas," setting off a public war of words.[9] Fellow country singing icon Toby Keith engages in a "war of words" with Maines and retorts that she is "miserable" and "irresponsible."[10] Meanwhile, a musical rap subculture degrades women, debases human sexuality, and glamorizes violence. Daily talk shows—including some political news shows—increase ratings by fomenting shouting matches as the audience and callers join the fracas. Talk show guests strain to make the most extreme point in the shortest amount of time.

In commerce, the American workplace suffers from incivility. A University of North Carolina study shows that work performance drastically drops in an increasingly uncivil workplace. Of 800 people who had faced incivility at work, 53 percent lost work time worrying about it, 37 percent lost commitment to their work, and 22 percent decreased their work effort.[11]

Incivility in government, media, and commerce caters to our lesser nature and becomes a vicious cycle. People interrupt one another; they shout over each other; they laugh derisively and shake their heads in sarcasm while someone else speaks. George Washington would be astounded. His 34th axiom of civility states, "It is good manners to prefer them to whom we speak before ourselves."

A fundamental notion of civility is that "life is a relational experience," an assertion made by P. M. Forni, a professor in the Department of Romance Languages and Literatures at Johns Hopkins University and co-founder of the Johns Hopkins Civility Project. Forni notes,

> Civility is linked to the Latin word *civitas*, which meant "city" and "community." Thus, civility implies a larger social concern. When we are civil we are members in good standing of a community, we are good neighbors and good citizens. Whether we look at the core of manners or at that of civility we discern not only pleasant form but ethical substance as well.[12]

There is "an understandable and widespread frustration with the current tenor of political debate," state Dr. Guy Burgess and Dr. Heidi Burgess, co-directors of the Conflict Research Consortium at the University of Colorado. They add, "There is a growing realization that our inability to deal with a broad range of problems is largely attributable to the destructive ways in which the issues are being addressed." The two professors call for an "increasingly vocal campaign for civility in public discourse."[13]

The Burgesses reflect many social leaders' concerns over today's potent mix of hot-button issues, unfettered media, and partisan politics. The present political and cultural challenges are increasingly difficult because of their "social" nature. Sexuality, abortion, and race are front and center, not only locally, but in the halls of Congress. "Tough social issues"—because they address the very core of people's values—always strain civility, asserts the National Civility Center, a not-for-profit begun in 2000 "to help people make their communities better places to live."[14]

We need a common consent to return to the rules championed by George Washington—the one indispensable individual in the formation of our country. Washington understood that being considerate of others, being kind in your arguments, and being caring of the outcome not only was right, but also led to the best results. Ultimately, we need to check our personal motives before we speak or act.

Washington's 58th and 59th rules noted, "Let your conversation be without malice or envy, for it is a sign of a tractable and commendable nature: And in all causes of passion admit reason to govern. Never express anything unbecoming, nor act against the rules moral."[15]

What we face today in our nation is not unlike the times and climate William Wilberforce faced in Great Britain during the early nineteenth century. He had two great passions: the end of British involvement in slavery and slave trade and the restoration of civility among the British peoples. Before we think that the return to civility is beyond possibility, consider that Wilberforce in his own lifetime succeeded in both missions, which were joined in the respect of person-hood that we must recapture in our country.

Likewise, respecting persons goes beyond being polite. Among our efforts to restore civility should be the advancement of better race relations. Conflict based on race is the epitome of incivility, for the only separating measure is the outward appearance of individuals. Reconciliation among races requires both creative and corrective measures. We must be creative, active in expressing our commonalities and shared values and respect. We must be corrective, refusing to embrace race baiters and divisive elements who gain by keeping our peoples apart.

Race is an issue that has divided our nation from the time of its birth. The issue of African slavery almost doomed the efforts to draft a Constitution that could be ratified. While our Founders eloquently wrote, "We hold these Truths to be self evident, that all Men are created equal, that they are endowed by their Creator with certain unalienable Rights, that among these are Life, Liberty, and the Pursuit of Happiness," this principle of equality would not become the practice of our nation for many years. Eventually, Congress and the states amended the Constitution to ensure equal rights for women and for non-whites. It took another century afterward to realize these constitutional protec-tions in everyday law and life. Our country is a better and stronger America for this progress. We still have far to go.

The Bible and most major religions teach that God is no respecter of persons and that he sees all of us as his children, regardless of the color of our skin. Common religious principles include practicing kindness and respecting the feelings, rights, and property of others. The idea of "treating others as we would like to be treated" has been taught by religious leaders, Sunday school teachers, and parents since the beginning of time. The teachings of Christianity, Judaism, and most other major religions clearly condemn racial prejudice. Promotion of racial harmony is morally the right thing to do.[16]

If the morality of good race relations is not sufficient to motivate one, pragmatic necessity dictates that we confront and solve the racial dilemmas that we face. Statisticians predict that by 2050 America will have no majority population. In other words, we will all be in a minority. Unless racial differences can be resolved in a positive and constructive manner, our nation and children face an uncertain future.

World history and current global events are persuasive teachers in demonstrating the consequences of unresolved conflicts fueled by hatred and ill will of one cultural, religious, ethnic, or racial group directed toward another. One only has to look at the violence, death, and destruction that have occurred in Northern Ireland, the Middle East, Bosnia and Kosovo, Rwanda, and elsewhere to realize what unresolved racial and ethnic conflict can produce. We think it can't happen here. They thought it couldn't happen there either.

We must address racial reconciliation in a constructive and positive way, not in a divisive manner. It takes people of all races willing to leave their comfort zones and move into a biracial environment, often perceived to be hostile, where they may have little understanding to take on a problem difficult of solution. Racial reconciliation will not occur in the legislative halls or courtrooms of America but in the hearts and communities of blacks and whites, all Americans, as we come together in good will with an intentional, genuine, and meaningful commitment to better race relations.

One of the most logical places to start improving race relations is through our churches. People who share a common faith should have no problem in working together. People who share their faith experiences with one another should be able to discuss racial problems without rancor or bitterness.

As we come together to form unity among the races, we must reject those who would wish us not to succeed. Just as it was wrong for right-wing Southern politicians to use racial demagoguery during the 1950s and 1960s to gain and maintain political power, it is wrong in the twenty-first century for liberal northern politicians to use racial demagoguery to drive a wedge and divide our people to gain and maintain political advantage. Playing the race card is not just destructive to the political battle—in the case of this book, judicial confirmation—but it is destructive to our society by undermining racial reconciliation.

None of us can change the past. But we must recognize the reality, pain, and aftereffects of the past, or we will have difficulty moving into the future. The wounds of the past still have unhealed aspects today, and those present concerns cannot be relegated to history. All of us are affected by our culture and our past experiences, but obsession with the past and a failure to address current problems realistically will help no one. We must reconcile the past but focus on the future.

No one likes pain. No one likes to think about things that are depressing or disturbing. Slavery by its very institution was designed to crush the human spirit, to compel submission, and its consequences will not easily be overcome. Many whites hate to think about or acknowledge the terrible consequences of Jim Crow and slavery. When we do not challenge and help those descended from slavery do their best, we fail them, and we fail ourselves.

I am convinced that, regardless of color, we all want the same things out of life. We want to feel respected, valued as individuals, and to have equal opportunities to achieve our full potential. Each of us wants to feel good about who we are and take pride in the things we do. We all wish for a good education, a nice home, and above all, the best for our children. I believe these are universal desires. If that is true, and since our destinies are intertwined, we ought to be willing to put aside differences and work to make this possible in my state—all Mississippians—and in our country—all Americans.

We find ourselves in the frustrating position of seeking civility while responding to incivility and seeking reconciliation while responding to divisiveness. On the one hand, leaving false attacks unanswered and malicious lies unchallenged yields the field of debate and public discourse to those who would take us to the lowest form of speech. On the other hand, it becomes difficult to respond rationally, civilly, and politely to the ravings of shouting talking heads that make for good television but bad democracy and community. Our challenge then is a measured and appropriate response to incivility, a personal and community-based effort to promote civility, and a consistent and unwavering commitment to reconciliation.

Two instances from Mississippi's past demonstrate how this can be done. First, women at Columbus, Mississippi, marked the first anniversary of the Civil War by placing flowers on the graves, not only of Confederate soldiers, but Union soldiers as well. This was the start of Memorial Day.

And second, L. Q. C. Lamar, a Mississippian who served as secretary of the interior under President Grover Cleveland before the Civil War, became the first person from a Confederate state appointed to the Supreme Court after the Civil War—a tremendously symbolic event. How was Lamar able to gain Senate confirmation after fighting for the Confederacy and against the Union under General Robert E. Lee? Upon the death of Charles Sumner of Massachusetts, who was the North's staunchest abolitionist, Lamar, then in the Senate, rose to praise this nemesis of the South. He won respect of both North and South when he said, "My countrymen, know one another and you will love one another." We need again to find ways to be civil to those with whom we have tremendously large disagreements. Lamar did, and it helped bring a badly divided nation together, to move beyond the Civil War.

Restoring civility, respecting one another, and being decent to one another regardless of ideology, political party, and especially race, will go a long way in improving the judicial confirmation process, our government in general, and our own communities. This alone will not resolve the problems facing the judiciary—but in all reality if we succeed in civility and reconciliation, we will come close to solving the confirmation battle, and the benefits to our nation will be incredible. While we seek to change our interpersonal relationships, we must also seek a change in how the Senate handles judicial confirmations.

CHAPTER EIGHTEEN

End the Filibuster:
The Constitutional Option

DEMOCRATS LAUNCHED AN unprecedented filibuster of ten appellate judges with the threat to filibuster six more during 2003 and 2004, essentially requiring a super majority approval of nominees in contrast to the Constitution's requirement of a simple majority. In *Supreme Chaos*, I discuss in detail the history of the filibuster and its unprecedented and unconstitutional use as to judges. For continuity, I will share some of this information again.[1]

Neither the Framers of the Constitution nor the Senate "created" the filibuster. The filibuster may be "considered Congress's most famous procedural tool," but it is one with a disgraceful heritage as the means employed for nearly a century to defend Jim Crow laws and prevent the enactment of civil rights legislation.

The term "filibuster" originated in the Dutch word *vrijbuiter*, which means "looters and robbers." The English anglicized *vrijbuiter* into "freebooter," a term for "pirate." The Spanish translated it into *filibusteros* to describe pirates who looted the Spanish West Indies. Americans adopted the word in the mid-1800s as "a synonym for pro-Slavery mercenary pirates who would attack Latin America to try to spread the Slave system." Opponents of the procedure in Congress applied the term to "legislative minorities who used what the majority deemed piratical, disorderly, [and] lawless methods of obstructing business in the Senate."

From 1789 until 1806, the Senate maintained a rule allowing debate to be ended by majority vote. This rule was omitted in 1806 (perhaps because it had been invoked only once) thus creating the possibility of a filibuster ever since.

No senator engaged the procedural option for filibuster until the 1840s. In 1841, Senator John C. Calhoun of South Carolina originated the filibuster to defeat legislation he viewed as a threat to the rights of individual states and the institution of slavery. From 1841 until 1917, there was no way to end debate, no way to stop a filibuster, no way to invoke cloture. Even then, senators applied the filibuster only against legislative measures, not against judicial nominees.

On March 4, 1917, President Woodrow Wilson—exasperated by the filibuster's use to prevent Congress from doing the work of the country—declared, the "Senate of the United States is the only legislative body in the world which cannot act when its majority is ready for action. A little group of willful men, representing no opinion but their own, have rendered the great government of the United States helpless and contemptible."

For more than 200 years of American history, the Senate used the filibuster—for good or for ill—only to block legislation. The Senate never used the filibuster to block the confirmation of judicial nominees with majority support until 2002 during George Bush's first term. As described by Professor Steven Calabresi, "for the first time in 214 years of American history a minority of Senators is seeking to extend the tradition of filibustering from legislation to judicial nominees who [the minority of senators] know enjoy the support of a majority of the Senate. This is a change of constitutional dimensions and amounts to a kind of coup d'etat."

A non-partisan coalition called the Lawyers' Committee on Supreme Court Nominations—a group comprised of the deans of most major law schools and the past presidents of the American Bar Association—stated the impropriety of filibustering judicial nominees in 1968:

> If . . . nominations do not win the support of a majority of the Senate, they will fail. If they do win such support, they deserve the Senate's consent. Nothing would more poorly serve our constitutional system than for the nominations to have earned the approval of the Senate

majority but to be thwarted because the majority is denied a chance to
vote . . . .

Historian Joseph Harris noted the limited role of the Senate in the
confirmation process:

> . . . the debates of the Convention indicate that "advice and consent"
> was regarded simply as a vote of approval or rejection. The phrase was
> used as synonymous with "approbation," "concurrence," and
> "approval," and the power of the Senate was spoken of as a negative on
> the appointment by the President.

Prior to the administration of George W. Bush, Democrats
vehemently opposed denying judicial nominees an up or down vote
before the full Senate. Senator Patrick Leahy emphatically declared,

> I have stated over and over again on this floor that I would . . . object
> and fight against any filibuster on a judge, whether it is somebody I
> opposed or supported; that I felt the Senate should do its duty. . . .
> Those who delay or prevent the filling of these vacancies must under-
> stand that they are delaying or preventing the administration of
> justice. . . . A President should be given a great deal of latitude on who
> he nominates to the Federal court. If we disagree with a nomination,
> then we can vote against it. But, frankly, Mr. President, not only does
> it damage the integrity and the independence of the Federal judiciary
> by just holding judicial nominations hostage where nobody ever even
> votes on them, but I think it damages the integrity of the U.S. Senate.
> . . . Every Senator can vote against any nominee. Every Senator has
> that right. . . . They can vote against them in this committee and on
> the floor. But it's the responsibility of the U.S. Senate to at least bring
> them to a vote.

Unfortunately, when George W. Bush became president, the
Democrats changed their tune with no explanation, no apology, no
shame. It was as if they never addressed the issue. They took action in
direct contravention of what they had advocated.

Not only was the filibuster of judicial nominees with majority support without precedent, it was unconstitutional. The Constitution clearly provides federal judges shall be confirmed by majority vote.

Our Founding Fathers were the most able group of people ever assembled to draft a governing document for any nation at any time in history. Article II, Section 2 of the Constitution provides the president shall have the power

> by and with the Advice and Consent of the Senate to make Treaties, provided two-thirds of the Senators present concur; and shall nominate, and by and with the Advice and Consent of the Senate shall appoint . . . Judges to the supreme Court, and all other Officers of the United States, whose Appointments are not herein otherwise provided for . . . .

The Constitution spells out that treaties must be ratified by a two-thirds vote of the Senate. The next clause in the Constitution provides judges of the Supreme Court shall be nominated by the president and appointed by the president with the "Advice and Consent" of the Senate. There is no requirement of a super majority vote for judges. Our Founders knew what they were doing. They knew how to require a super majority vote, and they did in several instances. The Constitution specifically requires a super majority vote for impeachment conviction (Article I, Section 3), expulsion of a member (Article I, Section 5), overriding a veto (Article I, Section 7), approving treaties (Article II, Section 2), proposing a constitutional amendment (Article V), and removing certain disqualifications to public service (Amendment XIV, Section 3), but not for judges. Just as it would be unconstitutional for the Senate to adopt a rule that requires unanimous approval for a treaty—while the Constitution states it is a two-thirds vote—so it is unconstitutional for the Senate, by rules of debate, to prevent majority confirmation of judicial nominees.

Republicans became so frustrated in 2005—after ten nominees had been filibustered and other nominees threatened with filibuster—that they threatened to invoke the "Constitutional Option," to obtain a parliamentary ruling that the Constitution only requires a majority vote for confirmation of judges. Some referred to this as the "nuclear option" because Democrats threatened to cause nuclear fusion, a meltdown in the Senate, if the Republicans insisted the Constitution be followed. Following the Constitution should not be controversial or cause for disruption of the Senate.

To implement this procedure, a Republican senator would, following the filibuster of a nominee, make the point of order that such action is unconstitutional. The presiding officer would submit that point of order to the Senate for a decision, but would rule the point is not debatable (otherwise, a filibuster on the point of order could occur). At this point, a Democratic senator could appeal the ruling that the motion is not debatable. A Republican would move to table or indefinitely suspend the Democratic appeal. By approving the motion to table (under Senate rules only a simple majority is necessary to table, and it is not debatable), the Senate would sustain the ruling that the original Republican point of order is not debatable. Then a simple majority of the Senate could decide that the filibuster against judicial nominees is unconstitutional.

This procedure was never invoked or implemented. The Senate avoided the Constitutional Option when seven Democrats and seven Republicans, dubbed "The Gang of Fourteen," entered into an agreement that allowed most of Bush's most controversial nominees to receive an up or down vote before the full Senate without a filibuster. The seven Democrats in the group agreed they would not filibuster any judicial nominees absent "extraordinary circumstances." Without a filibuster, the seven Republicans agreed not to support the Constitutional Option. This meant that most of George Bush's appellate nominees would be confirmed. It also assured that Chief Justice John Roberts and Justice Sam Alito would be confirmed. But the underlying problem was left hanging by this subjective and temporary agreement; the Gang of Fourteen memo relies on each signatory's own understanding and interpretation of "extraordinary circumstances," and it expires in January 2007.[2]

There is ample precedent for utilizing the constitutional option. Four times when he served as Senate majority leader, Senator Byrd used a simple majority to change Senate procedures apart from altering the standing rules: (1) ending post-cloture filibusters (1977); (2) limiting amendments to appropriations bills (1979); (3) governing consideration of nominations (1980); and (4) governing voting procedures (1987). Two of these overturned standing precedents and two reinterpreted the language of an existing standing rule.

Democrats dispute that these occasions serve as precedent for the constitutional option, but each of these changes was made by a point of order and sustained with a simple majority vote. The constitutional option would follow this exact process.

In 1975, Democratic senator Ted Kennedy also argued the case for majority rule in the Senate:

> [The filibuster] is a rule that was made by the Senate, and it is a rule that can be unmade by the Senate. . . . Mr. President, the immediate issue is whether a simple majority of the Senate is entitled to change the Senate rules. Although the procedural rules are complex, it is clear that this question should be settled by a majority vote.

Some conservatives caution Republicans not to invoke the constitutional option. They say in the future, conservatives might want to filibuster a judge. It is wrong for conservatives to advocate following the Constitution when it serves their purposes but disregard the Constitution when it conflicts with their goals. The Constitution provides for confirmation by a majority vote, not a super majority vote. The Constitution should be interpreted as written, regardless of whether we favor the outcome as a matter of public policy.

It is not necessary to filibuster judges who are truly out of the mainstream. History shows us the Senate can discuss, vet, and even defeat contentious Supreme Court nominees without the need of a filibuster. In fact, the Senate has defeated twelve Supreme Court nominees by majority vote without filibuster. Certainly if we can resolve the Supreme Court nominations without filibusters, we can do the same for appellate nominees.

The Democrats resorted to the filibuster because the Bush nominees were not the extremists the left wing labeled them. Bush's nominees enjoyed mainstream and majority support, so the only way Democrats could block them was to employ the filibuster—a tool of the minority to thwart the majority. In fact, the Gang of Fourteen's agreement that preserved the filibuster for "extraordinary circumstances" specifically agreed not to filibuster three of President Bush's most controversial nominees—admitting the nominees were not extraordinary nor out of the mainstream.

From 1960 until 2003, the Senate fought over contentious and high-profile Supreme Court nominees and even some court of appeals nominees. But the Senate never denied confirmation by filibuster of any nominee to the federal courts with majority support during this period or at any time in history. In the past, whenever the escalation reached the point of filibuster, senators backed off to maintain the tradition and comity of the Senate. Cases in point were the nominations of Richard Paez and Marsha Berzon, two very liberal Clinton nominees to the Ninth Circuit. When there was a conservative attempt to filibuster these two nominees, the Republican leadership under Trent Lott refused. Lott told the Associated Press, "My feeling is that we should not start filibustering these nominations." He joined Democratic Minority Leader Tom Daschle and filed for cloture before the filibuster attempt could get off the ground. When it came to President Bush's nominees, history changed and the Senate changed with it.

In the event another judicial nominee faces obstruction on the Senate floor, consistent with the Constitution, a statesman senator should invoke the Constitutional Option and end the filibuster. However, implementing the Constitutional Option is neither a comprehensive nor a permanent solution. To protect the judiciary and prevent irreparable harm, we must devise a permanent solution.

Procedure for Confirmation

WE CANNOT FIND a permanent workable solution to the problems facing the confirmation of federal judges unless we understand and appreciate the causes of the conflict. A three-part collision—procedural, political, and cultural—caused the current battle over judicial confirmations: (1) There is no detailed binding and controlling process for the confirmation of federal judges; (2) Democrats are retaliating against Republicans for not confirming some of President Bill Clinton's judicial nominees; and (3) The liberal philosophy of a "living Constitution" transfers the hot-button social issues from the legislative forum to the judicial arena.

This chapter will address the first two causes. I must confess I was amazed to learn neither the Constitution, nor statute, nor Senate rule has established a controlling procedure for confirming federal judges. With no defined process, fairness is in the eye of the beholder. With no outside restraints, human nature encourages escalation, leading to retaliation, ad infinitum.

Most agree that President Ronald Reagan's nomination of Judge Robert Bork to the U.S. Supreme Court in 1987 marked the turning point in the politicization of the judicial confirmation process and a triumph for unrestrained partisan attack on a nominee. Bork, a conservative nominee with ties to Republican administrations since President Richard Nixon, became the first trophy of groups like People for the American Way, who lambasted him with such ferocity his name became a term synonymous with mistreatment of an individual in the nomination process. Today nominees are said to be "borked" when so attacked.

But Judge Bork was not filibustered; the Senate rejected him on an up or down vote.

A few years later, in 1991, President George H. W. Bush nominated Clarence Thomas to the Supreme Court. The special-interest groups, emboldened by their success with Bork, lashed out again, and Senate Democrats paraded indecent charges, allegations, and innuendo against Thomas, who called the fiasco a "high tech lynching." Justice Thomas was not filibustered; the Senate confirmed him on an up or down vote.

When President Bill Clinton nominated Ruth Bader Ginsberg and Stephen Breyer to the Supreme Court, Republicans and conservatives did not respond in kind to the treatment of Bork and Thomas. Ginsberg was as liberal as Bork and Thomas were conservative—if not more so. And Breyer's liberalism trailed not far behind. Yet the Senate confirmed Ginsberg 96 to 3 and confirmed Breyer 87 to 9. Republicans did not engage in the bruising confirmation tactics Democrats employed during the previous Bush and Reagan administrations. Conservative groups criticized Republican senators for rolling over and not opposing Ginsberg and Breyer as liberal Democrats and Far Left groups had opposed Bork and Thomas.

But Republicans did take aim at Clinton's lower court nominees. They blocked eighteen Clinton appellate nominees in committee by refusing them a hearing. These nominees were not attacked and did not become high profile like those Bush would choose; nevertheless, they too were denied confirmation and prevented from serving on the judiciary. Further, Republicans obstructed these nominees during the last two years of the second Clinton administration, which allowed the vacancies to carry over into the new George W. Bush administration.

However, Republicans did not take this obstruction outside the committee, and the Senate Judiciary Committee, under Republican leadership, sent two of Clinton's most controversial nominees—Richard Paez and Marsha Berzon—to the full Senate for a vote. As mentioned, when conservatives considered a filibuster on these two nominees, more than twenty Republicans who opposed the nominations and voted against them nonetheless joined with Senators Trent Lott and Tom Daschle to vote for cloture to prevent a filibuster and allow these nominees an up or down vote. Senate Republican leadership refused to support filibusters against judicial nominees during the Clinton administration.

When President George W. Bush began his first term, the Democrats sought payback. First, many of the more partisan and liberal Democrats viewed Bush as illegitimate. Still furious over the Supreme Court's decision in *Bush v. Gore*, these Democrats were bitter that now President Bush would fill the judicial appellate vacancies blocked by Republicans during the Clinton administration.

President Bush did make an overture to Democrats by re-nominating Roger Gregory. President Clinton had given Gregory—the first African American to serve on the Fourth Circuit Court of Appeals—a recess appointment, but his appointment expired before Bush came into office. President Bush re-nominated Gregory and the Senate confirmed him. But Democrats ignored the gesture.

When Democrats took control of the Senate Judiciary Committee, they responded to the Republicans' blocking of Clinton nominees and systematically blocked nominees opposed by the liberal special-interest groups. Democrats and their special-interest groups made blocking of the Bush nominees high profile, and they escalated the battle by making the fight personal and mean spirited. Following the 2002 election, Republicans retook control of the Senate. No longer able to block nominees in the committee, Democrats now took their fight and frustration to the full Senate.

Smarting from their losses in 2002—a net decrease of two seats as well as loss of Senate control—the Democrats grew in outrage when several nominees they thought they had killed in committee reemerged. President Bush re-nominated me, Priscilla Owen, and other blocked nominees in early 2003. Republicans on the committee reported us to the full Senate.

Democrats made an agreement with the liberal special-interest groups that unless at least one Democrat joined the Republicans in committee to support a "controversial" nominee, then they would block the nominee on the floor. The downward spiral of civility and comity in the Senate continued and the battle escalated to a new high—the never before used filibuster of judicial nominees who enjoyed majority support. The tenor of the fight had never before been so highly partisan, strident, and personal for lower court judges.

Democrats in the Senate utilized what they thought was the ultimate weapon to block nominees—the filibuster. The filibuster communicated to President Bush: we will not even consider these nominees. President Bush responded with his ultimate weapon to install nominees—the recess appointment. In January 2004, he used the constitutional powers of the executive to appoint me to the Fifth Circuit Court of Appeals by recess appointment. The following month, he repeated the action with William Pryor to the Eleventh Circuit. While not lifetime appointments, these recess appointments did not require Senate approval; in fact, the Senate has no input whatsoever on such an appointment.

Some Republicans called for an even stronger response. They urged the administration to escalate the battle another notch and declare that every nominee deserved an up or down vote on the Senate floor, and any nominee filibustered would immediately, at the next possible opportunity, receive a recess appointment. Of course, the Democrats would respond in kind and almost certainly never confirm those nominees, and we would have a judiciary of temporary, transient, and unsure judges. Further escalation is not the answer; instead, we should look to fairness, reasonableness, and procedure.

As mentioned, the powder keg of judicial politics received a temporary reprieve in May 2005 with the "Gang of Fourteen" compromise. This compromise—closer to a ceasefire than a peace treaty in the confirmation war—provided a temporary solution to some of the symptoms. It halted the filibuster, but the agreement did not even touch the root cause, nor did it provide any correction beyond 2006.

This review of the escalation of the fight over judicial nominees demonstrates the consequences of the lack of established and controlling rules for the confirmation of federal judges. One of my law partners, Brad Clanton, and I wrote "A Proposal: Codification by Statute of the Judicial Confirmation Process," published in the *William & Mary Bill of Rights Journal*.[1] This piece elaborates on how judges are now confirmed, the lack of established procedures, and accurately details my concerns and recommended solutions. I will be sharing some of that material in the following paragraphs.

Judges are now confirmed based on senatorial courtesies, historical precedents of the Senate, and sometimes the whims of those in power at the time. All chairs of the Judiciary Committee since the 1960s have interpreted these precedents and courtesies somewhat differently, allowing each side to claim unfair treatment by the opposite party.

These traditions and precedents empower a small group of senators (or even an individual senator) to delay interminably the confirmation of judicial nominees. One of the oldest of these precedents is known as "senatorial courtesy," which allows a senator from the home state of a nominee to block a nomination to an office in that state. Although senatorial courtesy has generally been granted to senators of the president's party, senators from the opposition party have also successfully blocked nominations on numerous occasions.

Similar to senatorial courtesy, the "blue slip" is a tradition whereby the chairman of the Senate Judiciary Committee sends a blue slip to a judicial nominee's home state senators seeking their position on the nominee. Whether or not a home state senator's disapproval kills the nomination has depended on who was chairman of the Judiciary Committee at the time. For example, Mississippi senator James O. Eastland, judiciary chairman from 1956 to 1978, refused to allow a nomination to proceed without approval from both home state senators. During segregation in the South, this allowed Eastland to ensure his Southern Democratic colleagues would only have federal judges they approved—with race and civil rights often being the defining issue.[2] Other chairmen have given negative blue slips strong consideration but did not always allow a negative blue slip to defeat a nomination.

A third device used by senators to delay or block judicial nominees is the "hold," which allows an individual senator to hold indefinitely and prevent consideration of a nominee or legislation for any reason at all. Some suggest this power developed to allow senators to prevent a matter from being decided in their absence. But today it is employed to block

nominees and as a negotiation tactic with other senators or the administration to advance an often unrelated issue.

Senators and the press refer to another Senate tradition as the
"Thurmond Rule." Senator Patrick Leahy in summer 2004 took the
position that no more judges would be confirmed that year, based on the
Thurmond Rule. *The Hill*, a Capitol Hill newspaper that follows action
in Congress, reported,

> A true definition of the Thurmond Rule is almost impossible to ascer-
> tain. The Senate parliamentarian's office doesn't keep track of
> committee rules, and Judiciary Committee precedents have been
> subject to multiple interpretations and applications, depending on
> who was chairman over the years. . . . Even some of the most skillful
> senators aren't quite sure whether the Thurmond Rule is really a rule
> at all. Some call it a "precedent." Others term it a "general understand-
> ing." Some have never even heard of it. . . . The rule, according to one
> senior Democratic senator . . . is as follows: "In election years, judges
> are not normally brought up after July first." . . . Even some individual
> interpretations of the Thurmond Rule have changed over time. In
> 1997, Leahy said on the Senate floor that the "so-called" Thurmond
> rule kicks in "about the last few months of [the president's] term in
> office." . . . In October of 2000, Leahy said the rule "cuts off judicial
> nominations after about midyear."[3]

Senator Dick Durbin referred to the Thurmond Rule as "legend and
lore."[4]

Not only have different committee chairmen interpreted this precedent differently, but the current judiciary chairman, Senator Leahy, has
interpreted this precedent differently depending who is in the White
House. On July 12, 2000, near the end of the Clinton administration,
Leahy said on the floor, "We cannot afford to follow the Thurmond
Rule and stop acting on these nominees now in anticipation of the presidential election in November."[5] In 2007, with George Bush in the
White House, Leahy announced "he would observe the 'Thurmond
rule,'" understanding that meant "no judicial nominations will be

considered in the latter part of a presidential election year without the consent of both sides."[6]

Confirming judges without a detailed and controlling process according to "legend and lore" is like administering justice with no fixed rule of law, no written constitution. For the integrity of the Senate, respect of the nominees, and the quality and independence of the judiciary, we badly need comprehensive confirmation reform. I suggest a statute codifying the procedure for the confirmation of federal judges. Such a statute should include specified times within which a nominee would receive a respectful hearing before the Senate Judiciary Committee, a vote in committee, and a debate and a vote on the Senate floor. The statute should also include procedures to extend the deadlines in extraordinary circumstances for reasonable but limited periods of time.

I believe the Constitution authorizes Congress statutorily to codify the procedure for confirming federal judges; Congress should exercise that authority. Article II, Section 2 of the Constitution provides that the president "shall nominate, and by and with the Advice and Consent of the Senate, shall appoint . . . Judges of the Supreme Court, and all other Officers of the United States, whose Appointments are not herein otherwise provided for, and which shall be established by Law."

Although this provision obviously requires the Senate to confirm appointees to the U.S. Supreme Court, it does not specify how the Senate is to carry out that responsibility. While the Constitution gives the Senate and the House the authority to adopt rules to govern proceedings in each body, there is no impediment to the Senate choosing to adopt such a procedure by statute, consistent with the Constitution.

The Constitution established the Supreme Court. But Congress—not the Constitution—created the federal district courts and courts of appeals. These courts were established pursuant to Article III, Section 1 of the Constitution, which vests the judicial power "in one supreme Court, and in such inferior Courts as the Congress may from time to time ordain and establish." Furthermore, Article II, Section 2 of the Constitution authorizes Congress to vest the appointment of "inferior

Officers . . . in the President alone, in the Courts of Law, or in the Heads of Departments." Accordingly, under the Constitution, judges appointed by the president to these "inferior" courts could theoretically be appointed without confirmation. However, because lower federal court judges are given lifetime appointments, it is certainly wise policy for the Senate to exercise advice and consent with respect to these nominees. Yet, if Congress has the authority, under the Constitution, to create the lower federal courts and to vest the appointment of these judges in the "President alone," or in the "Courts of law," it logically follows that Congress has the authority to specify the procedures whereby the Senate is to confirm (or not confirm) nominees to these judgeships.

Legislation regulating the process of judicial confirmation has been introduced (albeit unsuccessfully) numerous times in the past. In 1998, Senator Dick Durbin offered an amendment to S. 2176, which provided that after any nomination had been pending for 150 days, the nominee would be deemed discharged from the committee and reported favorably to the Senate. Durbin also proposed an amendment requiring a vote in the Senate within five calendar days following the 150th day the nomination was pending. During that same Congress, Senator Patrick Leahy introduced S. 1906, the Judicial Emergency Responsibility Act of 1998. That legislation would have prohibited the Senate from recessing during any session for more than nine days when a judicial nomination had been pending for more than sixty days in a circuit in which a judicial emergency had been declared.

In 1991, Senators Bob Graham and Connie Mack introduced S. 910, the Judicial Nomination and Confirmation Reform Act. That legislation would have required the Senate Judiciary Committee to review and report on a judicial nominee no later than ninety days after receiving the nomination. Failing to do so, the nomination would be discharged automatically from committee without recommendation for a full vote in the Senate. The legislation further required a full Senate vote within thirty days after receiving the nomination from committee.

I recommend legislation to accomplish the following. First, the Senate Judiciary Committee should hold hearings on a judicial nominee within 120 days after the president submits the name to the Senate. Second, within thirty days of any such hearings (no more than 150 days after the nomination is received), a nomination should be reported out of the Senate Judiciary Committee: with a favorable recommendation, an unfavorable recommendation, or no recommendation at all. If the Senate Judiciary Committee fails to report the nomination, it would be automatically discharged from committee without recommendation. Third, within sixty days after receiving the nomination from committee (no more than 210 days after the nomination is received), the full Senate should hold an up or down vote; any judicial nominee receiving majority support would be confirmed.

As a pragmatic consideration, this established and clearly defined process for confirming judges should become effective at the beginning of the next presidential administration following its adoption. That way neither Democrats nor Republicans will know which party will immediately benefit by establishing the procedure. This should make it easier to pass such a measure. In the long run, both parties, the Senate, the judiciary, and the American people will all benefit.

All those involved will benefit from a statutory solution. First, statutory procedures will provide stability and predictability in the confirmation process, ensuring all presidents—regardless of party affiliation—that their nominees will be treated the same as nominees of the other party. Second, statutory procedures will provide senators and prospective nominees with clear and predictable rules for the confirmation process. Nominees will know that, regardless of which party is in control of the Senate, within a specified time they will either be confirmed or rejected. In any event, the nominees will be allowed to move on with their lives. Third, codifying the rules for the confirmation process will stop the endless cycle of retaliation in the Senate when control of the Senate changes hands or when different parties control the Senate and the presidency. Statutory procedures will provide both parties with a fresh start in confirming judges, leaving behind actual or perceived mistreatment of past nominees.

Codifying the procedures for confirmation of judges will not cure all the ills caused by the politicization of the judicial selection process. It will at least bring stability, predictability, and order to a chaotic and almost intolerable process.

I recognize this proposal would diminish the power of an individual senator or a minority of senators. But some senators have abused traditions and precedents, resulting in the current judicial confirmation chaos that threatens the quality, integrity, independence, and diversity of the federal judiciary. The conflict also undermines the collegiality of the Senate and weakens the ability of the Senate to fulfill its responsibilities. A problem of this magnitude resulting from the previous abuse of power demands a solution and justifies some concession of power.

I believe a statutory solution is preferable to a permanent Senate rule; it gives more credibility and stability to the process, and there are numerous precedents for codifying legislative process.[7] For those who are reluctant to establish procedures by statute rather than a Senate rule, then a permanent Senate rule would be far preferable to no solution at all.

This statutory proposal will cure some of the procedural problems and reduce retaliation. Such a statute will provide consistency, continuity, and stability to the confirmation process. In addition to addressing the procedural quicksand, we must address the root cause of the confirmation catastrophe: the politicization of the judiciary. As long as the "living Constitution" is part of the judicial landscape, we will continue to have battles over judicial confirmations.

Protect the Amendment Process

THE PREVIOUSLY DISCUSSED solutions to the confirmation struggle—civility, Constitutional Option, corrective procedural statute—treat the symptoms, not the primary cancer jeopardizing not only the confirmation process, but the entire judiciary as well, the "living Constitution" that has transformed the judiciary into a political branch of government. Some federal judges overreach their authority and abuse the doctrine of judicial supremacy to impose their own political and social values onto society without respect to the rule of law. This creates a supreme government of judges, more powerful than the executive branch or legislative branch, chosen only indirectly by the people and not authorized by the Constitution to exercise such unfettered power. Thus, judicial confirmation effectively becomes an election for the ultimate power in government, and the campaign in this election plays out in the Senate in response to White House nominations.

How did we get to this point? Liberals and many Democrats decided that what they could not win at the ballot box they could achieve through the courts. About two months before my first hearing—when I first discovered that my nomination was somehow controversial—Joseph Califano wrote a guest opinion column in the *Washington Post* titled "Yes, Litmus-Test Judges." Califano, who served as assistant for domestic affairs to President Lyndon Johnson and as secretary of health, education, and welfare to President Jimmy Carter, presents the liberal argument for politicizing the judiciary:

In considering presidential nominees for district and appellate judgeships, professional qualification alone should no longer be considered
a ticket to a seat on the bench. For years partisan gridlock and political pandering for campaign dollars have led to failures of the Congress
and White House, whether Democratic or Republican, to legislate
and execute laws on a variety of matters of urgent concern to our
citizens. As a result, the federal courts have become increasingly
powerful architects of public policy, and those who seek such power
must be judged in the spotlight of that reality. . . . What's new is the
growing role of federal courts in crafting national policies once considered the exclusive preserve of the legislature and executive. As gridlock
and big money have stymied the House and Senate and shaped the
way laws are executed, concerned citizens have gone to court with
petitions they once would have taken to legislators and executive
appointees. As the federal courts have moved to fill the public policy
vacuum, conservatives, liberals and a host of special interests have
developed a sharp eye for those nominated to sit on the bench. So
should the Senate. . . . Environmentalists, prison reformers and
consumer advocates have learned that what can't be won in the legislature or executive may be achievable in a federal district court where a
sympathetic judge sits. . . . Who sits in federal district and appellate
courts is more important than the struggle over the budget, the level
of defense spending, second guessing the tax bill and whose fingers are
poised to dip into the Social Security and Medicare cookie jars. . . .
Both sides know that many of the individuals who fill these seats will
have more power over tobacco policy, prison reform, control of
HMOs, the death penalty, abortion, environmental issues, the constitutionality of redistricting for House elections, gun control and the
rights of women and minorities than the president or congressional
leaders, and for a longer period of time. . . . That's why professional
qualifications should be only the threshold step in the climb of
judicial nominees to Senate confirmation . . . . the Senate must take
enough time to give these men and women the kind of searching
review their sweeping power to make national policies deserves.[1]

This guest editorial is a clear acknowledgment that the Court is now
making policy decisions that our Constitution vests entirely in either the
legislative or executive branches. Reacting to Califano's article, Roger

Pilon with the CATO Institute wrote that for many Democrats the Supreme Court is now "something akin to another legislative branch." He points out that the Democrats are looking not for a "judge applying the law, but a 'sympathetic judge.' That's politics, not law." I agree with Pilon that we need justices who know "the difference between politics and law—and respect it."[2]

Consistent with the desire of liberal Democrats that judges should make political policy decisions and create new rights, there has evolved over the years a theory of interpreting the Constitution as a document that changes meaning over time, referred to by those who support or utilize this theory as a "living Constitution." They reject the notion we are a government of laws, not of men; they reject the notion that the Constitution means what it says and says what it means; and they reject the notion that our Constitution is a contract between the government and its people. What they have created is a mystery Constitution, the meaning of which is unknown to average citizens and can only be revealed by a majority of the Supreme Court.

Liberals who want the court to "create rights," who seek "sympathetic judges," find allies with judges committed to interpreting the Constitution as a changing, evolving, "living," "mystery" document. Judges who utilize this method of interpreting exercise their "independent judgment" to determine the "sense of decency" of a modern evolving society. Unable to justify their decisions with the text or original understanding of the Constitution as ratified, they look to whatever trend in state law—or even foreign law—currently comports with their "in vogue" political view. These judges look to Sweden or to France or Zimbabwe and "interpret" our laws according to foreign decisions. Most Americans do not want to be governed by the laws of Europe or any other continent; they want to be governed by the rule of law as established by duly elected representatives in America. That was the foundational reason for the American Revolution: to be governed by the rule of law as established by "We the People" and not laws adopted across the ocean. The battle cry was "no taxation without representation." Today the battle cry should be "no legislation except by elected representation." Let the people, not judges, change the Constitution.

Interpreting the Constitution as a living, changing, mystery document transferring the social and domestic policy disagreements of our nation to the judiciary has created one of the major fronts in the culture war: the judicial confirmation battle. Culture warriors like People for the American Way, the Alliance for Justice, the National Organization for Women, NARAL Pro Choice America, and others brought this fight to judicial confirmation. These culture warriors seek to promote judges who will provide victories in a court of law when they lose in the court of public opinion at the ballot box. They seek to defeat judges who practice restraint imposed by respect for the rule of law. Interpreting the Constitution as parchment that changes meaning over time creates a battle in judicial confirmations for the future of our laws in a branch of government never intended to be politicized. This produces a judge with the power to rule decisively on issues deeply dividing Americans without the compromise and consensus necessary in legislative deliberations.

Interpreting the Constitution as a changing document contradicts the truest meaning of "the rule of law." The rule of law requires first that the law be clearly understood and second that those bound by the law know in advance what the law requires so they will know what is expected of them.[3] The concept of an evolving Constitution violates both these fundamental principles.

A changing Constitution provides neither understanding nor advance knowledge of what is required. An evolving Constitution does not provide clarity. You cannot have clarity about that which is unknown. Since the law can be created or changed by five members of the Supreme Court, the American people and their elected representatives cannot know what the law requires of them in advance. If the Constitution can be changed by litigation, the litigants are given no advance notice of what the Constitution compels. A mystery Constitution does not conform to the rule of law and provides little assurance of consistency—no more than that of a king or dictator.

Interpreting the Constitution as a changing, political document is contrary to the leading case relied upon as the basis for judicial supremacy, the power of the Supreme Court to be the final arbiter of constitutional law. In 1803, the case of *Marbury v. Madison* established the doctrine of judicial supremacy.[4] Speaking for the Court, Chief Justice John Marshall wrote, "[i]t is emphatically the province and duty of the judicial department to say what the law is," thus providing that between the three branches of government, the Supreme Court would determine when either of the other two branches exceeded their constitutional authority. But the *Marbury* Court ruled neither that the judiciary had power to change the Constitution, nor that the Court had the power to create law. To the contrary, the Court ruled the judiciary— just as the executive and legislative branches of government—was bound by the Constitution. Therefore, if the Supreme Court is going to apply *Marbury* for the principle of judicial supremacy, it should also follow the rest of the *Marbury* decision.

In *Marbury*, the Supreme Court exercised considerable judicial restraint not to exercise power it did not have. The Court also expressed great respect, deference, and appreciation for the Constitution as a written and permanent document. In *Marbury*, the Court had before it an act of Congress that gave the Supreme Court original jurisdiction in instances not specifically mentioned in the Constitution. Since the Constitution gave the Supreme Court original jurisdiction as to certain cases, did that negate original jurisdiction for the Supreme Court in all other situations, including the ones then authorized by Congress?

The Court reasoned "it cannot be presumed that any clause in the constitution is intended to be without effect . . . ." The Court concluded, "affirmative words are often, in their operation, negative of other objects than those affirmed; and in this case, a negative or exclusive sense must be given to them or they have no operation at all." The Court then held that Congress overstepped its authority in granting the Supreme Court original jurisdiction over other areas not designated by the Constitution.

Writing for the Court, Justice Marshall recognized as a "well established" principle "the people have an original right to establish for their future government, such principles as, in their opinion, shall most conduce to their own happiness" and that this was "the basis on which the whole American fabric has been erected. The exercise of this original right [adopting the Constitution] is a very great exertion; . . . The principles, therefore, so established, are deemed fundamental." Marshall further found that since these principals were derived from the supreme authority—the people—"they are designed to be permanent." Marshall found the Constitution to be permanent, not an evolving document.

He extolled the Constitution as "a superior, paramount law, unchangeable by ordinary means," saying that if the Constitution "is alterable when the legislature shall please to alter it . . . then written constitutions are absurd attempts, on the part of the people, to limit a power, in its own nature illimitable. Certainly all those who have framed written constitutions contemplate them as forming the fundamental and paramount law of the nation" and it is "to be considered by this court" as such.

Marshall expressed the view that those "who controvert the principle that the constitution is to be considered, in court, as a paramount law . . . would subvert the very foundation of all written constitutions" and reduce "to nothing what we have deemed the greatest improvement on political institutions—a written constitution." Marshall continued,

> . . . it is apparent that the framers of the constitution contemplated that instrument, as a rule for the government of *courts* as well as of the legislature. Why otherwise does it direct the Judges to take an oath to support it? . . . How immoral to impose it on them, if they were to be used as the instruments . . . for violating what they swear to support? . . . Why does a Judge swear to discharge his duties agreeably to the constitution of the United States, if that constitution forms no rules for his government? . . . *[C]ourts*, as well as other departments, are bound by that instrument [the Constitution]." (emphasis in original)

Marshall clearly recognized the Supreme Court is bound by the Constitution.

He noted that "in such a case as this" some might view the Court's action, at first impression, "without much reflection" as an "attempt to . . . intermeddle with the prerogatives of the executive . . . an extravagance so absurd and excessive, [it] could not have been entertained for a moment." Marshall emphatically stated his respect for the separation of powers. He further stated the Court would not consider questions "which are, by the constitution and laws, submitted to the executive."

Marshall in clear language wrote "questions, in their nature political . . . can never be made in this Court." Marshall specifically proclaimed and enunciated the principle the Supreme Court should not, and could not, address political issues or enter the political arena. Yet, that is exactly what some members of the Court are doing today, making political decisions, value decisions, the "sense of decency" not only of the U.S. but also of the world, and imposing those views on all Americans. In such cases, a majority of the Court seizes upon the *Marbury* pronouncement of judicial supremacy, while ignoring its declaration that the Constitution is a permanent written document, ignoring its pronouncement that the Court is not to enter the realm of politics, disregarding its proclamation of the separation of powers doctrine, and leaving the system of checks and balances carefully crafted by our Founders in shambles.

The Court, in traveling out of its judicial role, voyages over into the spheres of responsibility given by the Constitution to the legislative and executive branches. The Court legislates by changing the Constitution, adjudicates on the change the Court itself has made, and then requires obedience to its fiat, thus intruding into the executive responsibilities. Our Founders never intended one branch of government to exercise judicial, executive, and legislative powers.

Over the years, judicial supremacy to interpret the Constitution has been accepted almost without question. But only during the last half century has the Court openly, plainly, and on a wide-scale basis declared that it also has the power to change, add to, or alter the Constitution when a majority of its members exercise their "independent judgment" to determine that the Constitution no longer comports with their determination of the "sense of decency" of an evolving world.

Under this power, five judges now claim for themselves the right to do something even the American people themselves cannot do by majority vote, or by super majority vote. Congress alone cannot change our written Constitution, not by majority vote, not by super majority vote, or even by unanimous consent. No president—not George Washington,

Abraham Lincoln, Franklin Roosevelt, John Kennedy, or Ronald Reagan—could alter the Constitution. Nevertheless, some judges now assume for themselves power that neither Congress, the elected representatives of the people, the people themselves, the president, nor anyone else can exercise.

At the start of the American Revolution, the Continental Congress declared our independence from Great Britain, boldly proclaiming the only "just powers" that can be exercised by government are derived from the "consent of the governed." While the Declaration of Independence is not a part of the Constitution, it does give reference as to how the founding generation viewed the power of government. When the Supreme Court makes a decision that goes beyond the scope of the Constitution, it does so without the consent of the governed. The "governed" have only consented that their Constitution be changed by the amendment process. The violation of this rule of law—the restraint of our government by our Constitution, a blurring of the checks and balances of our separate but equal branches—has politicized the judiciary, created a constitutional crisis, and brought on confirmation chaos.

Let me share a real-life experience that makes several points. In 1982, Chip was playing football at Mississippi College. Margaret Ann and I drove down to New Orleans to watch Chip and his team play against Tulane. The sun shown brightly in our faces, and Margaret Ann developed a severe headache. When we started to return home, Margaret Ann told me she did not feel well, and she got into the backseat of the car and lay down, the only time in our marriage I can remember this happening. As we crossed the Pontchartrain Bridge on our return home, I tried to engage her in conversation. She reiterated she was sick and did not feel like talking. When I reached the Mississippi hospitality station at the Mississippi/Louisiana line, I stopped to go to the restroom. While I was inside, she woke up and decided to go to the restroom.

I came back and, assuming she was still asleep in the backseat, got in the car and drove home, an hour and forty-five minutes away. As I drove across the parking lot into our backyard and carport, I noticed the station wagon was not under the carport. I said, "Sweetheart, do you feel like going back to the office to get the car?" No answer. With more emphasis, I said, "Margaret Ann, wake up; we're home." Still no answer. As I was driving under the carport, I reached back and felt on the backseat. She was not there. I felt on the floorboard and she was not there either. I was flabbergasted. I got out of the car and walked up to the back door to read a note that our middle daughter Allison had written, "Daddy, you left mother at the Louisiana rest station." I walked into the house and the phone rang; it was Margaret Ann. She told me she was inside the rest stop, had a place on a sofa and could sleep for the night—I could arrange to get her the next morning. My response was, "I'm not about to do that." It did not take me as long to go back as it had taken me to come home.

At my swearing in ceremony as a district judge, Charles Clark, the then chief judge of the Fifth Circuit encouraged Margaret Ann to have me carry out the garbage for the sake of humility. While I was on the bench, Margaret Ann, likewise, insisted that from time to time I tell the story of leaving her at the Mississippi/Louisiana line, also for the sake of humility. I had a different motive for telling the story. I thought it demonstrated how well I did forty-seven years ago when I selected my life mate. Leaving Margaret Ann at the rest area happened twenty-four years ago, and we're still married. It also makes two other points that are more pertinent to this book. First, it demonstrates that judges are just like other people—they make mistakes and face the problems of everyday life. Second, individuals frequently get off on the wrong track or at the wrong station in life. When this happens, it can be disastrous for that individual, for family, and sometimes for others who encounter that individual. I saw it often as a trial judge. However, when nations get off on the wrong track, it is disastrous for millions of people.

Consider two nations that experienced revolution and got off on the wrong track, at the wrong station. Though near in time, the French Revolution diverged far from our American experience. The essential difference between the American Revolution and the French Revolution is that the American Revolution was a religious event, whereas the French Revolution was an antireligious event. The French Revolutionists submitted to no faith outside of themselves. They possessed no moral constraints to curb their vengeance, and blood ran like a river through the streets of Paris with Napoleon Bonaparte emerging to devastate Europe. The French Revolution established no rule of law, no checks and balances. Their failure bred a disaster.

In 1917, the Communists—the Bolsheviks—revolted in Russia. Their philosophy espoused materialism and atheism. They rejected the rights of individuals and derided the importance of the human spirit. They instituted a totalitarian regime, murdering millions of Soviet citizens. Like the French, the Soviets permitted no checks and balances for their leaders and thus established no rule of law. Their imprudence spawned a catastrophe.

These examples illustrate the importance of moral constraints woven into a system of government, the necessity of a clearly established rule of law, and the wisdom of checks and balances among the three branches of government.

We Americans are fortunate indeed that our Founders got us off on the right track, at the right station. Our Founders gave us a government deeply committed to the rule of law. They formed our government based on two premises: the worth of each individual person—"all Men are created equal"—and the imperfection of man, even a king. The tyranny of King George III taught them what Lord Acton would verbalize years later: "Power tends to corrupt and absolute power corrupts absolutely." They recognized the necessity of checks and balances to prevent the three independent and co-equal branches of our government from engaging in excesses. The Founders carefully limited the powers of each branch.

A violation by any branch of this carefully crafted system of checks and balances threatens the stability and vitality of the system. The concept of a living Constitution does not comport with these principles: specifically, it does not provide a clearly established rule of law and is in conflict with the system of checks and balances. To allow the judicial branch to cross over into the jurisdiction of the legislative and executive branches increases the power of judges, but violating the separation of powers over time will erode confidence in the courts and thus ultimately weaken the judiciary—indeed it will undermine the power of all branches of our government.

About the time I graduated from law school, I heard the story of a Supreme Court justice who was hearing arguments in a case. A young lawyer was arguing strenuously that the Court had to rule in his favor based on *Stare Decisis*: the legal doctrine that rules and principles established by prior controlling case law must be followed. The justice leaned forward and asked the young lawyer, "But is it right?"

There was a time when I might have thought this a great question: a judge concerned about what is right rather than the niceties of the law. But who will we give—for the rest of their life and regardless of how they might decide—the power to determine what is right or wrong for America? Will it be a Democratic or a Republican? A conservative or a liberal? Will it be a Christian, someone of the Jewish faith, someone of another belief, or an atheist? Will it be someone from the Christian Coalition, or will it be a member of the ACLU or the People for the American Way? These rhetorical questions answer themselves. We should fight to uphold the principle that we have: "A government of laws, and not of men."

Unlike the leaders of England or Rome, our Founding Fathers gave us a written Constitution so we would not be compelled to rely on the sense of justice or the sense of decency of a particular judge, or even five judges, for our life, liberty, or property. Instead, we could rely on our Constitution as written and ratified by the people through their duly elected representatives.

James Madison argued in Federalist No. 51,

> If men were angels, no government would be necessary. If angels were to govern men, neither external nor internal controls on government would be necessary. In framing a government which is to be administered by men over men, the great difficulty lies in this: you must first enable the government to control the governed; and in the next place oblige it to control itself.

Madison recognized that requiring the government to exercise restraint, "to control itself," was "a great difficulty." He was right.

The carefully crafted system of checks and balances—the unique concept so wisely given to us by our Framers—has allowed Americans to live under one governing document longer than any republic in the history of all mankind, and provided our people more freedom, more liberty, and more opportunity than any people have ever enjoyed in the entire history of civilization.

The structure of governance given to us by our Founders is more important than the Bill of Rights. The constitution of the now defunct Soviet Union promised grandiose rights, but we all know they did not exist because they had no carefully crafted system of checks and balances, no rule of law in its truest sense. Without the structure, without the safeguards, the Bill of Rights is an illusion, not a reality. When the Court exceeds the structure of the judiciary and goes beyond the Constitution, it threatens the Bill of Rights—and all our rights.

Another reason for rejecting the concept of interpreting our Constitution as a "living" document is that the courts are ill equipped to make political decisions. Their debate is private; it is not public. Judges cannot develop a consensus, cannot compromise, and have no process to collect data or to receive public input. Judges simply have no process to formulate public policy as do legislative bodies. Courts are not an appropriate branch of government to make political decisions. When judges start exercising their "independent judgment" to determine the meaning of the Constitution, rather than following the text and precedent, they cease being judges and have moved into the arena of policy. They are making political decisions. They are creating law rather than interpreting law. They have politicized the judiciary.

There are a number of areas where the courts have intruded into the political arena and changed the meaning of the Constitution.

The First Amendment prohibits "Congress" from making any "law respecting an establishment of religion" and prohibits "Congress" from passing any law "prohibiting the free exercise" of religion. For more than 150 years, the Establishment Clause was interpreted to prevent designation of a state church, a government-preferred religion, and to prohibit the expenditure of tax dollars to support religion. References to God in the public arena, in the public square, at public buildings, at institutions and ceremonies, was not considered an establishment of religion. Prayer at the beginning of congressional and legislative sessions, Scripture passages on public buildings, displays of the Ten Commandments at public sites, prayer in school settings, none of these were considered an establishment of religion.

The First Amendment has not changed—the protections it gives to religion, speech, and the press have not been altered by the amendment process. But the Court has made changes, and that should concern not just those of faith, but all those who value free speech and freedom of the press. If the Court can change the meaning of the First Amendment in religious matters, an activist Court can also threaten our speech rights and our tradition of a free and independent press.

Chief Justice William Rehnquist wrote that the decisions of the court "breathe with hostility to all things religious in public life." The Court has held that prayers cannot be offered in the classroom, invoked at high school graduation ceremonies, or given at high school football games. The Court has prohibited the display of the Ten Commandments and nativity scenes in public venues. The Ninth Circuit declared the phrase "One Nation under God" in the Pledge of Allegiance unconstitutional. The court has taken sides in the culture war, favoring secularism. This is a tragedy for our nation and for people of faith. But if we allow an activist judiciary to act without reining them in, who knows what other rights will be threatened in the future.

If America's traditional view of issues relating to freedom of religion and the establishment of religion clauses needs to be reexamined, that is a matter for the people and their elected representatives, not five members of the Court who view "We the People" as insufficiently enlightened, as insufficiently intelligent to consider these issues for themselves.

John Meacham in his book *American Gospel* has carefully documented that our Founders

> consciously allowed a form of what Benjamin Franklin called "public religion" to take root and flower at the same time they were creating a republic that valued private religious liberty. . . .
>
> The nation's public religion, then, holds that there is a God, the one Jefferson called the "Creator" and "Nature's God" in the Declaration of Independence. The God of public religion made all

human beings in his image and endowed them, as Jefferson wrote, with sacred rights to life, liberty, and the pursuit of happiness. What the God of public religion has given, no king, no president, no government can abridge—hence the sanctity of human rights in America. The God of public religion is interested in the affairs of the world. . . .

Public religion is not a substitute for private religion, nor is it a Trojan horse filled with evangelicals threatening the walls of secular America. It is, rather, a habit of mind and of heart that enables Americans to be at once tolerant and reverent—two virtues of relevance to all, for the Founders' public religion is consummately democratic. When a president says "God Bless America" or when we sing "America! America! God shed His grace on thee," each American is free to define God in whatever way he chooses. A Christian's mind may summon God the Father; a Jew's, Yahweh; a Muslim's, Allah; an atheist, no one, or no thing. Such diversity is not a prescription for dissention. It is part of the reality of creation.[5]

On July 3, 2005, an article by Noah Feldman, professor at New York School of Law, appeared in the *New York Times* magazine. Feldman proposes a solution to the state/church conflict: allow more public religious symbols, but expend no funds for religion. Both Meacham and Feldman take a position that is somewhere in between the Christian right and the secularist left, clearly demonstrating Americans have the capacity of grappling with this issue without having to have a solution imposed outside the Constitution and the democratic process.[6]

Religion is not the only area in which the Court has made political decisions. The Court has injected itself into policy considerations as to both legal and illegal aliens, in respect to education, welfare, and college tuition assistance. It matters not whether these decisions are good or bad, rather that the Supreme Court should not be resolving these issues that by the Constitution are both conceptually and specifically left to the discretion of Congress.

The Supreme Court declared the Texas Law prohibiting sodomy— anal intercourse—unconstitutional, thus holding that the right to commit acts of sodomy is a fundamental, basic right. Justice Byron

White earlier addressed this same question, writing, "The Court is most vulnerable and comes nearest to illegitimacy when it deals with judge-made constitutional law having little or no recognizable roots in the language or design of the Constitution."[7]

The issue that drives the engine of opposition against conservative judicial nominees is abortion: partial birth abortion, abortion without parental or spousal consent, abortion without even parental or spousal notification, in other words, abortion on demand. The Supreme Court held unconstitutional a federal statute prohibiting partial birth abortion. As previously mentioned, this same act if accomplished by a teenage mother and her boyfriend without the assistance of a medical doctor performing the abortion could result in murder charges.

The Court has crossed over on issues involving criminal rights, the death penalty, education, welfare, college assistance, and nearly any policy matter you can consider. The trouble comes not in addressing these issues that sometimes present constitutional questions, but when going beyond the Constitution and the jurisdiction of the Court to make policy decisions. Furthermore, the concern is not whether the outcome was positive or negative, but whether the judiciary should have the power to make these decisions at all.

In the above areas, the court has added to, altered, or changed the meaning of the Constitution. In changing the Constitution, the Court has impinged upon a right the Constitution reserves to the people or their elected representatives through the amendment process.

I discussed four cases in *Supreme Chaos* to demonstrate how a living Constitution affects the average American. First, in the Kelo case, Susette Kelo and Wilhelmina Dery's families lost their homes when the Court decided another private entity could take their private property—their homes—to build a shopping mall. Second, when the Ninth Circuit held the Pledge of Allegiance was unconstitutional, the court prohibited 10.6 million students in the public schools of nine western states from voluntarily reciting the Pledge of Allegiance. Third, the Massachusetts Supreme Court redefined marriage in that state to include homosexual relationships that, under the full faith and credit statute, could spread same-sex marriage to other states. Fourth, the Supreme Court ruled that the citizens of McCreary County and Pulaski County, Kentucky, cannot display the Ten Commandments in their courthouses despite thousands of such displays across the United States. Simultaneously, the Court specifically protected a public display of the Ten Commandments in Texas, treating Kentuckians and Texans separate and unequal.

How will it affect you and me in the future? We do not know. We cannot solve that mystery until five members of the Supreme Court make a decision. There will be no public debate. You and I will have no say. Nine judges will meet in secret and then tell us what the Constitution means and how it will affect all Americans.

A recent case, decided just before this book went to press, graphically demonstrates how liberal judges who do not feel bound and constrained by a written unchanging Constitution can impact and endanger the lives of ordinary Americans. Judge Anna Diggs Taylor ruled unconstitutional the National Security Agency's Terrorist Surveillance Program used to intercept international communications of those suspected of involvement in terrorist activities. She permanently enjoined the government from continuing the surveillance.

Judge Taylor went even further, declaring the Fourth Amendment "requires prior warrants for any reasonable search based upon prior—existing probable cause." Security screening at airports are considered Fourth Amendment searches and because "in 1989 the Supreme Court noted firearms were only detected in 0.0004% of airport searches—hardly the 'probable cause' needed for a warrant." A University of Virginia Law School professor warned, "If last week's decision in *ACLU v. NSA* is left standing, America may have to decide to shut down its commercial passenger airline industry or leave passengers totally at the mercy of terrorists armed with guns, knifes, and liquid explosives."[8]

A Wisconsin law professor described the opinion as demonstrating "petulance, an outrage and antipathy toward President Bush."[9] Even liberal Harvard Law School professor Laurence Tribe said the judge seemed intent "to poke a finger in the President's eye."[10] Even the *Washington Post* Editorial Board criticized the opinion.[11] Further, Judge Taylor failed to disclose she serves as a trustee for a nonprofit organization that gave $125,000 to the ACLU, a plaintiff in the case.[12]

This is only a lower court decision, and the final holding in this case will not be known until the appeals process is finalized. But it clearly illustrates how far afield judges can travel if they do not feel constrained by precedent or the wording of the Constitution and how it was understood when the relevant provision was adopted. The safety and security of Americans is endangered by decisions like *ACLU v. NSA*. If judges are not restricted by a written Constitution with a fixed meaning, we can expect more judges—sympathetic, activist judges—to create rights not found in the Constitution and further endanger our nation.

Judge Robert Bork pointedly said, "the truth is that the judge who looks outside the Constitution always looks inside himself and nowhere else." *ACLU v. NSA* confirms Bork's statement.

Judges on the Left departing from a Constitution with a fixed meaning can threaten our security and fail to protect us from crime by expanding the Constitution. So also could judges on the Right, if they should embrace the concept of a living Constitution, limit and restrict our rights by diminishing the Constitution. Make no mistake, if the ACLU pushes the judiciary to the Left to create new rights that cause the American people to feel threatened in their security, the American people will respond to ensure their safety. The pendulum will swing back and rights will be restricted according to the severity of the perceived threat. Having judges change the Constitution is not a good idea; five judges should not have that much power, and the unintended consequences of their actions could have those on the Left complaining about judges on the Right diminishing and restricting constitutional rights in the future.

If you think no activist judges would actually try to remove the protections of our most sacred rights, do not look across the ocean, just look at the past record of the Court. Chief Justice Roger Taney, seeking to advance his own personal political views and impose on others his views of what the law ought to be, wrote the egregious opinion in *Dredd Scott v. Sandford*[13] that held that a black person was not a "citizen" and thus could not bring an action in court.

Taney wrote that citizenship "was perfectly understood to be confined to the white race." That was not true. When the Constitution was ratified, five free states extended citizenship to blacks. If he had interpreted the Constitution as meaning what it meant when adopted, he would have agreed with Justice Benjamin Curtis, who in his dissent correctly adhered to the Constitution's original understanding and wrote,

> All free native born inhabitants of the states of New Hampshire, Massachusetts, New York, New Jersey, and North Carolina, though descended from African slaves, were not only citizens of those states, but such of them as had the other necessary qualifications possessed the franchise of electors, on equal terms with other citizens.

Writing for the majority, Taney went even further and held that the Congressional act making free territory out of the land acquired by the Louisiana Purchase was unconstitutional. Taney reached that conclusion despite the fact that the Constitution expressly provided, "The Congress shall have power to . . . make all needful Rules and Regulations respecting the Territory . . . belonging to the United States." The only way Taney could reach this determination was to ignore the plain language of the Constitution. Mark Levin writes in *Men in Black*, "With typical activist flare, Taney overruled Congress's power to ban slavery in the territories and imposed his views on the Nation."[14]

This is precisely what Justice Curtis argued in his dissent:

> When a strict interpretation of the Constitution, according to the fixed rules which govern the interpretation of laws, is abandoned, and the theoretical opinions of individuals are allowed to control its meaning, we have no longer a Constitution; we are under the government of individual men, who for the time being have power to declare what the Constitution is according to their own views of what it ought to mean.

Curtis, distressed at the outcome of the case and the activism of the Taney majority, resigned from the Supreme Court on principle, the only person ever to do so for that reason.

Dredd Scott was a political, not a legal decision. The Supreme Court's ruling was wrong and inconsistent with the rule of law. In making its decision, the Supreme Court ignored the Constitution and superimposed its own independent judgment on the parties. President Abraham Lincoln refused to recognize this case as the law of the land and so the executive branch ignored the judicial branch: an example of judicial activism creating a constitutional crisis.

In 1896, despite the Equal Protection Clause clearly providing that "no state shall . . . deprive any person of equal protection of the laws," another activist Supreme Court ignored the text of the Constitution's Fourteenth Amendment in *Plessy v. Ferguson* and adopted a "separate but equal" policy. The majority upheld a Louisiana statute that required all railway companies transporting passengers within the state of Louisiana to provide separate accommodations for white and black passengers. While the majority's reference to the fact that separate but equal facilities existed at the time the Fourteenth Amendment was adopted was true, it ignored the most basic principle of statutory and constitutional construction: if the text is unambiguous and clear, you never look to intent or circumstances surrounding the adoption, you simply apply the language as written. Furthermore, the Fourteenth Amendment was adopted to remedy such circumstances, and had these circumstances not existed, there is little reason to believe the amendment would have been necessary.

Justice John Marshall Harlan, in his dissent, grasped the basic premise when he argued that the Thirteenth and Fourteenth Amendments

> removed the race line from our governmental systems . . . they declared . . . that the law in the states shall be the same for the black as for the white, that all persons, whether colored or white, shall stand equal before the laws of the states . . . that no discrimination shall be made against them by law because of their color. . . . the constitution of the United States in its present form, forbids, so far as civil and political rights are concerned, discrimination by the general government or the states against any citizen because of his race. . . . Our Constitution is color-blind, and neither knows nor tolerates classes

among citizens. In respect of Civil Rights, all citizens are equal before the law. The humblest is the peer of the most powerful.[15]

In the give and take that comes in writing opinions on a multi-judge court, Harlan (in *Plessy*) pointed out the ruling of the majority could produce absurd results. The majority countered they would simply rule that such absurd laws were "unreasonable" and thus unconstitutional. Harlan countered and decried "a dangerous tendency in these latter days to enlarge the functions of the court" by determining what is and is not reasonable. Harlan said, "the Court exceeds its powers when it starts making such determination." In 1896, in *Plessy*, the Court said it would determine what was an "unreasonable law." In 2003, the Massachusetts Supreme Court determined there was no "rational basis" for a law defining marriage as between a man and woman. The Massachusetts Court reached its decision on same-sex marriage not by finding that the marriage statute conflicted with either the Massachusetts or U.S. Constitutions, but by using the same justification the Supreme Court used to defend its "separate but equal" decision: judges determining what is not "rational" or what is "unreasonable," not following the language of the Constitution.

In years past, judicial activism denied to blacks access to the courts and then created a separate but equal status for black Americans, denying them the rights enjoyed by white Americans and prolonging Jim Crow for almost seventy years. Today judicial activism denies people of faith rights understood for more than 150 years to be protected by the "free exercise" of religion clause of the First Amendment. Today judicial activism grants rights in numerous cases never contemplated by the drafters of our Constitution, rights not condoned by the majority of the American people.

Today, most who support a living Constitution are liberal. The rights they create, or seek to create, are liberal, but that has not always been true, as evidenced by *Dredd Scott* and *Plessy*. Consider the possibilities that in the future judges on the Right might embrace the concept of a changing Constitution and hold that freedom of the press or freedom of speech is more limited than understood for the past 200 years, or that the free exercise of religion clause trumps the establishment clause and that the government can pay for religious instruction or programs to instill in children a belief there is a Creator and the earth was created. The roof would blow off the Capitol. Liberals would descend on Washington demanding impeachment of judges. The opposition to judges who change the Constitution is entirely dependent on whose ox is being gored. It was wrong when judges on the Right disregarded the Constitution, and it is wrong when judges on the Left do the same.

Not only is interpreting the Constitution as a changing, evolving document bad policy, but the overwhelming majority of the American people want judges who interpret the law, not judges who make up the law. Though the cornerstone of the current debate over a living Constitution in the culture war is *Roe v. Wade*, even some abortion rights supporters today are beginning to question the obsession and dedication of pro-choice advocates to *Roe*. Benjamin Wittes, self-proclaimed pro-choice editorial writer at the *Washington Post*, wrote:

> The Democratic Party's commitment to preserving *Roe v. Wade* has been deeply unhealthy for the cause of abortion rights, for liberalism more generally, and ultimately for American democracy. . . .
>
> All would benefit if abortion rights proponents were forced to make their arguments in the policy arena (rather than during Supreme Court nomination hearings), and if pro-lifers were actually accountable to the electorate. . . .
>
> Since its inception *Roe* has had a deep legitimacy problem, stemming from its weakness as a legal opinion. . . . But thousands of pages of scholarship notwithstanding, the right to abortion remains constitutionally shaky, abortion policy is a question that the Constitution—even broadly construed—cannot convincingly be read to resolve.
>
> Consequently, a pro-lifer who complains that she never got her democratic say before abortion was legalized nationwide has a powerful grievance. And there's nothing quite like denying people a say in policy to energize their commitment to a position. This point is not limited to abortion. For instance, the host of gay-marriage ballot initiatives in November came in direct response to the decision by the

Massachusetts Supreme Court to treat same-sex unions as a judicial matter rather than a legislative one. . . .

So although *Roe* created the right to choose, that right exists under perpetual threat of obliteration, and depends for its vitality on the composition of the Supreme Court at any given moment.

In short, *Roe* puts liberal in the position of defending a lousy opinion that disenfranchised millions of conservatives on an issue about which they care deeply.

[If *Roe* were overruled] the right to abortion would most likely enjoy a measure of security it does not now have. Legislative compromises tend to be durable, since they bring a sense of resolution to divisive issues by balancing competing interests; mustering a working majority to upset them can be far more difficult than rallying discontent against the edicts of unelected judges. In short, overturning *Roe* would lead to greater regional variability in the right to abortion, but this would be a worthwhile price for pro-choice voters to pay in exchange for greater democratic legitimacy for that right and, therefore, greater acceptance of and permanence for it.

The right to abortion remains a highly debatable proposition, both jurisprudentially and morally. The mere fact that liberals have to devote so much political energy to pretending that the right exists beyond democratic debate proves that it doesn't.

But the costs of defending *Roe* have grown too high, and I'm just not willing to pay them anymore.

A liberal fear of democratic dialogue may make sense regarding social issues on which the majority is conservative. But it is a special kind of pathology that would rather demand a loyalty oath to a weak and unstable Court decision than make a case before one's fellow citizens on a proposition that already commands majority support. The insistence on judicial protection from a political fight that liberals have every reason to expect to win advertises pointedly how little they still believe in their ability to persuade.[16]

It also demonstrates how little respect abortion rights apologists have for the rule of law, checks and balances, and the democratic process.

Jeffrey Rosen, a law professor at George Washington University and Legal Affairs editor at the *New Republic*, has also written an exhaustive article on what would happen if *Roe* should be reversed.[17] He agrees with Wittes that the abortion issue as presently framed favors Republicans. "With *Roe* on the books, the focus of the abortion debate has tended to be on issues like partial-birth abortion, which is a huge political winner for Republicans."

He also agrees with Wittes that

> at some point after *Roe* fell, the country would reach some kind of political equipoise on abortion. It's difficult, in America, to deny the wishes of majorities for too long, and whether it takes years or decades, the state legislatures and Congress will eventually come to reflect the popular will.

I agree with Wittes and Rosen; if *Roe v. Wade* were reversed tomorrow, there would not be a great deal of difference in the availability of abortion in the blue states. That may be disappointing to those who believe in the sanctity of life, as I do; nevertheless, it is true. In most red states, abortion would be greatly limited: probably allowing for abortion when the mother's life is in jeopardy, likely for rape or incest, and in some states, when the mother's health would be affected. But in the blue states, abortion would probably be allowed with little or no constraint. But at least the decision would be made by legislative bodies, not by the courts.

Judicial activism has caused a loss of confidence in the judiciary. Yet, confidence in the administration of justice is essential for a representative form of government. The ABA survey of more than 1,000 voters in September 2005 revealed by an almost two-to-one margin voters feel judicial activism has reached a crisis stage. The extent of dissatisfaction surprised legal experts, with one saying, "These are surprisingly large numbers" and another, "the results are simply scary."[18] Judicial activism is the reason the judiciary is held in lower esteem than ever before. This is not good for the judiciary or the American people.

What is the remedy? What is the solution? If a living and mystery Constitution threatens our branches of government and our individual rights, what, if anything, can we do about it? For every word discussing the problem there has been a published word offering a solution. The most extreme recommendation is impeachment of federal judges. But impeachment would be perceived as an assault by political forces on an "independent judiciary" and could result in empowering activist judges while further removing confidence in the judiciary. Furthermore, the Constitution does not explicitly spell out a required theory of interpretation for judges who "shall hold their Offices during good Behavior. . . ."

Many other less extreme solutions have been proposed. Shortly after the filibuster was first utilized against judicial nominees, President Bush called for a permanent Senate Rules change to ensure timely consideration of judicial nominees no matter who is president or which party controls the Senate.

Senator Kay Bailey Hutchison suggested a rule change that would stop filibusters in exchange for prohibiting "holds" on nominees. Senator Chuck Schumer suggested the creation of a nominating commission in every state and the District of Columbia. Senators John Cornyn and Mark Pryor would change the confirmation process altogether. Senator Arlen Specter proposed changing the rules so that after a nomination is received, within a specified period of time, the Judiciary Committee would have to hold hearings, and if the nominee should be rejected on a party-line vote the nominee would still receive a vote by the full Senate. Senator Bill Frist recommended reducing the number of votes required to stop a filibuster over a progressive series of votes. After all the furor, nothing was done. Furthermore, these suggestions, by and large, addressed only the symptoms, the unprecedented unconstitutional filibuster of nominees.

Authors and commentators other than myself have suggested various other potential solutions: proposing amendments to the Constitution to address specific issues such as the definition of marriage, flag burning, the Pledge of Allegiance, and other areas of particular concern and controversy; divesting the court of jurisdiction in problem areas; term limits for judges; slashing court budgets; ignoring court mandates; shrinking or packing courts; prohibiting courts from relying on foreign law; prohibiting courts from imposing taxes; providing that single-member courts cannot invalidate laws; requiring a super majority of judges to invalidate laws as unconstitutional; and one of the most far reaching, acknowledging that the Judiciary has become politicized and suggesting that federal judges should be elected.[19]

But one recommendation advanced by both Judge Robert Bork and Mark Levin[20] deserves special attention. This proposal calls for a constitutional amendment to allow Congress to override Supreme Court decisions. Such an amendment could require a super majority vote of both Houses of Congress as is required for override of a presidential veto. This solution is compatible with the separation of powers doctrine and the system of checks and balances found in our Constitution. Just as the power of the president to veto an act of Congress is a check and balance on the power of Congress, and the power of Congress to override a presidential veto a check on the power of the executive, the amendment proposed by Judge Bork and Mark Levin would be a check on the power of the Supreme Court. The Bork/Levin proposal, however, will only address an issue after the Supreme Court has exercised its independent judgment to expand or diminish the Constitution contrary to the will of the overwhelming majority of the American people. Their proposed amendment does not address the theory of interpretation; it does not address the problem before judicial activism produces a decision expanding or diminishing the Constitution. Nevertheless, if their amendment were in place, it would have a salutary effect on Supreme Court judges who would know that if they go too far, they could be checked by the representatives of the people. The people's elected representatives could move to correct an egregious extension or diminution of the Constitution if there is sufficient sentiment among the voters.

A weakness in the Bork/Levin proposal is that liberals would continue to make incremental changes. They would change the Constitution as much as they perceived the public would tolerate. And after the public has accepted, grudgingly or otherwise, a change, they will then use that precedent to make additional changes to further the liberal agenda. As Levin quoted Robert Yates, an ardent anti-federalist, "One adjudication will form a precedent to the next, and this to a following one."[21]

I have an additional and different suggestion. The proper way—consistent with the consent of the governed—to expand, diminish, change, alter, or add to the Constitution is the amendment process. To remove the judiciary from politics, to prevent judges from changing the Constitution, we should simply and explicitly state through a constitutional amendment that the amendment process as stated in Article V of the Constitution is the only way to alter or change the Constitution. We must explicitly prohibit any other method, specifically judicial expansion or diminution.

The American people have consented to no other method of altering the Constitution. Thomas E. Baker suggests,

> When the Framers set out the sole constitutional way to amend the Constitution, they were not required to explicitly negate all other political theories for accomplishing change. . . . [O]riginalism is the one best method to keep judges from freelancing and imposing their own subjective policy preferences under the pretext of interpreting the Constitution.[22]

This amendment would enshrine originalism, not original intent but original understanding.

Baker is correct that the only appropriate way to change the Constitution is through the amendment process provided by the Constitution itself. It should not be necessary to explicitly state the negative. However, some activist judges contend that interpreting the Constitution as a living document is appropriate. They subscribe to a belief similar to that of Edward Bernays (1891–1995), nephew of Sigmund Freud and founder of modern public relations. Bernays told Marvin Olasky, "'We have no being in the air to watch over us' so we need 'human gods' to preserve us from 'chaos.'"[23] Judges who step in today to change the Constitution do not trust democracy. They believe that the masses and their elected representatives are not sufficiently enlightened, not sufficiently sensitive, not sufficiently intelligent to change the Constitution when it needs to be modified, so they assume for themselves the power to do so. In their view, they protect us from "chaos" as Bernays sought to do.

While the arrogance that they know better than the people and the Founders may be distasteful to the rest of us, it is not necessarily malicious. To be fair, there is no explicit prohibition for such activism in the Constitution. But I agree with Chief Justice John Marshall, who found an implicit and logical requirement for such judicial restraint. But if making the implicit explicit is the answer to depoliticizing the judiciary, then let us do it through the proper method and amend the Constitution. If adopted, even the most activist judges will find it difficult to ignore this explicit prohibition.

PROPOSED CONSTITUTIONAL AMENDMENT TO PROTECT THE AMENDMENT PROCESS

The Constitution, and the Amendments thereto duly adopted may be expanded, diminished, changed, modified, altered, or added to only by an amendment duly adopted as outlined in Article V of the Constitution. In the future, neither the Supreme Court nor the inferior courts will expand, diminish, change, modify, alter, or add to the Constitution and the amendments thereto duly adopted, but will interpret the Constitution and amendments thereto according to the common understanding of the relevant provision at the time it was adopted. This amendment does not affect the weight to be given prior decisions under the doctrine of *stare decisis*.

Our Founders realized we would need to change the Constitution over time. They intended the people and their elected representatives to change the Constitution through the amendment process, not by judges adding to or changing the meaning of the Constitution.

Our Founders intended that it should be difficult to change the Constitution. In fact, the provision giving each state equal representation in the Senate can never be changed. But in all other respects, the Constitution can be changed, but only by the agreement of two-thirds of both Houses of Congress, and three-fourths of either the state legislatures, or state constitutional conventions convened for that purpose; or, in the alternative, by two-thirds of the state legislatures calling for a constitutional convention that may propose changes, which must still be ratified by the legislatures or conventions in three-fourths of the states.

The amendment process worked well until 1971, but the Constitution has not been amended by any amendment initiated since 1971. Far Left special-interest groups found that under the concept of a changing, evolving, "living," "mystery" Constitution, it is easier to convince five members of the Supreme Court that the Constitution should be changed than to do it the old-fashioned way, the amendment process, where the people and their elected representatives have a say. That was when liberals started arguing that the process is too difficult and the Constitution too sacred to amend. In reality, liberals don't think the Constitution is too sacred for the Supreme Court to change or alter; they just think it is too sacred for the people to change.

The Constitution is not too sacred to amend, for the Founders created a process to do so. From the time the Constitution was adopted in 1788 until 1971, the Constitution was amended twenty-six times. (Additionally, an amendment originally proposed in 1789 relating to congressional pay was finally ratified in 1992 and became the 27th Amendment.) The twenty-six amendments adopted between 1789 and 1971 constitute an average of one amendment every seven years. From 1933 until 1971, we amended the Constitution seven times, an average of one amendment every five years. No amendment proposed since 1971—during the thirty-five years since the living mystery Constitution became a prevailing legal theory—has been adopted.

Up until 1971, our nation decided major policy issues through the amendment process: abolishing slavery, requiring states to give equal protection and due process to all citizens, providing the right to vote could not be denied because of race, authorizing the income tax, providing direct election of senators, adopting and repealing prohibition, limiting the presidency to two terms, ensuring women the right to vote, eliminating the poll tax, and extending the right to vote to eighteen-year-olds. These amendments successfully addressed hot-button issues, and the people and their elected representatives were involved. These changes were not brought about by court decree. The amendment process can work again if we try. We must protect the amendment process if we want to ensure that democracy—not judgeocracy—drives the American political system.

The "Gang of Fourteen" agreement produced a temporary reprieve in regard to confirmation, but it is not permanent and it did not solve the underlying problem. This amendment is permanent and will address the underlying cause.

The legislative resolution of controversial issues creates national unity, while judicial resolution of controversial issues only increases division. For example, Congress passed the Civil Rights Act of 1964, extremely controversial at the time, but did so only after compromise, broad consensus, and the democratic political process. Within three decades of its passage, we lived in a different America where the vast majority of Americans view the denial of equal rights to anyone based on race as wrong and intolerable. The Civil Rights Act today is universally accepted.

Likewise, many Americans opposed abortion when the Supreme Court, in 1973, decided *Roe v. Wade*. Judges reached the decision in secret through private debates with no public input or participation. Now more than three decades later, abortion divides our nation even more than in 1973.

What is the difference between the acceptance of the Civil Rights Act of 1964 and *Roe v. Wade*? The Civil Rights Act was adopted by the correct political process by the appropriate branch of government. Conversely, *Roe v. Wade* was handed down by an inappropriate branch of government, inappropriately deciding a political issue.

Our Constitution will be changed over time. We must decide if those changes will be made by the people's elected representatives or by members of the Court. We should make changes through the proper method: legislative determination through the amendment process, not judicial decree.

Those liberal special-interest groups and Democratic senators decrying "conservative activist judges" should embrace this amendment as a means to prevent the activism they decry. My amendment would neither reverse nor lock in *Roe v. Wade* or any other "changes" to the Constitution made by prior judicial decisions. These decisions will be left subject to *stare decisis*. But in the future, we should return the writing or changing of laws to the purview of the legislature and should return constitutional changes to the amendment process.

If we fail to act, the judiciary is in serious jeopardy of irreparable harm. My sincerest hope is that Congress will act before it is too late. Passing such an amendment will not be easy, but we must do more than decry judicial activism. If our Founders could find common ground to adopt our Constitution with all of the controversial issues, differences of opinion, and competing theories of government that abounded in 1787, surely our leaders today can come up with a solution. Hopefully statesmen can emerge and find a way out of the present quagmire and depoliticize the judiciary.

The Constitution should be as alive as our democracy and as static as the rule of law. When the people demand constitutional changes, we have a proscribed method of doing so, and whenever there is broad desire and support, those changes—however radical or however reasonable; whether foundation shaking or of slight consequences—can be made as our living democracy might demand. However, unless the people speak through their elected representatives consistent with the constitutional plan, our Constitution must otherwise remain static, fixed, and certain to provide the protections of the rule of law both to individuals and to the institutions of government.

A return to civility will benefit our communities and government and will ease the political rancor that prevents progress—including judicial confirmations. A statute or Senate rule proscribing the proper and unchanging way to conduct judicial confirmations will return the desire to public service by nominees, protect the fairness of the process, and increase comity in the Senate. But even with both of these successes, we could continue to see a politicization of the judiciary. Requiring the amendment process to change the Constitution and prohibiting any other methods (including judicial activism) will return hot-button social issues from the judicial realm that has no jurisdiction to the legislative arena where democracy works and the people speak.

Epilogue

As I was finalizing this book, a pastor friend related that he wrote all members of the Judiciary Committee in support of my confirmation and that Democratic senator Diane Feinstein of California had responded she could not support my confirmation because of my "strong convictions." This statement was an obvious reference to my religious convictions and my personal view on abortion and this echoed the secularist charges that I was a dangerous theocrat. This criticism comes close to applying a "religious test" for one who would serve as a federal judge, something clearly prohibited by the Constitution.

I do have strong convictions. I have strong convictions as to my faith, but this does not disqualify me from sitting as a federal judge. My faith does not make me a threat to those who do not believe or to those who believe differently than I do. The Constitution guarantees the same rights to all Americans and permits all to be involved in government and politics, Christians included.

Since the Left challenged my convictions and my faith, let me share firsthand what I believe. My faith is not complex; it is rather simple. I believe the Bible is God's word. I believe that through the Bible, God reveals himself to mankind. I believe God created the heavens and the earth and that he created mankind in his own image. I believe God seeks to draw all people to himself and provides a path for reconciliation: "For God so love the world that he gave his only begotten Son, that whosoever believeth on him should not perish, but have eternal life."[1]

The Bible reveals God's commandments as to how we should live our lives, what we should do and what we should not do. The Bible teaches Christians are to be compassionate, generous, loving, and caring citizens, concerned about the needs of their fellow man, particularly those who are the "least."

Being a Christian does make one perfect; none of us are. Fortunately, God is faithful to forgive.

I believe God is no respecter of persons; God loves all of his children equally. Thus, I believe we ought to respect our fellow man without regard to race, color, station in life, or country of origin.

Although the Bible teaches that there are dire consequences for rejecting God, every American is free to accept or reject the Bible as God's word. The Bible teaches that faith comes only by an individual's free choice. The Bible and the Constitution both teach that religion should not be established nor coerced by government. However, neither should government interfere with any citizens expressing their faith and exercising their freedom of religion, and no religious test should be directly or indirectly applied to those who hold office or seek to hold office. Under our Constitution, Christians have a right to believe the Bible just as nonbelievers have the right not to believe Scripture.

The faith I claim is a positive and loving faith, a sensitive faith responsive to the needs of others: "He hath showed thee, O man, what is good; and what doth Jehovah require of thee, but to do justly, and to love kindness, and to walk humbly with thy God?"[2]

I believe God's grace is sufficient for man's needs. It has sustained Margaret Ann and me through difficult periods as well as joyous times. We are deeply grateful to so many who encouraged and prayed for us during my confirmation battle.

Consistent with my faith, I also have a strong conviction that an appellate judge who takes an oath to uphold the Constitution of the United States is bound by that Constitution and Supreme Court interpretations thereof. I believe in a government of laws, not a government of men. I believe the Constitution means what it says and says what it means. I do not believe five judges should change or reinterpret the Constitution, whether they be liberal or conservative. I believe all judicial nominees should be judged not on their personal and religious views but on whether they will follow the rule of law.

In addition to religion, the ghosts of Mississippi's past haunted my nomination. While other senators raised the issue implicitly, Senator Chuck Schumer raised it explicitly. This attack was unfair to me and unfair to Mississippi of the twenty-first century.

Mississippi has made tremendous progress in race relations in recent years, perhaps more than any state in the Union. We had far to come and still have far to go, but in that, we are not unlike the rest of the nation.

Today, Mississippi has the highest number of black elected officials in the country, despite a smaller population than many states. In a number of instances, African American have won where the majority votes are white. Robert Clark, the first African American elected to the Mississippi legislature, was elected president pro tempore of the House of Representatives from 1992 through 2004 by a majority white legislature. The overwhelmingly white First Circuit Court District of Mississippi elected my colleague Barry Ford, an African American attorney, circuit court judge three times. The voters of Forrest, Perry, and Marion counties—also a majority white area—have elected my friend, Johnny Williams, another African American attorney, as chancery judge.

In 2005, while I was serving on the Fifth Circuit Court of Appeals, I spoke to the American Legion's Mississippi Boys State program and participated in the swearing in of their officers. More than 60 percent of the delegates to Boy's State that year were white, but the three top elected state officials were all African Americans.

In recent years, Mississippi has corrected many injustices from the civil rights era. I earlier shared the prosecution of Sam Bowers for the fire-bombing death of Vernon Dahmer, and the exoneration of Clyde Kennard who was wrongfully prosecuted to prevent him from integrating the University of Southern Mississippi. Mississippi also prosecuted Byron De La Beckwith for the 1963 slaying of Medgar Evers; Beckwith recently died in the state penitentiary. Mississippi prosecuted Edgar Ray Killens for his role in the death of three civil rights workers in Philadelphia; Killens is also now in the state penitentiary. Ernest H. Avants was prosecuted and convicted in federal court for the 1967 murder of Ben Chester White; he died in prison in 2004 while serving time for his civil rights era crime.

Recently the people of Neshoba County and its principal city of Philadelphia formed a committee to memorialize the death and courage of the three civil rights workers—James Chaney, Andrew Goodman, and Michael Schwerner—slain in Mississippi during the civil rights era. Jim Prince, the white editor of the local *Neshoba Democrat*, and African American Leroy Clemons, president of the Neshoba County NAACP, co-chaired the coalition that helped heal racial scars in that community.

In December 2004, the predominately white town of Newton— hometown of slain civil rights leader Medgar Evers—spearheaded the multiracial Newton County Medgar Evers Committee to celebrate his birth and life and designated a key local crossroads as the "Medgar Evers Memorial Interchange." About that same time, the Jackson City Council renamed the state's largest airport as the Jackson-Evers International Airport.

The University of Mississippi (Ole Miss) created the William Winter Institute for Racial Reconciliation to promote racial harmony and understanding. Jackson State University, the state's largest predominately black university, created 1 Mississippi for the same purpose.

The Reverend Dolphus Weary wrote about his struggles during the civil rights era in his book *I Ain't Coming Back*. But he did come back to Mississippi and now leads Mission Mississippi, a statewide Christian biracial group seeking racial reconciliation and unity through common faith. John Perkins moved beyond the beatings and injuries of the civil rights movement to form the Foundation for Reconciliation and Development, which partners with Mendenhall Ministries and Voice of Calvary Ministries and others to address the spiritual, physical, and economic needs of Mississippians by reconciling the races and using their united skills and resources. They reach into university classes, civic organizations, poverty communities, and churches to build bridges between blacks and whites.

Countless churches, organizations, and individuals across Mississippi are finding ways to bridge the racial divide. It is time for the rest of the nation to see Mississippi through the perspective of our progress, not through the lens of the past.

Mississippi, like the rest of America, was settled by immigrants. There were Spanish and French influences, but most Mississippians came from Western Europe or Africa. In recent years, the Hispanic population has increased. We must continue to find common ground if we are to prosper and move forward.

No other country has prospered as has the United States. Our unity of purpose, common ideals, and shared goals have eluded many of our neighbors. While other nations have been ripped apart by their internal cultural differences, we have shown an ability to become a whole greater than the sum of our parts.

America's diversity is growing, and soon there will be no majority race; we will all be minorities. The American values are not dependent upon any race, ethnicity, or color; the American tradition transcends people differences to form a civic unity. For America to maintain our unity and purpose where so many other countries have fractured, we must recommit ourselves to the principles of our nation: a government of laws and not men; respect for the rule of law; respect for one another. These principles have allowed our people more freedom, liberty, and opportunity than any civilization has ever experienced.

On the Great Seal of the United States is the phrase *E pluribus unum*, meaning "out of many, one." I'm afraid today we emphasize "we are many from one," not "one from many." That does not strengthen our union. Although we should celebrate our diversity, we should emphasize our unity. We must recognize that different as we may be, we are all Americans.

In America there will always be disagreements. That is a by-product of our freedom, a consequence of our diversity. But we must not destroy each other in our discussions and debates.

I am not suggesting that anyone give up deeply-held convictions; nor am I suggesting that Christians should not boldly proclaim the love, compassion, commands, and redemption of God. The Bible requires such testimony, and the Constitution guarantees the right to do so both under freedom of speech and freedom of religion. We can and should exercise these rights and compete in the marketplace of ideas. However, Christians will win no converts shouting louder or with a voice more shrill than the secularist. Secularists may silence opposition for a time, but such will be short-lived and the price far greater than any advantage gained. Under our Constitution, we can and should have these debates, yet remain united against threats both foreign and domestic.

The solutions I have proposed are reforms over which there is tremendous disagreement. Regardless, these are issues that need to be addressed. Hopefully, for the sake of our children and grandchildren and the future of America, we can address them with reason, respect, and civility.

We all have a responsibility—Democrat or Republican, liberal or conservative, Christian or non-Christian—to make our nation better and stronger, for this land is your land, this land is my land, and this land is our land. Our futures are intertwined.

Acknowledgments

I OWE SO much to so many, it is difficult to know where to begin and impossible to name everyone. I am deeply grateful for every word, letter, statement, e-mail, travel to Washington, or other effort made on behalf of my confirmation, and for every word of encouragement and prayer made on my behalf and on behalf of my family.

My greatest debt of gratitude goes to my wife, Margaret Ann, who stood with me every step of the way. She is an inspiration, an encourager, and an awesome prayer partner. Margaret Ann is a wonderful mother to our four children—they could have no better mother or me a better wife. She has been my loving and faithful wife for more than forty-seven years and a significant contributor to anything good I have accomplished. Words cannot express the gratitude and appreciation I have for her.

My son, Congressman Chip Pickering, worked the hardest to secure my confirmation. He did everything honorably and humanly possible. He would not give up. I can never sufficiently convey appreciation to Chip for his actions to defend my name and reputation. Our three daughters, Paige Dunkerton, Allison Montgomery, and Christi Chapman, were equally supportive with their words and prayers. The families of my children gave strength to us all as well. I appreciate my only brother Gene, his wife Karon, and my only sister Ellen Walker, and her husband, Jimmy, for traveling to Washington for my second hearing.

Senators Trent Lott and Thad Cochran recommended my appointment to the district court in 1990 and to the Fifth Circuit Court of Appeals in 2001. I appreciate their recommendations and am thankful for their warm friendship and strong support over the years. President George H. W. Bush appointed me to the district bench. I have always had the highest respect for him and Barbara. President George W. Bush showed loyalty and determination by nominating me, re-nominating me, and giving me a recess appointment. For his confidence and support, I will always be grateful.

Ed Haddon served on the staff of the Senate Judiciary Committee for Senator Jeff Sessions. He worked tirelessly for my confirmation and was indispensable to my confirmation fight. I am grateful to Ed as well as Senator Sessions, who allowed him to work so hard on my behalf.

I am grateful to Senator Orrin Hatch, chairman of the Judiciary Committee; all the Republican senators on the Judiciary Committee and their staffs who worked and supported my nomination; Senators Zell Miller and John Breaux, who both broke rank with the Democrats, supported my nomination and voted to stop the filibuster; the only Independent in the Senate, Jim Jeffords, who also supported my nomination and voted to stop the filibuster; Senator Ben Nelson of Nebraska who supported my nomination; and for the Republican senators, all of whom supported my nomination and voted to end the filibuster.

Thanks to the following who worked on my confirmation: Steven Wall and Brad Prewitt, assistants to Senators Lott and Cochran, respectively; Susan Butler, Stanley Shows, Mike Chappell, and Brian Perry on Chip's staff; staffs in the Justice Department, White House, and at the Judiciary Committee.

Working with me over the almost five years I was facing confirmation, my staff took the brunt of the battle as they helped me prepare documents and materials to respond to the various requests of the Senate Committee and charges of special-interest groups—hard work for which I'm deeply grateful: Paul Walters, career law clerk; Sonja Gatlin, secretary; Margaret Seal, court reporter; Stephen King, Brian Petruska, Lorraine Walters Boykin, and Jeff Williams, law clerks; and Sharon Potin, courtroom deputy.

Thanks to my fellow district judges with whom I served for thirteen years; members of the Fifth Circuit Court of Appeals, who accepted me and worked with me during the eleven months that I had the privilege of serving on the Fifth Circuit; and the staffs and the other support personnel of both courts as well as the leadership and personnel at the Administrative Office for the Courts.

I was humbled by the editorial endorsement of every major newspaper in Mississippi, the local television station WDAM, and numerous columnists and editorial writers inside and outside Mississippi. I appreciate the near unanimous support of past presidents of the Mississippi Bar, and the broad base of support I received from Mississippians with whom I have lived and worked over the years, both Democrat and Republican, both black and white.

The Democratic support included former governor William Winter; Frank Hunger; all of the then statewide elected Democratic officials in Mississippi: Governor Ronnie Musgrove, Lieutenant Governor Amy Tuck, Attorney General Mike Moore, Secretary of State Eric Clark, Commissioner of Insurance George Dale, and Commissioner of Agriculture Lester Spell; former governor Bill Waller; former lieutenant governors Brad Dye and Evelyn Gandy; Wayne Dowdy, chairman of the Mississippi Democratic Party; Danny Cupit, chairman of the Democratic Party in the 1970s when I was chairman of the Mississippi Republican Party; Mayor Phillip West; former state representative David Green; Mayor Melvin Mack; Mayor Johnny Dupree; city council members Anne Clayton, Rev. Arthur Logan, Johnny Magee, and Henry E. Naylor; Forrest County supervisor Charles Marshall; and numerous others who identified themselves as Democrats in their letters of support.

Two of my closest friends, James Huff and Wesley Breland, did so many things to be supportive in my confirmation battle. Charles Evers, Deborah Gambrell, Charles Lawrence, Judge Henry Wingate, Judge Johnny Williams, Mike McMahan, and Frank Montague were most helpful.

I am very appreciative of my partners, colleagues, and staff at Baker Donelson Bearman Caldwell & Berkowitz who have been my friends and encouragers since I left the court.

Thanks to Craig Shirley and Dianne Banister of Shirley and Banister, who put me in contact with Stroud and Hall and gave me advice and counsel along the way; Randy Evans, who represented me in negotiations; and Dr. Cecil Staton and the rest of staff at Stroud & Hall. Thanks to Joe Maxwell, who greatly contributed to the chapter on civility; Clint Pentecost, who provided solid research; Rich Campbell, who volunteered to proofread *Supreme Chaos*, my companion book on confirmation; Brian Perry, who took a leave of absence for this project, helped research, write, and edit, and without whose capable assistance I could not have written this book; Cindy Hosey, my administrative assistant, who typed every page of this book numerous times with good cheer and efficiency; and to Magnolia State Bank (where I serve on the board of directors) and Thomas Brown.

A special thanks to former justice Reuben V. Anderson; Robert (Bob) Anderson; Rev. Cecil Ashford; Herman and Patsy Aycock; Reverend George Barnes; Angela Barnett; Ken Bassinger; Charles Bolton; Lillian Breland; Tucker Buchanan; Mr. and Mrs. Stan Burton; W. O. "Chet" Dillard; Melvin Daniels; Gus DeLoach; Don Dornan; Jennifer Drawdy; James K. Dukes; Donnie Ray Fairly Sr.; Rev. Kenneth E. Fairley; Milton Gavin; Pamela Gerity; Early M. Gray; Mr. and Mrs. Louis Griffin; Ellen Gunn; Steve Guyton; Dr. and Mrs. Eddie Hamilton; Charles Harrison; Mr. and Mrs. Carey Hauenstein; Dr. and Mrs. Gene Henderson; John Holiday; Pat Holifield; Dr. and Mrs. Mark Horne; Scott Howell; Marilyn Huff; Dr. and Mrs. Doug Jefcoat; Tammi Jenkins; Judge Grady Jolly; Nora J. Jones; Rev. Nathan Jordan; Judge Damon J. Keith; the late Dr. Larry and Mrs. Kennedy; J. W. (Judy) King; James King; Dr. and Mrs. Eric Linstrom; Chris McDaniel; Dr. Joe McKeever; Dr. and Mrs. Robert Marsh; Rev. and Mrs. Jim Ormon; the late Judge Fred Parker and Mrs. Parker; Dr. John Perkins; Joe Phillips; Justice Mike Randolph; Joy Roberts; Al Rosenbaum; Stephanie Schmitt; Senator and Mrs. Vincent Scoper; Rev. Arthur L. Siggers; Ralph Simmons; Raymond Swartzfager; Rena Pittman Temple; Larry Thomas; Ginny Traylor; Dr. and Mrs. Randy Turner; Jennifer Selby; Mayor Susan Vincent; the late Dr. Jimmy Waites and Mrs. Waites; Rev. Dolphus Weary; Mr. and Mrs. Williams Wells; Charlote Whitehead; and others whose names I cannot list because of space limitations.

Notes

CHAPTER ONE

[1] Audrey Hudson, "Feminist Groups Target Bush Nominees," *The Washington Times*, 11 December 2001.

[2] Chip continues to serve in Congress and in January 2007 began his sixth term.

[3] Amy Tuck would later switch to the Republican Party. I believe the anger from her own Democrat Party over her fair redistricting plan contributed to her decision.

[4] John Nowacki, "The left targets Pickering . . . again," *Free Congress Foundation*, 11 February 2002.

[5] As the proceedings dragged on, I was reversed once more and the cases I handled exceeded 5,000.

[6] Hudson, "Feminist Groups Target Bush Nominees."

[7] Audrey Hudson, "GOP Set to End Judicial Backlog," *The Washington Times,* 11 November 2002.

CHAPTER TWO

[1] For a more comprehensive look at the history of Jones County during the Civil War years, see Victoria E. Bynum, *The Free State of Jones: Mississippi's Longest Civil War* (Chapel Hill: University of North Carolina Press, 2002), and Ethel Knight, *The Echo of the Black Horn: An Authentic Tale of 'the Governor' of 'The Free State of Jones* (Baton Rouge: Franklin Press, 1951). I knew Ethel Knight well, and a friend and I purchased her farm on the Leaf River a few years ago. Many in Jones County disagree with a number of conclusions in both books.

[2] *Times of London*, 25 May 1998.

[3] *Nightline*, ABC News, 29 May 1998.

[4] Adam Cohen, "Widow and the Wizard," *Time Magazine*, 18 May 1998.

[5] *Baton Rouge Advocate*, 8 March 1994.

[6] Ben Bryant, "Backers: Judge Fought Klan," *Biloxi Sun Herald*, 7 February 2002.

[7] W. O. "Chet" Dillard, *Clear Burning: Civil Rights, Civil Wrongs* (Jackson, Mississippi, Persimmon Press, 1992), 108.

[8] Bettie E. Dahmer, "I Awoke to the House Being on Fire," *Voices of Civil Rights* (http://www.voicesofcivilrights.org/Approved_Letters/1717-Dahmer-MS.html).

[9] Mary K. Garber "Justice Delayed, Justice Served," Joint Center for Political and Economic Studies, *Focus Magazine*, October 1998.

[10] *Sam Bowers v. Mike Moore and the State of Mississippi*, U.S. District Court, S.D. Miss., 2; 00-CV-54PG.

[11] George E. Curry, "Kerry Regrets Limited Civil Rights Involvement," *Atlanta Daily World*, 28 April 2004.

[12] Durbin fundraising letter, 12 April 2002.

CHAPTER THREE

[1] Boyden Gray was referring to comments made by Aron at the Federalist Society debate on Judicial Confirmations (Hon. C. Boyden Gray; Wilmer Cutler Pickering; Nan Aron, President, Alliance for Justice; Leonard Leo, Moderator), 20 February 2003. The colloquy was as follows:

AUDIENCE PARTICIPANT: "Ms. Aron, you seem to rely on the confirmation process to accomplish what Congress can do through other means. For example, if Congress wants to protect individuals, they can expand federal court jurisdiction, create new federal causes of action, and if they don't like the way a judge is behaving, they can simply impeach him. Is this not evidence of weak political will?"

MS. ARON: "I can't think of—I guess I can. I can think of the last time a judge was impeached, but it's more than ten years ago. And these are for high crimes and misdemeanors. It's almost impossible to impeach a federal judge for the commission of a high crime and misdemeanor. And what I always found quite amusing was statements by people like Tom Delay in the House. Any time a judge issued a ruling with which he disagreed, the Delay would be right on the floor of the House saying 'impeach that judge.' It's not done, and it shouldn't be done unless there's a real valid reason for that to occur. Congress isn't about to expand in large causes of action. You know that; I know that. This is not a Congress that necessarily, at least with a majority party, sees its role as expanding its capacity to meet the needs of the people of this nation. And neither house sees this role as its role. Therefore, I think that that notion would simply fail, given the current makeup in leadership in both the House and Senate today."

MR. GRAY: "I hope you're not suggesting that because the majority party, in your view, won't expand rights, the court should do it?"

MS. ARON: "No. But I say that the courts are there to interpret those rights and interpret those statutes. And certainly, you want to have courts that do it in a way that respect and respond to what Congress is doing, not simply overrule what it's done."

[2] "Fresh Air," National Public Radio, 16 February 2005.

CHAPTER FOUR

[1] Jason Straziuso, "Bush Judicial Nominee Pickering Accused of False Senate Testimony," Associated Press, 23 January 2002.

[2] Helen Dewar, "Miss. Judge Is Latest Focus of Confirmation Fights," *Washington Post*, 27 January 2002.

[3] David Freddoso, "Democrats Bork Pickering as Test Run For Bush Supreme Court Nominations," *Human Events*, 25 February 2002.

[4] People for the American Way, "Opposing the Confirmation of Charles W Pickering, Sr., to the U.S. Court of Appeals for the 5th Circuit," 24 January 2002.

[5] *National Review*, 8 April 2002.

[6] Roger Clegg, "Politics, Pickering, and Philosophy: The Role of the Political Branches in Judicial Selection," *Nexus, A Journal of Opinion* (Anaheim: Chapman University School of Law, 2002): 49.

[7] Confirmation hearing on the nomination of Charles W. Pickering Sr. to be circuit judge for the Fifth Circuit, 7 February 2002, serial no. J-107-57, pp. 89, 90.

[8] Clegg, "Politics, Pickering, and Philosophy," 56.

[9] Confirmation hearing on the nomination of Charles W. Pickering Sr., pp. 89, 90.

[10] Michael D. Cooke, letter to Sen. Leahy, hearing, serial no. J-107-57, p. 225.

[11] *Greenwood Commonwealth*, 7 February 2002.

[12] Sam R. Hall, *Natchez Democrat*, 5 February 2002.

[13] Ana Radelat, "Senate urged to oppose Pickering," *Clarion Ledger*, 7 February 2002.

[14] *Clarion Ledger*, 8 February 2002.

CHAPTER FIVE

[1] Although a juvenile at the time, Jason Branch's name is now a matter of public record reported by the national press. So I will use his name here as well.

[2] *United States v. Daniel Swan*, criminal action #2:94CR3PR.

[3] 18 USCA, section 3553 (a)(6).

[4] *United States v. Clark*, 4th Circuit, no. 05-4274, 12 January 2006.

[5] Swan sentencing transcripts, 15 August 1994, 15 November 1994, 23 January 1995.

[6] Under federal guidelines, a defendant receives a slightly higher sentence if he does not plead guilty and goes to trial. In this situation the increase would have been nine months—exactly the increase in sentence I imposed on Swan.

[7] Byron York, "The Cross Burning Case: What Really Happened, Part II: The Facts are Far Different From the Democratic Spin," *National Review*, 13 January 2003.

[8] Attorney Ed Pittman Jr., letter to Sen. Patrick Leahy, hearing, serial no. J-107-57, p. 355.

[9] Attorney Carol Ann Estes Bustin, letter to Sen. Patrick Leahy, p. 214.

[10] Attorney Scott J. Swartz, letter to Sen. Patrick Leahy, p. 361.

[11] *Atlanta Journal Constitution*, 9 March 2003.

[12] *Fort Wayne News—Sentinel*, 23 February 2003.

CHAPTER SIX

[1] After Republicans dismissed Miranda under pressure from Democrat senators over this incident, Miranda launched back at the Democrats alleging corruption. One memo he cited reads, "Elaine Jones of the NAACP Legal Defense Fund (LDF) tried to call you [Senator Kennedy] today to ask that the Judiciary Committee consider scheduling Julia Scott Gibbons, the uncontroversial nominee to the 6th Circuit at a later date. . . . Elaine would like the Committee to hold off on any 6th Circuit nominees until the University of Michigan case regarding the constitutionality of affirmative action in higher education is decided by the en banc 6th Circuit. . . . The thinking is that the current 6th Circuit will sustain the affirmative action program, but if a new judge with conservative views is confirmed before the case is decided, that new judge will be able, under 6th Circuit rules, to review the case and vote on it." The memo's author admitted concern "about the propriety of scheduling hearings based on the resolution of a particular case but "Nevertheless we recommend that Gibbons be scheduled for a later hearing: the Michigan case is important . . . ." This was an example, an instance of one of the special-interest groups putting pressure on the Democrats in the Senate Judiciary Committee to postpone a confirmation hearing of someone who was not controversial to affect the outcome of a specific case before the court. Certainly this was taking the politicizing of the judiciary to a new low.

[2] Stephen Henderson, "Racial furor over judicial nomination questionable when Pickering's record studied," *Clarion Ledger*, 9 March 2003.

[3] Joan Biskupic, "Bush Nominees Hearings May Start Judicial Battles," *USA Today*, 7 February 2002.

[4] Byron York, "The Next Big Fight," *National Review Online*, 6 February 2002.(http://www.nationalreview.com/york/york020602.shtml)

[5] Neal A. Lewis, "Fight Over Judicial Nominee Resumes," *New York Times*, 6 February 2002.

[6] David Freddoso, *Human Events*, 25 February 2002.

[7] York, "The Next Big Fight."

[8] *USA Today*, 7 February 2002.

[9] *Human Events*, 25 February 2002.

[10] Confirmation hearings on the nomination of Charles W. Pickering Sr. to be circuit judge for the 5th Circuit, 7 February 2002, serial no. J-107-57, p. 3.

[11] Ibid., 77.

[12] Ibid., 84.

[13] Based on data from the clerk of the Fifth Circuit Court of Appeals and data from my chambers.

[14] Information from staff, Department of Justice, Office of Legal Policy.

[15] Chart developed by Republican staff, Judiciary Committee of the Senate.

[16] Confirmation hearings on the nomination of Charles W. Pickering Sr. to be circuit judge for the 5th Circuit, p. 92.

[17] *Clarion Ledger*, 8 February 2002.

[18] *Laurel Leader Call*, 7 February 2002.

[19] Bill Minor, "Charles Pickering background reveals no 'racial extremism,'" *Clarion Ledger*, 23 February 2003.

[20] Transcript, confirmation hearing on the nomination of Charles W. Pickering Sr. to be circuit judge for the Fifth Circuit, 7 February 2002, serial no. J-107-57, pp. 110-11.

[21] When I could not get a response from the Justice Department attorneys as to the inquiry I had made, I called Frank Hunger, a friend from Mississippi, who headed up the Justice Department Civil Litigation Division during the Clinton Administration. He is a brother-in-law to former Vice President Al Gore. I expressed my frustration over my inability to get a response from the government attorneys as to my inquiries and asked as a matter of process whether this was standard. Frank told me this was a matter outside of his responsibilities. Later when I called Frank and asked his recollection of my call, he didn't even remember that I had called.

[22] Press release from the Mississippi Republican Party, 7 July 2004 (quoting CNN).

[23] Michael I. Krauss to Sen. Orrin Hatch, ranking member, Senate Judiciary Committee, 11 February 2002.

[24] Carl Cameron, "Backroom Deal Offered for Pickering Confirmation," *Fox News*, 6 March 2002.

[25] Jessie J Holland, *Associated Press*, 7 February 2002.

[26] *Roll Call*, 8 February 2002.

[27] *Roll Call*, 21 February 2002.

[28] *Washington Post*, 17 February 2002.

[29] *Human Events*, 25 February 2002.

[30] Ibid.

[31] "Judicial Nominees Set for Fight That's 'Nastier Than Ever,'" *Clarion Ledger*, 8 May 2005.

[32] Ibid.

[33] Ibid.

[34] Ibid.

[35] *Clarion Ledger*, 8 February 2002.

[36] *National Review*, 19 March 2002.

[37] Byron York, "The GOP's Post Pickering Strategy?" *National Review Online*, 1 March 2002. (http://www.nationalreview.com/york/york031202.shtml)

CHAPTER SEVEN

[1] *Clarion Ledger*, 26 February 2002.

[2] *Associated Press*, 11 February 2002.

[3] Ibid.

[4] Neil Lewis, *New York Times*, 28 February 2002.

[5] John Machacek and Ana Radelat, *Hattiesburg American*, 28 February 2002.

[6] Neil Lewis, *New York Times*, 6 March 2002.

[7] *Wall Street Journal*, 7 March 2002.

[8] Ibid.

[9] Ana Radelat, *Clarion Ledger*, 7 March 2002.

[10] *Clarion Ledger*, 8 March 2002.

[11] James Charles Evers, *Wall Street Journal*, 7 February 2002.

[12] Press conference by President George W. Bush, 13 March 2002.

CHAPTER EIGHT

[1] In addition to civil rights activist Charles Evers, I had twenty-five letters of support from African American leaders with whom I had worked and lived over my lifetime. Eight of these leaders were present or former elected officials, four were former NAACP officials, and four were church leaders. I had the support of every statewide elected Democrat official including the governor, the lieutenant governor, the secretary of state, the attorney general, the commissioner of insurance, and the commissioner of agriculture. I had the support of two former Democrat governors, three former Democrat lieutenant governors, and the chairman of the Democratic Party when I was chairman of the Republican Party. My nomination was endorsed by all of the major newspapers in Mississippi, as well as the then current and eighteen former presidents of the Mississippi Bar Association.

[2] All quotes from the Senate Judiciary Committee Debate from 14 March 2002 are taken from a transcription of the C-SPAN recording of the event.

[3] Statement on the Senate floor, 9 January 2003.

[4] CBS News, 8 January 2003.

[5] Gannett News Service, 9 January 2003.

[6] Senator Dick Durbin fundraising letter, 12 April 2002.

[7] Gannett News Service, 9 January 2003.

[8] *Laurel Leader Call*, 1 March 2002.

[9] Denis Steven Rutkus, "Senate Judiciary Committee Votes on Judicial Nominations Other than Those Approving Motions to Report Favorably, 1943 to the Present," Congressional Research Service Memorandum, 5 March 2002.

[10] *Clarion Ledger*, 15 March 2002.

[11] Associated Press, 15 March 2002.

[12] Statement on the Senate floor, 15 March 2002.

[13] *Washington Post*, 15 March 2002.

[14] *Roll Call*, 15 March 2002.

[15] *The Hill*, 20 March 2002.

[16] Helen Dewar, *Washington Post*, 25 March 2002.

[17] Robert E. Thompson, *Chattanooga Times Free Press*, 24 March 2002.

[18] *New York Times*, 15 March 2002.

[19] Ibid.

[20] *London Daily Telegraph*, 15 March 2002.

[21] Neal A. Lewis, "First Punch in the Revived Bench-Tipping Brawl," *New York Times*, 17 March 2002.

[22] Associated Press, 27 March 2002.

CHAPTER NINE

[1] Paul Kane, "GOP Senate Hopefuls Expect Boost From Pickering Nomination Battle," *Roll Call*, 21 March 2002.

[2] Tom Curry, "GOP Senate Majority Would Solve Impasse Over Judicial Nominees," MSNBC, 29 March 2002.

[3] Amy Goldstein, "Senate's Committee's Rejection of Pickering Turned into GOP Campaign Theme," *Washington Post*, 15 April 2002.

[4] Paul Kane, "Democrats Foresee No Fallout On Judges," *Roll Call*, 13 May 2002.

[5] Donald Lambro, "GOP chief sees tight battle for Senate," *Washington Times*, 13 May 2002.

[6] David Van Drehle, "New GOP Group to Push for Judicial Nominees," *Washington Post*, 23 July 2002.

[7] Duncan Currie, "Bench Warfare; The coming battle over President Bush's Supreme Court nominee," *Weekly Standard*, 27 June 2005.

[8] Julie Mason, "Democrats reject Owen nomination," *Houston Chronicle*, 6 September 2002.

[9] Ibid.

[10] Ibid.

[11] "'He Is Latino': Why Dems borked Estrada, in their own words," *Wall Street Journal Opinion Journal*, 15 November 2003.

[12] Memo to Senator Ted Kennedy, 28 February 2002.

[13] Audrey Hudson, "GOP Set to End Judicial Backlog," *Washington Times*, 11 November 2002.

[14] Neil A. Lewis, "Bush Places Senate's Delays on Judicial Appointees at Core of Campaigning," *New York Times*, 16 October 2002.

[15] *Hattiesburg American*, 7 November 2002.

[16] Audrey Hudson, "GOP set to end judicial backlog," *Washington Times*, 11 November 2002.

[17] Sean Rushton, "Judge Pickering's Revenge: The judicial confirmation battle has already hurt Democrats," *National Review Online*, 6 November 2003. (http://www.nationalreview.com/comment/rushton200311060941.asp)

[18] Neil A. Lewis, "Stalled Nominations to the Bench Suddenly Get a New Life," *New York Times*, 7 November 2002.

[19] *Washington Post*, 7 November 2002.

[20] Neil A. Lewis, "Stalled Nominations to the Bench Suddenly Get a New Life."

CHAPTER TEN

[1] *Laurel Leader Call*, 12 & 14 December 2002.

[2] *MSNBC News*, 8 January 2003.

[3] Associated Press, 7 January 2003.

[4] Byron York, "Schumer on the Attack," *National Review*, 9 January 2003.

[5] Jonathan Karl, "Bush To Reintroduce Judicial Nominees Rejected Last Year by Senate," *CNN Inside Politics*, 8 January 2003.

[6] Matt Volz, Associated Press, January 2003.

[7] Stuart Taylor Jr., "Who's Worse? Race-Baiting Democrats or Class Warring Republicans?" *National Journal*, 18 January 2003.

[8] Byron York, "Schumer on the Attack," *National Review*, 9 January 2003.

[9] Paul M. Weyrich, *Toogood Reports*, 28 April 2003.

[10] *Wall Street Journal*, 10 January 2002.

[11] Josh Benson and Greg Sargent, "Chuck's Game: Plans to Block Bush's Judge," *New York Observer*, 15 January 2003.

[12] *Laurel Leader Call*, 13 January 2003.

[13] *Clarion Ledger*, 2 February 2003.

[14] Byron York, "Schumer's Campaign Violations," *National Review Online*, 5 May 2003.

[15] Paul Kane, "Pickering Makes Fight Personal," *Roll Call*, 18 February 2003.

[16] Charlie Mitchell, "Chip Ready to Knock Some Blocks Off," *Northeast Mississippi Daily Journal*, 4 March 2003.

[17] Matt Volz, "Pickering Says His Father's Fight for Post Bigger Than One Person," Associated Press, 30 May 2003.

[18] *Clarion Ledger*, 25 January 2003.

[19] Emily Wagster Pettus, Associated Press, 11 February 2003.

[20] Rosalyn Anderson, WLBT News, 10 February 2003.

[21] Editorial, *Clarion Ledger*, 12 February 2003.

[22] While these legislators did personally support me, they never formally followed through on the action.

[23] *Clarion Ledger*, 7 May 2003.

[24] Statement of Phillip "Bucket" West.

[25] *Knight Ridder*, 23 February 2003.

[26] *Atlanta Journal Constitution*, 9 March 2003.

[27] Jonathan Groner, *Legal Times*, 5 March 2003.

[28] Stephen Dinan, "Hispanics tune out Estrada filibuster," *Washington Times*, 19 June 2003.

[29] Donald Lambro, "Republicans draw Hispanic voters from Democrats," *Washington Times*, 12 July 2003.

[30] Personal conversation between the author and Miguel Estrada.

[31] Tom Perrault, "Reaction to Miguel Estrada's Withdrawal," *Crosswalk.com*, 5 September 2003.

[32] Randy E. Barnett, "Benching Bork, How to End the War Over Judges," *National Review Online*, 29 April 2003.

CHAPTER ELEVEN

[1] Jessie J Holland, Associated Press, 5 September 2003.

[2] Byron York, "Why Estrada Quit," *National Review Online*, 4 September 2003.

[3] Paul Kane, *Roll Call*, 29 September 2003.

[4] *Feminist's Daily News Service*, 12 September 2003.

[5] Stephen Henderson, *Knight Ridder*, 2 October 2003.

[6] Ibid.

[7] Ibid.

[8] Charles Hurt, *Washington Post*, 3 October 2003.

[9] Transcript of C-SPAN archives tape of proceedings before the Judiciary Committee, 14 March 2002.

[10] Jesse J. Holland, Associated Press, 2 October 2003.

[11] Neil A. Lewis, "Senate Panel Approves Judge's Nomination," *New York Times*, 3 October 2003.

[12] Ibid.

[13] Byron York, *National Review Online*, 30 October 2003.

[14] Neil A. Lewis, *New York Times*, 3 October 2003.

[15] Nat Hentoff, 19 October 2003.

[16] Hentoff, 17 October 2003.

[17] Hentoff, 19 October 2003.

[18] *Washington Post*, 3 January 2004.

[19] *CQ Today*, 30 October 2003.

[20] *Roll Call*, 22 October 2003.

[21] Nick Anderson, *LA Times*, 30 October 2003.

[22] *Washington Times*, 30 October 2003.

[23] Ibid.

[24] *Los Angeles Times*, 30 October 2003.

[25] John Cornyn, "Restoring our Broken Judicial Confirmation Process," *Texas Review of Law and Politics*, vol. 8.

[26] *Clarion Ledger*, 31 October 2003.

[27] Ibid.

[28] WDAM, NBC affiliate in Hattiesburg.

CHAPTER TWELVE

[1] Katherine Mangu-Ward, "Picking on Pickering," *Weekly Standard*, 1 December 2003.

[2] "President's Statement on Appointing Judge Charles Pickering to Fifth Circuit Appeals Court," 16 January 2004.

[3] Jack Elliot Jr., *Associated Press*, 18 January 2004.

[4] Ibid.

[5] All Politics, CNN.com, 18 January 2004.

[6] Sam Hananel, Associated Press, 17 January 2004.

[7] *Burlington Free Press*, 17 January 2004.

[8] Stephen Henderson, *Philadelphia Inquirer*, 17 January 2004.

[9] "Point of View," WLBT, 29 January 2004.

[10] Bill Rankin and Eunice Moscoso, *Atlanta Journal Constitution*, 17 January 2004.

[11] Chad Groening and Jody Brown, Agape Press.

[12] *Hattiesburg American*, 17 January 2004.

[13] Stephen Henderson, *Philadelphia Inquirer*, 17 January 2004.

[14] *Atlanta Journal Constitution*, 18 January 2004.

[15] *Clarion Ledger*, 31 January 2004.

[16] *Laurel Leader Call*, 22 January 2004.

[17] *Mobile Press Register*, 17 January 2004.

[18] *National Journal*, 24 January 2004.

[19] *Mobile Press Register*, 17 January 2004.

CHAPTER THIRTEEN

[1] *Associated Press*, 27 March 2004.

[2] Jason Niblett, *Laurel Leader Call*, 27 March 2004.

[3] Paul Beston, *American Spectator*, 29 March 2004.

[4] Transcript of *60 Minutes* segment.

[5] Paul Beston, *American Spectator*, 29 March 2004.

[6] Ratings furnished by CBS.

[7] *Orlando Centennial*, 25 April 2004.

[8] Editorial, *Greenwood Commonwealth*, 2 April 2004.

[9] Editorial, *Meridian Star*, 30 March 2004.

CHAPTER FOURTEEN

[1] The history of the building is taken from Michael R. Smith, "The John Minor Wisdom United States Court of Appeals Building," updated October 1998.

[2] Cases before the Fifth Circuit are routinely heard by a three-judge panel. But several cases each year are heard before the entire court, referred to as an en banc hearing. Generally, these hearings result from a disagreement among the judges as to how the issues should be decided.

[3] The Fifth Circuit has seventeen authorized active circuit judges. Before my recess appointment, there were two vacancies and only fifteen active judges. There was still one vacancy while I was on the court due to the filibuster of Priscilla Owen. After Priscilla Owen was confirmed, there remained one vacancy due to my retirement.

[4] *McComb Enterprise Journal*, 23 May 2004.

[5] *US Newswire*, 3 July 2004.

[6] The information as to decisions rendered, opinions written, and orders entered was obtained from the clerk of the Fifth Circuit, Charles R. Fulbruge III.

CHAPTER FIFTEEN

[1] There have been additional developments since this book went to press. Both William Haynes who was nominated to the Fourth Circuit Court of Appeals and William Myers who was nominated to the Ninth Circuit Court of Appeals in 2003 asked that their nominations be withdrawn following the 2006 election when Democrats once again regained control of the Senate. President Bush nominated Mike Wallace of Mississippi to the Fifth Circuit Court of Appeals to fill my vacated seat in 2005, but by the following year, Wallace faced Democrat obstruction and also asked that his nomination be withdrawn. Just before the new Congress convened in 2007 under Democrat control, Senate Majority Leader Harry Reid announced, "President Bush must finally face reality and send us different candidates for these vacancies in January." He said the Senate would not confirm those nominees. (Keith Perine, "As Judicial Battles Loom, Leahy Revives Senate 'Blue Slip' Tradition," *CQ Today.* [4 January 2007])

[2] Evan P. Schultz, "Boom! Why Democrats should learn to stop worrying and love the 'nuclear option,'" *Legal Times*, 4 September 2006.

[3] Sean Rushton, "Judge Pickering's Revenge: The judicial-confirmation battle has already hurt Democrats," *National Review Online*, 6 November 2003.

CHAPTER SIXTEEN

[1] Virginia Thomas, "A Wakeup Call," *Wall Street Journal*, 5 September 2003.

[2] John Cornyn, "Restoring our Broken Judicial Confirmation Process," *Texas Review of Law and Politics*, vol. 8.

[3] *USA Today*, 14 July 2005.

[4] Neil A. Lewis, *New York Times*, 29 October 2003.

[5] David Von Drehle, *Washington Post*, 3 January 2004.

CHAPTER SEVENTEEN

[1] *Lend Me Your Ears: Great Speeches in History*, selected and introduced by William Safire (New York: W. W. Norton and Company, 2004).

[2] A special thanks goes to Joe Maxwell for his extensive work with me on this chapter.

[3] George Washington, *Rules of Civility & Decent Behaviour in Company and Conversation: A Book of Etiquette* (Williamsburg VA: Beaver Press, 1971).

[4] "Keys to Civility," National Civility Center, CivilityCenter.org, http://civilitycenter.org/keys.php.

[5] Aaron Brown, *CNN Newsnight*, 14 November 2003.

[6] "Rice spars with Democrats in hearing," CNN.com, 19 January 2005.

[7] Elsa Walsh, "Minority Retort," *New Yorker*, 8 August 2005.

[8] "NAACP chairman compares GOP to Nazis," *World Net Daily*, 2 February 2006.

[9] "Chicks defiant with interview, nude cover," CNN.com, 24 November 2003.

[10] "Toby Keith Says Natalie Maines Is 'Miserable,' 'Irresponsible,'" LAUNCH Radio Networks, 11 June 2003.

[11] Nicole Jacoby, "Employees say they've had enough of incivility, bad manners," CNNfn, 29 November 1999.

[12] P. M. Forni, "Ethical Action and Relational Competence: Why Manners and Civility are Good," *Protocol Today*, October 2003.

[13] Guy Burgess and Heidi Burgess, "The Meaning of Civility," Conflict Research Consortium, 1997. (http://www.colorado.edu/conflict/civility.htm)

[14] "Keys to Civility," http://civilitycenter.org/keys.php.

[15] George Washington, *Rules of Civility & Decent Behaviour*.

[16] Many of the observations in this chapter about promoting better race relations are taken from a column I wrote for the *Jackson Clarion Ledger* on 26 December 1999 while working to help establish the William Winter Institute for Racial Reconciliation at the University of Mississippi.

CHAPTER EIGHTEEN

[1] For original documented footnotes for this material, please refer to Charles Pickering, *Supreme Chaos* (Macon GA: Stroud and Hall, 2005); also see "A Proposal: Codification by Statute of the Judicial Confirmation Process," an essay one of my law partners, Brad Clanton, and I published in the *William & Mary Bill of Rights Journal* 14:807, February 2006.

[2] The Gang of Fourteen memo specifically singled out two pending nominees: "Signatories make no commitment to vote for or against cloture on the following judicial nominees: William Myers (9th Circuit) and Henry Saad (6th Circuit)." As an example of how this compromise failed to resolve the conflict, Henry Saad asked that his nomination be withdrawn in March 2006, while the nomination of Myers continued to languish in the Senate until January 2007, when he asked the president to withdraw his name.

CHAPTER NINETEEN

[1] Charles W. Pickering Sr. and Brad Clanton, "A Proposal: Codification by Statute of the Judicial Confirmation Process," *William & Mary Bill of Rights Journal* 14:807, February 2006.

[2] When Democrats retook control of the Senate in 2007, Senate Judiciary Committee Chairman Patrick Leahy announced he "would observe the 'blue slip' tradition: No nomination will advance without the consent of both home-state senators. The tradition had been discarded by his Republican predecessors" (Keith Perine, "As Judicial Battles Loom, Leahy Revives Senate 'Blue Slip' Tradition," *CQ Today*, 4 January 2007).

[3] *The Hill*, 21 July 2004.

[4] Ibid.

[5] Ibid.

[6] Perine, "As Judicial Battles Loom, Leahy Revives Senate 'Blue Slip' Tradition."

[7] See 2 U.S.C. §§ 631-45a (2000) (congressional budget process); 2 U.S.C. §§ 658d-658e (2000) (legislation containing unfunded mandates); 5 U.S.C. § 802 (2000) (legislation that nullifies agency regulations); 5 U.S.C. §§ 901-12 (2000) (executive reorganization plans); 8 U.S.C. § 1255a(h) (2000) (Senate rules for legislation adjusting the status of certain aliens); 15 U.S.C. § 719f (2000) (procedures for approving presidential determinations concerning Alaskan natural gas pipelines); 16 U.S.C. § 1823 (2000) (procedures for disapproving international fisheries agreements); 29 U.S.C. § 1306(b) (2000) (procedures for considering Pension Benefit Guaranty Corporation premium revisions); 42 U.S.C. § 2210(i) (2000) (procedures for nuclear accident compensation legislation); 42 U.S.C. § 6249c (2000) (legislation implementing certain

petroleum contracts); 50 U.S.C. § 1622 (2000) (procedures for terminating declared states of emergency); Amtrak Reform and Accountability Act of 1997, Pub. L. No. 105-134, § 205, 111 Stat. 2570, 2582 (1997) (Senate procedures for considering Amtrak restructuring and liquidation plans); Foreign Operations, Export Financing, and Related Programs Appropriations Act, Pub. L. No. 104-208, § 518A, 110 Stat. 3009-121-3009-145 (1996) (procedures for approving presidential findings regarding population planning funding); Defense Authorization Amendments and Base Closure and Realignment Act, Pub. L. No. 100-526, § 208, 102 Stat. 2623, 2632-33 (1988) (procedures for considering recommendations to close military bases); Anti-Drug Abuse Act of 1988, Pub. L. No. 100-690, § 7323, 102 Stat. 4181, 4467 (1988) (Senate procedures for habeas corpus reform legislation).

CHAPTER TWENTY

[1] Joseph A. Califano Jr., "Yes, Litmus-Test Judges," *Washington Post*, 31 August 2001.

[2] "Senate Battle Over Justices Begins Monday," *Fox News*, 10 November 2003.

[3] David F. Forte, "The Rule of Law and the Rules of Laws," 38 Cleveland State L Rev. 97, 1990.

[4] 1 Cranch 137, 5 U.S. 137 (1803).

[5] Jon Meacham, *American Gospel* (New York: Random House, 2006), 20, 22-23.

[6] Noah Feldman, "A Church-State Solution," *New York Times*, 3 July 2005.

[7] *Bowers v. Hardwick*, 478 U.S. 186, 194 (1986).

[8] Robert F. Turner, "Shaky surveillance ruling," *Washington Times*, 27 August 2006.

[9] Ann Althouse, "A law unto herself," *New York Times*, 23 August 2006.

[10] Balkin Blog, 19 August 2006.

[11] Editorial, *Washington Post*, 18 August 2006.

[12] Editorial, *New York Times*, 24 August 2006.

[13] 60 U.S. 393 (1856).

[14] Levin, *Men in Black: How the Supreme Court is Destroying America* (Washington D.C.: Regnery Pub., 2005), 15.

[15] 163 U.S. at 555, 556, 16 U.S. Ct. 1138 (1896).

[16] Benjamin Wittes, "Letting go of Roe," *Atlantic Monthly*, January/February 2005.

[17] Jeffrey Rosen, "The Day after Roe," *Atlantic Monthly*, June 2006.

[18] *ABA Journal and Report*, September 2005.

[19] See Levin, *Men in Black*, 195-203; Robert H. Bork, *Coercing Virtue: The Worldwide Rule of Judges* (Washington D.C.: AEI Press, 2003), 81-84; Larry D. Kramer, *The People Themselves: Popular Constitutionalism and Judicial Review* (New York: Oxford University Press, 2004), 249; Phyllis Schlafly, *The Supremacists: The Tyranny of Judges and How to Stop It* (Dallas: Spence Publishing Company, 2004), 113-44; Judicial Action Group Business Plan, and Richard Davis, *Electing Justice: Fixing the Supreme Court Nomination Process* (New York: Oxford University Press, 2005).

[20] Bork, *Coercing Virtue,* and Levin, *Men in Black.*

[21] Levin, *Men in Black,* 29.

[22] Thomas E. Baker "Constitutional Theory In a Nutshell," *William & Mary Bill of Rights Journal,* J. 57 at 78.

[23] Marvin Olasky, *World,* 29 July 2006.

EPILOGUE

[1] John 3:16.

[2] Micah 6:8 (American Standard Version).